The Republican Resistance

The Republican Resistance

#NeverTrump Conservatives and the Future of the GOP

Edited by
Andrew L. Pieper and Jeff R. DeWitt

LEXINGTON BOOKS
Lanham • Boulder • New York • London

Published by Lexington Books
An imprint of The Rowman & Littlefield Publishing Group, Inc.
4501 Forbes Boulevard, Suite 200, Lanham, Maryland 20706
www.rowman.com

6 Tinworth Street, London SE11 5AL, United Kingdom

British Library Cataloguing in Publication Information Available

Library of Congress Cataloging-in-Publication Data Available

Library of Congress Control Number: 2020942609

ISBN 978-1-7936-0745-4 (cloth)
ISBN 978-1-7936-0747-8 (pbk)
ISBN 978-1-7936-0746-1 (electronic)

The only thing necessary for the triumph of
evil is for good men to do nothing.

*Edmund Burke, paraphrased from "Thoughts on
the Cause of the Present Discontents."*

Contents

Preface

Donald Trump's victory made fools of many so-called "experts," including many of the subjects, and certainly the editors, of this volume. To describe Trump's candidacy as a "long-shot" gives it more credit than it received at its outset, and Republicans, Democrats, and independent political observers have spent the last four years trying to make sense of his victory. Some Republicans are less inclined to explain or justify what happened than to simply embrace the phenomenon of Donald Trump, bask in the sunlight, and relish the opportunity to lead the nation that his improbable victory imparted on their party. Other Republicans, detailed in this volume, wish his election was a fluke, hoping against hope that the next scandal will lead their fellow partisans to "see the light" and finally turn on their president.

Originally, this volume was conceived as a sort of "Profiles in Courage" wherein we would feature conservatives and Republicans who proudly stepped up and out in opposition, and who maintained their criticism, their defense of principles they hold dear, even after Trump secured the nomination and won the presidency. It soon became clear that such a volume would be too simplistic, overly black and white while, in fact, this story is in gray-scale. Most of the those who we might consider original #NeverTrumpers have morphed into what we might call #EventualTrumpers, or perhaps #OccasionalTrumpers. The story of intra-party and conservative opposition to Donald Trump is clearly more nuanced. This volume explores its evolution rather than glorifies its membership.

Unlike many studies of the Trump phenomenon, we are not focused on presenting a detailed profile of those supporters and loyalists who voted for Donald Trump, or appear at his rallies, or proudly wear his MAGA merchandise. A veritable mountain of academic articles, journalistic and scholarly ethnographies, and public opinion data analyses have pored over the evidence, attempting to explain how a draft-dodging, brash billionaire from New York known mostly for his garish taste in buildings and women won over veterans and religious working-class voters from the Rust Belt. Such studies are important and help us gain a better understanding of the appeal of Trump, and the challenges facing both traditional conservatives and Democrats. This volume, instead, rests upon the foundational idea that elites—from both the conservative intellectual movement and the establishment GOP in the United States—are also critical actors we must strive to understand. They have helped guide the Republican Party and American political culture, more broadly, for decades. It is unlikely they will simply disappear or abandon an intellectual movement they have shaped and identified with for years.

We explore Donald Trump's immediate impact on American democracy and public policy because it has fundamentally shaped both the nature of a 160-year-old political party and one of the most influential intellectual movements in American political history. That shift matters for all Americans, regardless of party affiliation or ideological orientation. The contributors to this volume explore #NeverTrumpers not because they oppose Donald Trump, support conservatism, sympathize with Trump voters, or out of any partisan or ideological motives. We study #NeverTrumpers because political parties matter, and the ideas and principles that drive people matter. Understanding #NeverTrumpers, rather than diminishing the supporters of Donald Trump, enhances our ability to analyze historical moments and provides opportunities to document shifts in social and cultural trends.

As editors of this book, we have been benefited from the help of many individuals. At Lexington Books, a variety of editors, including Emily Roderick, who guided us through the initial process, Alison Keefner, Bryndee Ryan, and Joseph Parry, who were invaluable during the latter stages of writing and editing. We are also indebted to the contributors, all of whom were solicited specifically for this volume, and embraced the challenge of numerous drafts, made difficult by the ever-shifting sands of the Trump administration and its critics. Our colleagues at Kennesaw State University were also helpful, providing real-time feedback in regular hallway consultations. We would be remiss if we did not mention our families. Andy would like to thank his kids, Jonah and Micah, who indulged excessive dinner-table shop talk and postponed ping pong battles so dad could proofread, and his talented wife Roxanne, whose level-headed problem solving and support saved more than a few hours of his sleep. Jeff would like to thank his lovely wife and daughter, Joyce and Madison, both of whom provided boundless and unyielding encouragement and demonstrated profound patience throughout this journey, his mom and dad for nurturing his inquisitive nature and appreciation for diligent determination, his sisters, Diana and Deborah, for their steadfast support, and his stepsons, Nicholas and Christopher, for always listening and for providing inspiration with their own life accomplishments.

Chapter 1

Resisting Trump

Origins of #NeverTrump and the Battle for the Soul of the GOP

Andrew L. Pieper and Jeff R. DeWitt

The election of Donald Trump as president of the United States in November 2016 was a political earthquake, one supporters and detractors alike agree has changed the course of history. The policy implications have been stark and will continue well beyond his presidency. The political implications have been perhaps even more drastic—for both political parties. Trump has shaken the forty-year-old coalition of traditional conservatives, orthodox religious voters, and free-market libertarians that has long-composed the Republican Party. This book explores the members of that coalition, especially traditional, establishment-oriented Republicans, and conservative intellectuals who opposed his candidacy, who generally still oppose his presidency, and who represent the elite-in-waiting within the segment of the conservative movement that believes it will have to rebuild the GOP when the Trump coalition implodes.

The chapters that follow describe and assess how the emergence of Donald Trump as a presidential candidate, and the aftermath of his election victory in 2016, has impacted the conservative movement and the Republican Party as well as the U.S. party system and American politics more generally. We argue that Trump's selection as nominee and his performance while president has resulted in a dramatic "intra-party dealignment," as prominent public figures have either drifted away from the GOP or severed partisan ties completely. #NeverTrump sentiment, our principal focal point, was succinctly encapsulated by conservative columnist George Will who proclaimed in August 2015 that "(Trump) is an affront to anyone devoted to the project William F. Buckley began six decades ago with the founding in 1955 of *National Review*—making conservatism intellectually respectable and politically palatable."[1] Trump's eventual nomination as the GOP candidate for president was the last straw for Will, who announced "I joined it [the Republican Party] because I was a conservative, and I leave it for the same reason: I'm a conservative."[2]

Forty years before Donald Trump's emergence as GOP standard-bearer, free-market libertarians, socially conservative Christians, international interventionists, and Burkean conservatives joined together to supplant the New Deal coalition of Democratic dominance. This Republican coalition remained relatively stable since the election of Ronald Reagan, even through the recent tumult of the insurgent Tea Party movement. It is plausible that the current, widening schism within the GOP could have been temporary if Trump lost the general election. His victory, however, while consolidating support among rank-and-file Republicans in the electorate, at least for the moment, also ensured continued opposition from conservative activists, elites, opinion leaders, and those within the GOP establishment who are concerned that his electoral win and behavior in office are antithetical to ideological and party principles and will likely result in a smaller, more marginalized base of Republican voters as time passes.[3] Tim Miller, Republican communication consultant and strategist who worked with President George W. Bush, GOP presidential nominee Mitt Romney, and also Jeb Bush, expressed this concern, and sounded a clarion call to action. "I think another very real potential right now—why it's important that people in the party speak out against Donald Trump and against Trumpism—is that the Republican Party moves to a period of minority status."[4]

Criticism of Trump by established party leaders, conservative interest groups, lawmakers, and members of the media has been rooted in various policy and ideological based differences, but is also triggered by negative perceptions of his personal demeanor and performance as president. This volume aims to assess how Trump's campaign and tenure has impacted those within the old coalition who oppose his policies, style, and character and whether these cleavages will survive and extend beyond his presidency. At the end of the day, we address two key questions for conservatives. First, what has been the nature, tenor, and sustainability of opposition to Trump? Second, what will the Republican Party look like after his presidency in terms of its leadership, issue positions, values, and electoral support?

AN ELECTORAL EARTHQUAKE

Few experts predicted Trump's triumph, including members of his own party. As is chronicled herein, much of the initial opposition to Trump was based on his perceived unelectability. For example, in July 2015, conservative pundit

Charles Krauthammer issued the following proclamation from his perch on FoxNews: "This is the strongest field of Republican candidates in 35 years. You could pick a dozen of them at random and have the strongest cabinet America's had in our lifetime and instead all of our time is spent discussing this rodeo clown."[5] Even Senator Lindsey Graham, who quickly became one of President Trump's most ardent defenders, said in February 2016 "I'm not going to try to get into the mind of Donald Trump, because I don't think there's a whole lot of space there." He added, "I think he's a kook, I think he's crazy, I think he's unfit for office."[6] Proving skeptics from all corners wrong, however, Trump managed to secure a 304-227 Electoral College victory over Democrat Hillary Clinton, even while losing the popular vote 46.1 percent to 48.2 percent.

There is no shortage of explanations for how a political novice with an unconventional, some would say "amateurish," campaign operation who was disliked by many elites within his own party and who destroyed age-tested norms of American electoral politics, was able to secure such an unimaginable victory. The simplest explanation is that depressed Democratic turnout, especially among minority voters, led to Trump's victory.[7] Both Clinton and Trump lacked broad appeal but, based on pre-election polls and media coverage, most assumed the Democrat would win in a landslide. Although lingering questions about email servers and Russian interference served to suppress enthusiasm and turnout, late deciding voters broke toward Trump, after the early election campaign dynamics had passed.[8]

Clearly, factors other than depressed Democratic turnout contributed to Donald Trump's surprise victory. Some of the most sophisticated analyses point to his inclination to launch into anti-immigrant appeals and his ability to activate latent racially charged attitudes among supporters.[9] Diana Mutz highlights how "status threat," rather than economic hardships, best predicted presidential candidate preferences in 2016. "(G)rowing domestic racial diversity and globalization contributed to a sense that white Americans are under siege by these engines of change" and these anxieties helped catapult Trump to the White House.[10] Party coalitions were changing before Trump's emergence onto the national political scene as "working class" whites had been migrating to the GOP for a decade or more.[11] In the end, a sizeable number of voters who supported Obama in 2008 and 2012 flipped to Trump in 2016, in large part based on attitudes about immigration and race.[12]

THE ORIGINS OF #NEVERTRUMPISM

Initially, most Republican Party leaders found the prospect of a Donald Trump presidency to be both humorous and implausible. Criticism or sheer dismissal of Donald Trump was not uncommon in the summer and fall of 2015. His candidacy was seen by many as nothing more than a novelty branding exercise—a vanity project doomed to failure. Once Trump began to gain electoral momentum, however, public opposition crystalized and criticism grew in certain quarters. By early 2016, as "establishment" candidates such as Jeb Bush, Marco Rubio, and Chris Christie withdrew from the race and polls suggested the New York developer-businessman and former reality-show host was surging toward the nomination, reality started to set in.

The "#NeverTrump"[13] movement was formally launched, one could say, with the publication of a February 15, 2016, issue of *National Review*, titled "Conservatives against Trump."[14] In the pages of this bedrock conservative media mouthpiece, prominent thought leaders systematically promulgated what many on the right had been discussing privately—Donald Trump was simply unfit to be president. *National Review* has been a central intellectual player since its inception in 1955, as William F. Buckley founded this bastion for "non-licensed nonconformist" conservatives.[15] It helped spearhead the long effort to unify disparate wings of the conservative movement and had generally represented a traditional orthodox conservative philosophy, one deeply skeptical of populist overtures.

As such, in some ways, it was not surprising that the editors and contributors of *National Review* would be reticent to support the inexperienced, uninformed, flamboyant, and seemingly unprincipled Donald Trump as president. What was stunning, however, was that one of the (if not *the*) most respected conservative media outlet would so openly and so stridently oppose the presumptive Republican nominee for U.S. president. To be accurate, the "Conservatives against Trump" issue of *National Review* was technically a collection of arguments for why he should not be the GOP nominee. Several contributors spent as much time disparaging Hillary Clinton as they did Donald Trump, with some staking out an important qualification, which foreshadows reconsiderations to come—were Trump to become the nominee, they would still support him over the Democrat.

A veritable "who's who" of the nation's most respected conservative thinkers presented a variety of reasons for opposing the Trump candidacy, but the editors of *National Review* were clear in an earlier piece published in January 2016 on one this overarching point—he was undeniably unqualified on virtually all counts. "Trump is a philosophically unmoored political opportunist who would trash the broad conservative ideological consensus within the GOP in favor of a free-floating populism with strong-man overtones." He was compromised by his relationship with foreign dictators and "knows approximately as much about national security as he does about the nuclear triad—which is to say, almost nothing." Trump is a "huckster" and a "menace to American conservatism who would take the work of generations and trample it underfoot in behalf of a populism as heedless and crude as the Donald himself."[16]

The reverberations in American conservatism would be stark if Trump were to be the nominee, and the contributors to *National Review* were unsparingly harsh in their criticism. Most were simply appalled that Trump had seduced so many primary voters. They believed his message contradicted conservative and, indeed, American values. David Boaz, for example, argued that his projection of nativism and authoritarianism ran counter to "American tradition and our founding principles," while L. Brent Bozell III claimed that although other Republicans had hoodwinked conservatives, "Trump might be the greatest charlatan of them all."[17] Mona Charen argued his temperament was fundamentally antithetical to conservatism, writing that Trump was a "con man" who "has demonstrated an emotional immaturity bordering on personality disorder" that disqualifies him from "being a mayor, to say nothing of a commander-in-chief."[18]

Others worried openly about Trump's impact, both short term and long term, on the Republican Party. Radio host Michael Medved wrote that "Trump is the living, breathing bellowing personification of all the nasty characteristics Democrats routinely ascribe to Republicans." If Trump were the nominee, he asked, "Will the Republican Party and the conservative movement survive?"[19] R. R. Reno likewise proclaimed that Trump was the culmination of a damaging trend in the Republican Party, which "has become home to a growing number of Americans who want to burn down our political and economic systems and hang our cultural elites."[20] Yuval Levin considered Trump a "direct challenge to conservatism, because he embodies the empty promise of managerial leadership outside of politics."[21]

OPPOSITION ENGAGED

National Review was, effectively, the canary in the coal mine. The establishment versus insurgency battle was engaged within the broader conservative movement and Republican Party. In the following months, Trump consolidated support among most elected officials and Republicans in the electorate but found himself publicly condemned by several prominent conservative intellectuals and GOP leaders. William Kristol, editor of *The Weekly Standard* (and contributor to the *National Review* issue), led a relentless barrage of attacks on candidate and then President Trump. Former Republican congressman and talking head Joe Scarborough, who had initially been welcoming of Trump's candidacy, eventually denounced Trump from his position as co-host of "Morning Joe" on MSNBC.[22] Several newspapers which had dependably endorsed only Republican presidential nominees for decades, like the *Arizona Republican*, the *Dallas Morning News*, and the *Cleveland Plain Dealer* advocated for Hillary Clinton, with the latter writing that "a Trump presidency threatens our national security and basic civic values."[23] The *San Diego Union Tribune* made Hillary Clinton the first Democrat it had endorsed in its 148-year history.[24] Perhaps most famously, George F. Will, the poster boy of modern American conservatism, announced in June 2016 that he was leaving the Republican Party and urged all principled conservatives to oppose the Trump candidacy.[25] The following month, Clare Malone of FiveThirtyEight.com analyzed numerous data points and arrived at the ultimate conclusion—we were witnessing "The End of a Republican Party." "Trump," she asserted, "is a one-man crisis for the GOP."[26]

The criticism came in longer forms as well. A series of books by conservative activists and authors supplemented anti-Trump commentary in newspapers, online, and on cable television. Republican operative Rick Wilson, conservative national security expert Max Boot, George W. Bush speechwriter David Frum, and radio host Charlie Sykes, among others, published books criticizing Trump the person, the candidate, and the president, lamenting his takeover of the Republican Party.[27] In both March and August 2016, over fifty national security policymakers, many of them conservatives of impeccable credentials who had served in Republican administrations, signed letters expressing their judgment that Donald Trump did not meet even the basic qualifications to serve as commander-in-chief. The August letter ended with the simple assertion that he would be "the most reckless President in American history."[28]

From the start, prominent legislative figures were also on the front lines of the #NeverTrump movement, speaking out in opposition to his candidacy. First-term Senator Ben Sasse (R-NE) was one of the first out of the gate, posting an "open letter" in February 2016 in which he cited ideological concerns. Sasse asserted: "If Donald Trump becomes the Republican nominee, my expectation is that I will look for some third candidate—a conservative option, a Constitutionalist . . . I do not claim to speak for a movement, but I suspect I am far from alone."[29] The longest serving Hispanic Republican in Congress, Ileana Ros-Lehtinen (R-FL), also objected with her voice and with her vote, announcing that she could not support a candidate who "started his campaign by calling Mexicans rapists." Instead, she would write in Jeb Bush's name for president.[30] Several months later, in October 2016, in the wake of release of the *Access Hollywood* tape, Senator Kelly Ayotte (R-NH) pledged to write in Vice Presidential nominee Mike Pence for president, proclaiming that "I'm a mom and an American first, and I cannot and will not support a candidate for president who brags about degrading and assaulting women."[31] Similarly, Senator Mike Lee (R-UT) cast a self-described "protest vote" for independent candidate Evan McMullin, referencing candidate Trump's support for banning Muslim immigrants.[32]

By late Summer 2017, Senator Jeff Flake (R-AZ), once a Tea Party darling, had also seen enough. His *Conscience of a Conservative* echoes fellow Arizonan Barry Goldwater's ideological sensibility expressed in his book of the same name from a half century earlier, only now with the subtitle—*A Rejection of Destructive Politics and a Return to Principle*—which assails the current president and politics of the day. Flake writes:

> Never has a party so quickly or easily abandoned its core principles as my party did in the course of the 2016 campaign. . . . We lurched like a tranquilized elephant from a broad consensus on economic philosophy and free trade that had held for generations to an incoherent and often untrue mash of back-of-the-envelope populist slogans.[33]

OPPOSITION FRACTURES

In the end, Republicans and conservatives reacted to Trump's nomination in myriad ways. Unsurprisingly, opposition to Trump was neither universal nor sustainable. Those who had served the party for decades were forced to readjust their expectations in terms of policy goals and executive temperament. Many of those GOP establishment figures and conservative elites who were initially skeptical would become born-again Trump supporters after he secured the position as the party's standard-bearer, and particularly after he prevailed in the general election. Over time, some #NeverTrumpers evolved into "#EventualTrumpers," as they were faced with a stark choice—picking a side ("us or them") in the binarily polarized political world.[34] They decided, some albeit reluctantly, to saddle up with Trump.

Early opponents hopped aboard the "Trump Train," in obvious contradiction to previously held convictions. Strategic embrace of Trump and his brand of populism seemed necessary in order to preserve their own political relevance. The president garnered unyielding support and sway among their, and his, constituents, especially GOP primary voters. On top of this, many grew fearful of his penchant for seemingly vindictive retaliation against those who question him. However, a select few lawmakers (among them Senators John McCain, Jeff Flake, Bob Corker (R-TN), Ben Sasse (R-NE) and Representatives Mark Sanford (R-SC), and Justin Amash (R-MI) continued to openly question his authority, his policies, and his demeanor. Of particular concern were revelations about Russian interference in the 2016 elections.

In October 2019, during the height of impeachment hearings, President Trump took to Twitter to lambaste his critics. "The Never Trumper

Republicans, though on respirators with not many left, are in certain ways worse and more dangerous for our Country than the Do Nothing Democrats. . . . Watch out for them, they are human scum!" Afterward, the White House Press Secretary Stephanie Grisham subsequently doubled down, seemingly expanding the label to anyone who opposes the president's agenda.[35] Jennifer Rubin, columnist for the *Washington Post* and Trump critic, proudly volleyed back: "I want a t-shirt."[36] Talk radio host and author Charlie Sykes similarly satirically embraced the "human scum" label and even referenced a "secret handshake" for the society of #NeverTrumpers in publicizing via Tweet a "Summit on Principled Conservatism."[37]

It has become an undeniable political reality—critical divisions in the movement and Republican Party were fully exposed after simmering under the surface for years. In chronicling the history of American conservatism, Matthew Continetti notes,

> Episodes of division and strife are far more common than moments of unity and peace. The more you study the history of American conservatism, the less willing you are to describe it in monolithic terms. There isn't one American right, there are multitudes, every one of them competing for the attention of politicians and policymakers. . . . The campaign and election of Donald Trump complicated this already cloudy picture. The debate over Trump's character and fitness for office opened, or poured salt on, wounds that have not and will not heal. Moreover, the varying opinions of Donald Trump the person became hard to disentangle from divergent assessments of his program.[38]

Tim Alberta, former *National Review* reporter, presents the current battle in historical context in *American Carnage: On the Front Lines of the Republican Civil War and the Rise of President Trump*, published in 2019. Trump's nomination forced Republican and conservative establishment-oriented elites to defend their turf against populist insurgents who initiated their efforts in the 1990s. Interestingly, some of the original players, such as John Boehner (R-OH), would eventually become the so-called establishment and were caught off-guard by the fiery anti-elite, uncompromising upstarts from the Tea Party, the Freedom Caucus, and, eventually, Trump and his supporters.

Populist overtones have been especially pronounced in rhetoric and proposed policies relating to race, immigration, and culture. Establishment conservatives grew fearful of alienating an increasingly diverse electorate, while at the same time defending their more "conservative" positions against insurgents who seemed more willing to use scorched earth rhetoric to mobilize supporters and advance its agenda. Peter Wehner, a veteran of three Republican administrations highlights profound intra-party, or co-partisan, shifts which began prior to Trump's candidacy. "But our base was changing.

Some of it was tied to 9/11. Some of it was tied to economic insecurity. Some of it was tied to a sense of lost culture for a lot of people on the right. Those attitudes on immigration were proxies for a lot of other things."[39]

In 2011, former president George W. Bush raised red flags about what might become lexical priorities of the Republican Party. In promoting the need for comprehensive immigration Bush proclaimed: "What's interesting about our country, if you study history, is that there are some 'isms' that occasionally pop up. One is isolationism and its evil twin protectionism and its evil triplet nativism . . . I'm a little concerned that we may be going through the same period. I hope that these 'isms' pass."[40] Five years later, as the GOP convention was celebrating the beginning of the Trump—Republican era, the Bush Family network found itself on the outside looking in, pained and dismayed over what had become of their party. "Representatives of the last Republican White House are effectively in exile from presidential politics these days, dispirited by their party's embrace of Donald J. Trump, the nominee, and feeling betrayed by former friends who are backing him."[41]

The Growth and Opportunity Project (GOPR), published by the Republican National Committee in the wake of 2012 election, represents exactly what President Bush had proposed and exactly what the Trump-led insurgency was rebelling against. The Task Force recommended that Republicans talk in more sensitive ways about immigrants and work for reform that addresses (in part) undocumented people. If enacted, this would effectively take the divisive immigration issue off the table and also bridge cultural and ethnic divides, putting the party on a stronger electoral foundation. Trump chose the alternate tack, however—lean in with vigor, deploy anti-immigration "Build a Wall" rhetoric and promote more extremist positions which had the twin effects of ginning up anxiety among supporters while also serving to further polarize the nation, and likely harming the greater interests of the party. This approach, of course, ran counter to the more pragmatic judgment of those within the GOP establishment.

Former vice-president Dick Cheney opines that this new breed of insurgents is so hostile to elites that it hampers the ability to make and implement policy. Cheney expresses confusion and disappointment at 2008 vice-presidential nominee Sarah Palin's popularity. "We went from wanting people who were experienced and qualified to wanting people who would throw bombs and blow things up."[42] Wehner agrees, saying "We went from glorifying excellence and achievement to embracing this anger and grievance and contempt."[43] Establishment-oriented figures have come to realize that Republican voters may not really be so conservative after all. "I'm not so sure the people who were voting for us as Republican were, on the whole, as ideological as we thought they were," said former Republican House Majority Leader Eric Cantor, himself a victim of co-partisan warfare.[44]

REALIGNMENTS, DEALIGNMENTS, AND MISALIGNMENTS

The #NeverTrump movement is a case study worthy of exploration, especially in light of the current and future status of the American political party system since parties remain the critical "intermediary institutions" which connect elite and mass publics.[45] Changing electoral coalitions are nothing new, of course. Realignment theory posits that every thirty to forty years party systems undergo semi-permanent shifts involving each party coalition, usually resulting in one becoming the dominant governing party for several decades.[46] Scholars point to "critical elections," which signal pivot points leading toward realigned party systems.[47] All the while, as Blum and Parker point out:

> Since the realignment of the late 1960s, American political parties have become both more internally coherent and more polarized from each other on race, economics, religion, and other issues. This is well known. We know less, however, about the implications of this partisan reordering and polarization for internal party conflict. Such a dispute seems to be happening in the current GOP, led by Donald Trump.[48]

A variety of factors have led some to question the contemporary application of realignment theory, suggesting that party coalitions have instead "dealigned," a concept we build upon in this book. Dealignment is characterized by diminished loyalty among party supporters, many of whom may ultimately abandon the party label and organization.[49] Research demonstrates that while dealignment may be best understood as an issue-driven phenomenon, attitudes toward presidential candidates also motivate shifting loyalties, resulting in short term and long term effects on individual-level party identification.[50] Frances E. Lee finds that "compared to most other democracies, the U.S. system offers much less opportunity for organized populist parties but more opportunity for populist candidacies."[51] Party system dynamics in the Trump era suggest a blend of top-down and bottom up causal flow whereby a principal elite political entrepreneur—President Trump—shapes loyalties and partisan dispositions, or lack thereof, within members of the mass public who subsequently project preferences onto elites within government and broader democratic institutions. As Gary Jacobson notes:

> If asked to choose, most Republicans put Trump ahead of his party. They invariably rate his favorability higher than that of the Republican Party generally or of its congressional wing and its leaders in particular, and a solid majority side with Trump when conflicts with other Republican politicians arise.[52]

As such, those inclined toward a #NeverTrump posture are presented with a stark choice—speak out in opposition and risk relegation to political exile or get on board with the Trump agenda, insofar as there is one.

Dealignment theory has significant import for both electoral politics and policymaking within the United States. Political parties, at times, coalesce around new constituencies, ideological orientations, and policy priorities. Only in the 1970s and 1980s was the GOP able to incorporate religious conservatives into its camp, while the centrist Democratic Leadership Council (DLC) consolidated its power with the election of Bill Clinton in 1992 by adding suburban "soccer moms." Given that these victories typically reverberate within electoral coalitions for some time, we explore the current and future state of the Republican Party, and question whether key players and principles of its Reagan coalition will remain on the outside looking in or realign the party with its core as it existed prior to events leading up to the 2016 election. Blum and Parker investigate foreign policy views of Trump supporters, and ask "What happens when members of a party are faced with competing messages from leaders within the party?"[53]

We call the apparent disconnect between various elites and rank-and-file partisans in the electorate "misalignment." From this perspective, while the priorities and values of conservative thought leaders, party establishment figures, and Republican voters are not necessarily in direct conflict (though they may be in some circumstances), they are also not aligned in ways that would tend to promote coherent, consistent messaging and efficient governing and policymaking. We have witnessed this in the Trump presidency as a unified government was unable, over the first two years of the Trump presidency, to enact any major policy initiatives other than rather sweeping tax cut legislation. Republican policy proposals in areas such as infrastructure, gun control, immigration and prescription drugs, seem to stall out nearly before they get started. Many leaders in government, media, think tanks, and otherwise are "wary of taking a firm stance that the president could contradict at any moment."[54] It is difficult, in other words, for conservative and GOP elites and the party base to be fully in sync when policy preferences may be deeply ingrained but also occasionally discordant, and public opinion easily moved in any direction by a 280-character presidential tweet.

CONCLUSION

The chapters that follow examine the contours of the "#NeverTrump" movement, led primarily by elites who find themselves "misaligned" with the presidential standard-bearer and the Donald Trump–era Republican electorate. We explore various themes relating to Republican Party and conservative opposition to the candidacy and presidency of Donald Trump, with chapters oriented around two overarching sections. The first section looks at *who* has opposed Trump and where they have expressed discontent. Chapters focus on the U.S. Congress (chapter 2), states and local governments (chapter 3), the media (chapter 4), think tanks (chapter 5), and the GOP establishment and conservative elites more generally (chapter 6). The second section delves into *why*, or on what basis, some Republicans and conservative elites have opposed President Trump. Chapters include critiques based on foreign policy/ national security (chapter 7), domestic policy (chapter 8), ideological purity (chapter 9), personal character and "decency" (chapter 10), and concerns over corruption and illegality (chapter 11).

Taken as a whole, this volume serves as a comprehensive academic interpretation of the #NeverTrump phenomenon. Each chapter may also effectively stand alone as an independent case study analysis of American politics, highlighting relevant concepts and theoretical perspectives within that subfield. Moreover, while each chapter addresses #NeverTrumpism from a particular thematic vantage, all authors touch three common criteria. The first criterion is the origin of #NeverTrumpism with regards to that particular topic. When did it begin, with which individuals and/or institutions, and on what basis? The second criterion addresses the impact of #NeverTrumpism on the party or greater political dynamics, including the conservative movement and the president's agenda. What are the political implications and is opposition sustained or does it whither and wane over time? Are intra-party critics viewed more as political enemies or wayward allies to be persuaded and/or cajoled, brought back into the fold? The third criterion requires an assessment of how the #NeverTrump movement has and will potentially impact the GOP and party systems in general, as well as the conservative movement in the coming years.

Unlike other critical analyses and commentaries on the Trump presidency, our objective is not to offer explicitly normative arguments about the relative benefits and drawbacks of Donald Trump and his presidential tenure.[55] Rather, this edited volume, and each of the chapters within, strive to tell the stories of how Trump and his presidency has cleaved off important thought leaders and policymakers from the Republican Party and American conservative movement, and how those divisions have impacted his presidency, and will shape American politics moving forward.

NOTES

1. George Will, "Donald Trump Is an Affront to Anyone Devoted to William F. Buckley's Legacy," *National Review*, August 13, 2015, https://www.nationalreview .com/2015/08/donald-trump-conservative-movement/.

2. Ian Schwartz, "George Will on Republican Exit: Like Reagan Said, I Didn't Leave the Party, The Party Left Me," *Real Clear Politics*, June 26, 2016, https://ww w.realclearpolitics.com/video/2016/06/26/george_will_on_republican_exit_like_rea gan_said_i_didnt_leave_the_party_the_party_left_me.html.

3. Alan Abramowitz, *The Great Alignment: Race, Party Transformation, and the Rise of Donald Trump* (New Haven: Yale University Press, 2018); Gary C. Jacobson, "Extreme Referendum: Donald Trump and the 2018 Midterm Elections," *Political Science Quarterly*, 134, no. 1 (Spring 2019): 9–38.

4. Clare Malone, "The End of a Republican Party: Racial and Cultural Resentment have Replaced the Party's Small Government Ethos," *FiveThirtyEight*, July 18, 2016, https://fivethirtyeight.com/features/the-end-of-a-republican-party/.

5. "Krauthammer on Trump: We Have the Best Republican Field in 35 Years and We're Talking About This 'Rodeo Clown,'" *Real Clear Politics*, July 6, 2015, https ://www.realclearpolitics.com/video/2015/07/06/krauthammer_on_trump_we_have_ the_best_republican_field_in_35_years_and_were_talking_about_this_rodeo_clown .html.

6. George F. Will. "Why Do People Such as Lindsey Graham Come to Congress?" *The Washington Post*, January 23, 2019, https://www.washingtonpos t.com/opinions/why-do-people-such-as-lindsey-graham-come-to-congress/2019/01 /23/9830a174-1e68-11e9-8e21-59a09ff1e2a1_story.html.

7. For instance, black voter turnout in Michigan and Wisconsin was more than 12 points lower in 2016 that it was in 2012, and in Ohio it was 7.5 points lower. See Osita Nwanevu, "Low Black Turnout May Have Cost Clinton the Election," *Slate*, May 8, 2017, https://slate.com/news-and-politics/2017/05/low-black-turnout-may-have-cost -clinton-the-election.html.

8. Seth McKee, Daniel A. Smith, and M.V. (Trey) Hood III, "The Comeback Kid: Donald Trump on Election Day in 2016," *PS*, 52, no. 2 (April 2019): 239–42.

9. Abramowitz, *The Great Alignment*.

10. Diana C. Mutz, "Status Threat, Not Economic Hardship, Explains the 2016 Presidential Vote," *Proceedings of the National Academy of Sciences of the United States of America*, 115, no. 19 (April 23, 2018): 4330–39.

11. Tim Alberta, *American Carnage: On the Front Lines of the American Civil War and the Rise of President Trump* (New York: Harper Collins, 2019); Alan Abramowitz, *The Great Alignment*; Larry Bartels, "Partisanship in the Trump Era," Working Paper prepared for "Parties and Partisanship in the Age of Trump" Symposium, 2018, https://www.vanderbilt.edu/csdi/includes/Workingpaper2_2108. pdf; John Sides, "Race, Religion, and Immigration in 2016: How the Debate over American Identify Shaped the Election and What It Means for a Trump Presidency," 2017, https://www.voterstudygroup.org/publication/race-religion-immigration-2016.

12. Tyler T. Reny, Loren Collingwood, and Ali A. Valenzuela, "Vote Switching in the 2016 Election: How Racial and Immigration Attitudes, Not Economics, Explain Shifts in White Voting," *Public Opinion Quarterly*, 83, no. 1 (2019): 91–113; Marc Hooghe and Ruth Dassonneville, "Explaining the Trump Vote: The Effect of Rascist Resentment and Anti-Immigrant Sentiments," *PS*, (April 2018): 528–34; Michael W. Sances, "How Unusual Was 2016? Flipping Countries, Flipping Voters, and

the Education-Party Correlation Since 1952," *Perspectives on Politics*, 17, no. 3 (September 2019): 668–78.

13. Throughout this volume, we use the "#NeverTrump" label to represent conservative and Republican (or formerly Republican) critics of Donald Trump. The hashtag acknowledges that much of the exchange between critics and defenders has played out on (i.e., trended on) social media platforms, Twitter in particular.

14. "Conservatives Against Trump," *National Review*, February 15, 2016, https://www.nationalreview.com/magazine/2016/02/15/conservatives-against-trump/.

15. William F. Buckley, Jr., "Our Mission Statement," *National Review*, November 19, 1955, https://www.nationalreview.com/1955/11/our-mission-statement-william-f-buckley-jr/.

16. The Editors, "Against Trump," *National Review*, January 22, 2016, https://www.nationalreview.com/2016/01/donald-trump-conservative-movement-menace/.

17. "Conservatives Against Trump," 27.

18. "Conservatives Against Trump," 28.

19. "Conservatives Against Trump," 34–35.

20. "Conservatives Against Trump," 37.

21. "Conservatives Against Trump," 32.

22. Patrick Doyle, "Joe Scarborough Details Trump Falling Out: 'He Screamed at Me,'" *Rolling Stone*, June 29, 2017, https://www.rollingstone.com/tv/tv-features/joe-scarborough-details-trump-falling-out-he-screamed-at-me-204793/.

23. Chris Quinn, "Using LeBron James as Endorsement Vehicle for Hillary Clinton a Perfect Fit for an Awkward Election," *Cleveland.com*, January 11, 2019, https://www.cleveland.com/opinion/2016/10/using_lebron_james_as_endorsem.html.

24. "Endorsement: Why Hillary Clinton Is the Safe Choice for President," *San Diego Union-Tribune*, September 30, 2016, https://www.sandiegouniontribune.com/opinion/the-conversation/sd-hillary-clinton-endorsement-for-president-20160929-story.html.

25. George F. Will, "Republicans: Save Your Party, Don't Give to Trump," *The Washington Post*, June 22, 2016, https://www.washingtonpost.com/opinions/republicans-save-your-party-dont-give-to-trump/2016/06/22/f56a8cda-37eb-11e6-a254-2b336e293a3c_story.html.

26. Malone, "The End of a Republican Party: Racial and Cultural Resentment Have Replaced the Party's Small Government Ethos."

27. Rick Wilson, *Everything Trump Touches Dies: A Republican Strategist Gets Real About the Worst President Ever* (New York: Free Press, 2018); Max Boot, *The Corrosion of Conservatism: Why I Left the Right* (New York: Liveright, 2018); David Frum, *Trumpocracy: The Corruption of the American Republic* (New York: Harper, 2018); Charlie Sykes, *How the Right Lost Its Mind* (New York: St. Martins Press, 2017).

28. David E. Sanger and Maggie Haberman, "50 G.O.P. Officials Warn Donald Trump Would Put Nation's Security 'at Risk,'" *The New York Times*, https://www.nytimes.com/2016/08/09/us/politics/national-security-gop-donald-trump.html.

29. Ben Sasse, "AN OPEN LETTER TO TRUMP SUPPORTERS to my friends supporting Donald Trump," Facebook, February 28, 2016, https://www.facebook.com/sassefornebraska/posts/561073597391141 (accessed March 1, 2020).

30. Alex Daugherty, "Miami Congresswoman Still Plans to Vote for Jeb Bush for President," *Miami Herald*, August 9, 2016, https://miamiherald.typepad.com/nak edpolitics/2016/08/miami-congresswoman-still-plans-to-vote-for-jeb-bush-for-pres ident.html.

31. Kelly Ayotte, @KellyAyotte, October 8, 2016, "I Will Not Vote for Donald Trump. Read My Statement Here," Twitter, https://twitter.com/kellyayotte/status/7 84779876796665857.

32. Dan Harrie, "Utah Sen. Mike Lee Voted for McMullin in Protest of Trump," *The Salt Lake Tribune*, November 6, 2016, https://archive.sltrib.com/article.php?id =4563854&itype=CMSID.

33. Jeff Flake, *Conscience of a Conservative: A Rejection of Destructive Politics and a Return to Principle* (New York: Random House), p. 66.

34. Jeremy Peters, "The 'Never Trump' Coalition That Decided Eh, Never Mind, He's Fine," *The New York Times*, October 5, 2019, https://www.nytimes.com/2019/1 0/05/us/politics/never-trumper-republicans.html?smid=nytcore-ios-share.

35. Hayley Miller, "White House Press Secretary: People Who Don't Like Trump 'Deserve' to Be Called Scum," *HuffingtonPost*, October 24, 2019, https://www .huffpost.com/entry/stephanie-grisham-donald-trump-scum_n_5db1bba4e4b01ca2 a859157c.

36. Jennifer Rubin, @JRubinBlogger, "On his way to the event, Trump wrote on Twitter that 'Never Trumper' Republicans who don't support him are 'human scum,'" Twitter, October 23, 2019, https://twitter.com/JRubinBlogger/status/1187 173624593170434.

37. Charlie Sykes, @SykesCharlie, "Human Scum," Twitter, February 19, 2020, https://twitter.com/SykesCharlie/status/1230354683082002432.

38. Matthew Continetti, "Making Sense of the New American Right," *National Review*, June 1, 2019, https://www.nationalreview.com/2019/06/new-american-right -schools-of-thought/.

39. Alberta, *American Carnage*, 18.

40. George W. Bush, Bush on Immigration in 2011, Video Clip, https://www.c-s pan.org/video/?c4654456/user-clip-bush-immigration-2011.

41. Jonathan Martin, "The Trump Convention: A Painful Moment for the Bush Family Network," *The New York Times*, July 19. 2016, https://www.nytimes.com/2 016/07/20/us/politics/bush-family-rnc.html

42. Alberta, *American Carnage*, 25.

43. Alberta, *American Carnage*, 39.

44. Alberta, *American Carnage*, 132.

45. Kara Lindaman, and Donald P. Haider-Markel, "Issue Evolution, Political Parties and the Culture Wars," *Political Research Quarterly*, 55, no. 1 (March 2002): 91–110.

46. V. O. Key, "A Theory of Critical Elections," *The Journal of Politics*, 17, no. 1 (February 1955): 3–18; Walter Dean Burnham, *Critical Elections and the Mainsprings of American Politics* (New York: Norton, 1970); Johnathan Knuckey, "Classification of Presidential Elections: An Update," *Polity*, 31, no. 4 (Summer 1999): 639–53.

47. Burnham, *Critical Elections*. While this volume does not take a position on the validity of realignment theory, we view it as a theoretical framework within which to analyze how modern elections, voting, and governing work.

48. Rachel Marie Blum and Christopher Sebastian Parker, "Trump-ing Foreign Affairs: Status Threat and Foreign Policy Preferences on the Right," *Perspectives on Politics*, 17, no. 3 (September 2019): 737–55.

49. Edward G. Carmines and James A. Stimson, *Issue Evolution: Race and the Transformation of American Politics* (Princeton: Princeton University Press, 1989); David R. Mayhew, *Electoral Realignments: A Critique of an American Genre* (New Haven: Yale University Press, 2002).

50. Edward G. Carmines, John P. Melver, and James A. Stimson, "Unrealized Partisanship: A Theory of Dealignment," *The Journal of Politics* 49, no. 2 (May 1987): 376–400.; Kara Lindaman, and Donald P. Haider-Markel, "Issue Evolution, Political Parties and the Culture Wars"; Ronald B. Rapoport, "Partisan Change in a Candidate-Centered Era," *The Journal of Politics*, 59, no. 1 (February 1997): 185–99.

51. Frances E. Lee, "Populism and the American Party System: Opportunities and Constraints," *Perspectives on Politics*, 17, no. 3 (September 2019): 1–19.

52. Jacobson, "Extreme Referendum: Donald Trump and the 2018 Midterm Elections," 9–38. As Jacobson (2019) points out, when "asked in an October 2018 NBC News/Wall Street Journal survey, "Do you consider yourself to be more of a supporter of Donald Trump or more of a supporter of the Republican Party?," 59 percent of Republicans chose Trump, 35 percent, the party; these results are typical."

53. Blum and Parker, "Trump-ing Foreign Affairs," 738.

54. Adam Cancryn and Sarah Karlin-Smith, "Trump Whipsaws GOP on Drug Pricing," *Politico*, September 24, 2019, https://www.politico.com/story/2019/09/24/trump-whipsaws-gop-on-drug-pricing-1763102.

55. Wilson, *Everything Trump Touches Dies*; Sykes, *How the Right Lost Its Mind*; Frum, *Trumpocracy*; www.thebulwark.com.

Part I

WHERE #NEVERTRUMP?

Chapter 2

A Dying Breed

#NeverTrumpism in Congress

Jeffrey Lazarus

While most of us were asleep at one o'clock in the morning of July 28, 2017, the U.S. Senate was bustling with activity, and all eyes were on Senator John McCain (R-AZ). After seven years of symbolic moves, congressional Republicans were finally ready to repeal the Affordable Care Act, popularly known as Obamacare. This latest effort had been in the works since Donald Trump was first elected president with a Republican-controlled House and Senate. The seven-month legislative process was tortuous but eventually a repeal bill passed the House and this morning the Senate would vote on whether to pass the bill. Even at this late stage, though, the outcome was still in doubt. All forty-six Senate Democrats opposed the bill, along with the chamber's two independents and two Republican senators, Lisa Murkowski (R-AK) and Susan Collins (R-ME). If the fifty remaining Republicans all voted to pass the bill, there would be a 50-50 tie, which Vice President Mike Pence would break in favor of repeal, and Obamacare would be history. Forty-nine of them had announced that they would vote yes; of 100 senators only John McCain had kept silent on how he planned to vote.

McCain reveled in the attention and in his reputation as a maverick. At alternate times during his career, McCain played the role of loyal Republican, moderate pragmatist, or party pariah. But McCain's relationship with the party had been strained since Trump became president. The two had never liked each other, and the feud escalated in June 2015 when McCain complained that Trump "fired up the crazies" at a rally in McCain's home state of Arizona.[1] In response Trump insulted McCain incessantly for several days, culminating at a campaign rally when Trump claimed that McCain—a prisoner of war for five years during Vietnam—is "not a war hero. He's a war hero because he was captured. I like people who weren't captured."[2] For the next two years the pair traded barbs in speeches, interviews, and (for Trump) over Twitter. So, when McCain became the deciding vote on Obamacare repeal the question became would he vote with his party or would he use it as an opportunity to settle a score with the president?

McCain chose to settle the score, and did so in dramatic fashion. The Senate takes votes by calling roll, and senators typically respond "aye" or "nay" when their names are called. But when McCain's name was called, he didn't say a word. Instead he walked to the front of the Senate chamber and, standing right in front of Majority Leader Mitch McConnell (R-KY), made a thumbs down gesture. Seven years of Republican efforts to repeal Obamacare were doomed in part by a feud between President Trump and a Republican senator.[3]

This was only the most dramatic example of the infighting that occurred between Trump and Republican members of Congress. Starting as early as 2015, dozens of lawmakers from Trump's party objected to his brash style, inflammatory rhetoric, personal scandals, and occasional direct insults. Certainly, #NeverTrump Republicans represented a minority of the GOP membership in Congress—at the time of Trump's election there were 300 GOP members of Congress, only fifty-two of whom publicly opposed him during the general election.[4] But even that small fraction was historically unprecedented. The opposition continued into Trump's presidency; it was enough to cost him significant support in many of his legislative efforts, and make it exceedingly more difficult for him to move his policies through Congress. The result was a massive lost opportunity for Republicans. Despite having gained control of the House, Senate and presidency during the 115th Congress (2017–2019), they managed to score remarkably few legislative victories. #NeverTrump Republicans in the Senate also limited Trump's ability to dictate the direction of special counsel Robert Muller's investigation into Russian election interference. During the 115th Congress, #NeverTrumpism had a significant effect on what both Congress and Trump could and could not do.

However, opposition to Trump among House and Senate Republicans diminished quickly and is now functionally extinct. Despite fairly low approval ratings overall, Trump enjoys consistent 90 percent or better approval among Republican voters. The Republican Party base in general strongly supports Trump, and these voters decide the outcome of Republican primary elections. This means #NeverTrump Republicans face the choice of getting on board with Trump or struggling to secure the GOP nomination in the party primary. The most vigorous #NeverTrumper Republicans have left Congress, although a few high-profile #NeverTrump senators, such as Lindsey Graham, Ted Cruz (R-TX), and Cory Gardner (R-CO), have converted and become full-throated Trump supporters. Taken together, the end result is that after the 2018 elections (which came near the end of the 115th

Congress), congressional Republicans have coalesced around Trump to the point that, when the House of Representatives voted on whether to initiate impeachment hearings in November 2019, not a single Republican voted in favor of it (Justin Amash of Michigan supported the measure, but had already left the GOP). It is increasingly apparent #NeverTrumpism does not have a viable future among congressional Republicans.

THE ORIGINS OF CONGRESSIONAL #NEVERTRUMPISM

When Donald Trump ran for president in 2015–2016, he was a difficult candidate for congressional Republicans to get behind because he brought with him an unprecedented amount of political baggage. Trump's campaign featured attacks on foundational aspects of American governance such as an independent judiciary, the First Amendment, and the United States' commitment to NATO. Trump attacked symbols of the U.S. military, such as John McCain and the family of a U.S. soldier who had been killed in action in Afghanistan. There was racially charged rhetoric aimed at Muslims and Hispanics, only slightly more veiled antisemitic references, and a highly publicized speech in which Trump mocked a reporter's physical disability in front of thousands of attendees at a campaign rally. In addition to these campaign incidents, Trump's personal history also featured accusations of racism and antisemitism, two divorces and several extramarital affairs, shady and secretive business deals, at least one rape accusation that was being adjudicated during the campaign, and close (and once again secretive) ties to Russia. In a nutshell, Trump was far from an ideal party standard bearer.[5]

Thus, when Trump captured the nomination, Republican politicians and candidates for office faced a conundrum. For Congress members endorsing the party's presidential nominee is de rigueur—not only is it an expected formality that maintains good relations within the party, it is also a standard move that helps the endorser as much as the presidential nominee. Many more voters have heard of the presidential nominee than any other politician in the party.[6] As such, endorsing the presidential nominee mean that one is not only trying to help the nominee win but is also an effort to latch on to the nominee's higher name recognition and help yourself win a few extra votes.[7]

On the other hand, Trump's controversial history and campaign meant his coattails might not help Republican politicians as much as a typical nominee. As a result, many Republican members of Congress chose to keep some distance from Trump. Throughout much of the primary season, this wasn't much of a risk—Trump was not a favorite to win the nomination until the late stages. However, as his candidacy gained momentum, and even after he won the nomination, many Republicans were still reluctant to endorse. Representatives Reid Ribble (R-WI) and Robert Dold (R-IL) announced as early as December 2015 that they would not vote for Trump if he became the party's nominee. In the coming months, a slow trickle of Republican members followed suit, and by early October 2016 eleven Republican House members and five Republican senators had announced that they would not support Trump that November.[8]

That changed in the second week of October when the "Access Hollywood tape" became public. Among other statements, these recordings feature Trump bragging about groping and kissing women without their consent. This incendiary video clip appeared to be the death knell of Trump's campaign. House Speaker Paul Ryan (R-WI) told Republican House members in a conference call that "I am not going to defend Donald Trump . . . Not now, not in the future," giving his members permission to break with the party's seemingly doomed nominee and do what they needed to win their own races.[9] In the end, a total of thirty-six sitting Republican House members and sixteen Republican senators announced that they would vote for a candidate other than Donald Trump in the 2016 elections.[10] This represented more than one out of every six sitting Republican members of Congress. That level of defection from the party's presidential candidate is unprecedented in American history; typically support for the party's nominee is virtually unanimous.[11]

The remaining Republican members—the vast majority of them—did endorse Trump, but, even so, several of these endorsements were less than full-throated. Some GOP politicians justified their support of Trump by comparing him to Democratic nominee Hillary Clinton. Representative Lee Zeldin (R-NY) gave a typical example: "Even though I don't agree with Donald Trump on everything . . . he is a better candidate by far than Hillary Clinton."[12] Others made simple statements of their intent to vote for Trump without elaborating on why, like Representative Peter King (R-NY): "I will vote for him and I will endorse him."[13] Still others leaned on the fact that as a Republican, they vowed to accept whoever Republican primary voters had chosen. Senate majority leader Mitch McConnell (R-TN) endorsed Trump by saying "I have committed to supporting the nominee chosen by Republican voters and Donald Trump . . . is now on the verge of clinching that nomination."[14] All of these make for tepid endorsements at best.

Thus, Trump began his term as president with historically low levels of support from his own party's congressional delegation. As with anything a politician does, it is difficult to tease out which congressional Republicans kept their distance from Trump because of principled opposition to his actions and words, and which members did so simply because they believed it was best for their careers—Congress members routinely justify principled moves by citing electoral concerns and vice versa.[15] For many members, it was likely a combination of both. However, this distinction between politics and principle undoubtedly played a critical role in determining whether members would maintain their opposition to Trump throughout their congressional tenure, such as Senator Jeff Flake (R-AZ) and Representative Justin Amash (I-MI), and those who would eventually come around to the idea of supporting Trump to save their careers once it became clear that Trump was so popular among Republican primary voters.[16] Senators Ben Sasse (R-NE) and Lindsey Graham (R-SC) are two who went that route.

LEGISLATIVE CONSEQUENCES OF THE #NEVERTRUMP MOVEMENT IN CONGRESS

Typically during unified government, the party in power can enact significant elements of their legislative program.[17] However, despite their control of the presidency and majorities in both the House and the Senate, Republicans achieved just one significant legislative victory during the 115th Congress—a major tax reform bill.[18] Against this came a slew of setbacks and defeats. Certainly, #NeverTrump Republicans were not the only reason Republicans had trouble legislating. Intra-party divisions, the Senate's sixty-vote filibuster requirement, and extreme polarization all played a role as well.[19] However, all of those conditions set up a situation in which GOP leadership in both chambers would need all the votes they could get just to pass bills with bare majorities. The thin tolerance Republicans were operating under meant that Trump's rocky relationship with congressional Republicans would prove especially costly.

Trump's political baggage made him unable to convince Republicans to take up his issues, and just as bad at lobbying them for votes when they did. This proved to be a devastating shortcoming. Despite the formal separation of powers built into the American political system, Congress, in practice, relies on the president to set the legislative agenda, rally public support for legislative proposals and provide the focal point for piecing together legislative coalitions with enough votes to get bills passed.[20] There were enough #NeverTrump Republicans in the 115th Congress to make Trump singularly ineffective at playing the president's informal but still very important role in the legislative process. Here are a few brief examples.

For one, Trump failed to convince Republicans to support his signature campaign promise, construction of a physical barrier along the Mexican border. Many were lukewarm on "the wall" to begin with, and Trump was unsuccessful in his efforts to lobby congressional votes for it. The issue even resulted in a high-profile government shutdown, as Trump refused to sign some 2019 spending bills unless Congress included $5.7 billion for wall construction. However, Republicans pointedly adjourned Congress without addressing the issue, leaving the issue to be decided by Democrats who would assume a majority a few weeks later. Trump never received the funding he sought for the wall, almost entirely because he could not convince Republicans in Congress to make the wall a priority.

Trump also proposed toughening controls on both legal and illegal immigration. The issue came to a head when the Senate voted on four different immigration plans in a single day. One of the plans came directly from the White House; the other three were authored by various senators. None of the four proposals got enough votes to pass, but Trump' proposal received the *fewest* Republican votes out of all four: fourteen of the fifty-one Republican senators voted against it. Moreover, the House never made a serious effort to pass an immigration bill—it was not a high priority issue for the GOP majority leadership in that chamber despite being Trump's highest priority.

A third issue Trump fell short on was a campaign promise to fund improvements to the nation's roads, bridges, and other physical infrastructure. Trump tried several times to roll out an infrastructure plan, but he had a tendency to be his own worst enemy on the issue. Most of his grand announcements *promised* a detailed plan for what a bill would look like, but these plans typically were incomplete or even nonexistent, and each time neither Trump nor anyone in the White House consulted with congressional Republicans. As a result, neither the House nor the Senate made any serious attempt to deal with the issue.

Separate from Trump's inability to lead Congress through the legislative process to pass bills, congressional Republicans were also willing to ignore or push back against Trump on non-legislative issues. For example, Trump repeatedly called on Mitch McConnell to abolish the filibuster in order to smooth the path toward enacting Republican legislation in the Senate. McConnell brushed aside those calls without a second thought, and no other Republican senator was willing to take up the issue either. Additionally, several Republican members were more than willing to rebuke Trump for some of his more egregious statements and policy missteps. When news leaked that Trump had referred to some nations as "shithole countries," for example, Representative Mia Love (R-UT) called the statements "unkind, divisive, elitist, and [they] fly in the face of our nation's values."[21] At one point, Trump abruptly decided to withdraw the military from Syria without consulting his own military leadership on the issue; Lindsey Graham (R-SC) derisively referred to the situation as "Iraq all over again," and Senator Bob Corker (R-TN) blasted the decision as "obviously . . . political."[22] When Trump unilaterally imposed tariffs on China, Representative Mark Sanford (R-SC) called the decision an "experiment with stupidity."[23] After Trump defended Saudi Arabia in the murder of journalist Jamal Khashoggi, Corker said he was "astounded," and Graham argued "When we lose our moral voice, we lose our strongest asset."[24]

This last episode even led Congress to invoke the War Powers Resolution—a law that limits the president's ability to send the military into battle when Congress has not declared war—for just the second time in the forty-five years since it was enacted. Congress used the resolution in an attempt to end the administration's weapons sales to Saudi Arabia (the Saudis were using the weapons in its war against Yemen). The effort was unsuccessful, but the fact that majority Republicans in Congress invoked the resolution at all against a same-party president was a significant public rebuke.

SENATE TRUMP SKEPTICS AND ROBERT MUELLER

A less visible result of the congressional #NeverTrump movement was that Trump was constrained in how he handled the investigation into Russian election interference. This constraint came from a group of #NeverTrump Republican senators and some who were less committed to their anti-Trump views but were still publicly skeptical about him; the group included McCain, Lindsey Graham (R-SC), Bob Corker (R-TN), Susan Collins (R-ME), Lisa Murkowski (R-AK), Ben Sasse (R-NE), Jeff Flake (R-AZ), and Dean Heller (R-NV). Despite their frequent public criticism of Trump, these senators regularly voted in favor of his legislative proposals and judicial nominees. Thus they appeared to be trying to have things both ways: they wanted the electoral benefit of criticizing an unpopular president's least popular statements, but at the same time to earn the approval of Republican partisans in the electorate that came from being loyal Trump partisans in Congress. This appearance was bolstered by the fact that the skeptics had real power. In 2017, Senate Republicans had a bare majority of only fifty-two senators (fifty-one after Democrat Doug Jones unexpectedly won the Alabama runoff to replace Jeff Sessions). If the skeptics voted against the party, Republicans would not be able to pass anything or confirm nominees.[25] It seemed to many that they were squandering the opportunity to use their leverage to punish Trump.

However, the skeptics' opposition to Trump was not entirely inconsequential. Their presence in the Senate answers a question, which is otherwise something of a mystery: why did Trump not fire Attorney General Jeff Sessions, Deputy Attorney General Ron Rosenstein, or special counsel Robert Muller during the 115th Congress, despite repeated threats to do so? Early in Trump's term, Robert Mueller was appointed as special counsel to oversee a Justice Department investigation into any ties Trump's presidential campaign may have had with Russia. Sessions recused himself from overseeing the investigation due to his own Russian contacts, which meant that Mueller's investigation would be overseen by Deputy Attorney General Ron Rosenstein. This was distressing to Trump—he had not appointed either Mueller or Rosenstein, but he had appointed Sessions. Trump had hoped to influence the investigation, but for that to happen it would have to be overseen by someone he had appointed. As a result, Trump spent the next eighteen months threatening to curtail the investigation and hinting that he would use his power to fire Mueller, Rosenstein, and possibly even Sessions in order to gain control over the investigation. However, Trump did not do any of these things despite technically having the ability to do so.

The most likely explanation for Trump's restraint is that interfering with the Mueller investigation was a red line for one or more of the Senate #NeverTrumpers and skeptics. There is no documentation of a specific threat, but the group was publicly very supportive of Mueller. Susan Collins, for instance, called for the Senate to pass the bill and stated repeatedly for months that "it is absolutely essential that [Mueller] be allowed to finish his work."[26] Likewise, Corker said "I think [Trump] needs to leave Mueller alone" and predicted "there would be total upheaval in the Senate" if Trump impeded Mueller from doing his job.[27] Implicit in these messages was the senators' support for protecting Mueller as well as the chain of command above him— Sessions and Rosenstein.

Graham even went so far as to introduce a bill that would have made it more difficult for Trump to fire Mueller or the others. The bill made it to a vote in the Senate Judiciary Committee, and it passed with Graham, Flake and two other Republicans voting in favor (along with all the Committee's Democrats). Flake in particular pushed hard to get the bill a vote on the Senate floor; at one point, he even threatened to stop voting to confirm Trump's judicial nominees and followed through on that threat a week later, blocking a slate of nominees from coming out of committee.[28] However, Majority Leader McConnell blocked the bill from coming up for a vote on the Senate floor. With the support of every Democrat in the chamber and the #NeverTrump Republicans as well, the bill was certain to pass if the Senate had voted on it, and McConnell wanted to protect Trump from the public rebuke which would have come from the Senate passing a bill so clearly and publicly written in opposition to him. However, the message that Trump would have trouble getting nominees through the Senate if he interfered with the Mueller investigation had already been sent (albeit in a somewhat weaker form) when the bill passed the Judiciary Committee with Republican support.

It's likely that if Trump had interfered with the Russia investigation, at least some of the Trump skeptics would have made a move against Trump. That move might have consisted of voting with Democrats on the Senate floor as Flake threatened, bringing a resolution of censure against the president, publicly calling for impeachment, or possibly even abandoning the Republican Party altogether (which Sasse publicly mused about, as I discuss below). The Senate's narrow majority meant Trump and Senate Republicans needed support from members of the "Furrowed Brow Caucus" to pass anything, so if they did privately tell Trump that firing any Sessions, Mueller, or Rosenstein was a red line for them, Trump would have to respect that.

The best evidence that this red line existed came after the 2018 elections. Flake and Corker retired and Heller lost his reelection bid, but despite these losses Republicans improved their position in the Senate to control of fifty-three seats. This meant that moving forward, the pivotal fifty-first vote in the Senate would no longer be a Trump skeptic but a more loyal Republican; thus Trump would no longer need the skeptics' votes to confirm judges or avoid a censure vote. The election that brought all of that change occurred on November 6, 2018; Trump fired Jeff Sessions the very next day.

PAUL RYAN AND THE #NEVERTRUMP MOVEMENT

Perhaps no single member of Congress had a more tortured relationship with Trump than House Speaker Paul Ryan. During the campaign, Ryan was a leading member of the Republican #NeverTrump movement. When Trump called for a "total and complete shutdown" of Muslim immigration, Ryan responded "This is not conservatism . . . not what this party stands for and more importantly not what this country stands for."[29] When Trump complained that a judge presiding over a case involving Trump's business was biased because of his Mexican heritage, Ryan described the criticism as a "the textbook definition of a racist comment."[30] And as noted above, after the Access Hollywood tapes became public Ryan claimed to be "sickened" by Trump's statements and released members of the Republican conference from publicly supporting Trump.[31]

With Trump as president, Ryan faced a difficult choice. He could continue to lead the anti-Trump wing of the Republican Party, criticizing Trump publicly and calling for a more moral approach to politics. Conversely, Ryan could get down to the business of legislating, working with Trump to pass what he hoped would be a historic series of conservative pieces of legislation. Doing both would be impossible—Trump is famously sensitive to criticism, lashing out at slights both real and perceived and refusing to work with anyone who he perceives as disloyal. As reporter Tim Alberta put it, Ryan "could not afford to be both the Speaker of the House *and* the conscience of the Republican Party."[32] Ryan chose the pragmatic route, and set out to work with Trump as best he could: "I felt a major onset of responsibility to help the institutions survive."[33]

What followed over the following two years was an uneasy truce between a political odd couple: a House Speaker who was a devout Catholic and a policy wonk, and a president who was contemptuous of moral limits on his behavior and largely ignorant of both policy and government processes. But the two of them (along with Senate Leader Mitch McConnell) would have to work together if they wanted to pass the Republican agenda. Ryan and Trump never grew to like one another, but they worked together, as Trump would later put it, "because it's life and we sort of need each other a little bit."[34] In public Ryan and Trump projected a good working relationship during the 115th Congress, with criticisms in either direction being rare. However, Ryan and Trump feuded often in private, and internally Ryan never reconciled himself to working with someone he still viewed as immoral. Ryan would later complain "We've gotten so numb to it all . . . Don't call a woman a 'horse face.' Don't cheat on your wife. Don't cheat on anything. Be a good person. Set a good example . . . We had more arguments with each other than pleasant conversations, over the last two years. And it never leaked."[35]

In the end, the relationship wore on Ryan. There were very few legislative successes in the House—as discussed above, Republicans scored only a single real legislative victory during the 115th, the 2017 tax reform bill. In the Senate, McConnell would see additional successes on judicial nominations but the House took no part in those. In the end, the trade-off was just too great: Ryan was sacrificing a lot of personal integrity to gain very little in policy victories for the Republican Party. As a result, Ryan announced in April 2018 that he would retire at the conclusion of the 115th Congress. Nonetheless, Ryan remains a loyal Republican, and predicted that Trump would win reelection in 2020 (though his comments fell short of endorsing him).[36]

#NEVERTRUMP REPUBLICANS ARE DISAPPEARING

Despite #NeverTrump Republicans' impact on the 115th Congress, they have since effectively disappeared from Congress. Some lost primary elections to pro-Trump Republican challengers; others lost in the 2018 general election, victims of a Democratic wave; and still others saved their careers by becoming Trump loyalists. Combined, this means that going forward, the #NeverTrump movement in Congress is effectively dead.

Although many Republicans in Congress withheld support from Trump during the 2015 Congress, opposing him was an electorally hazardous position within the Republican Party. That is because Trump enjoys tremendous support among Republican voters. Trump has consistently maintained at least a 90 percent approval rating among Republican voters.[37] During the height of impeachment hearings, despite strong evidence that Trump had solicited foreign help to tarnish the reputation of a political rival, only five percent of Republican voters report that they think Trump should be removed.[38] Dominant majorities of Republican voters support Trump-linked policies like building a wall along the Mexican border and increasing deportations of illegal immigrants.[39] Indeed, support for Trump has become a litmus test for Republican primary voters.[40] If a congressional candidate does not project strong support for the president and his goals, Republican voters will abandon them in a primary election for a candidate that does. Elected politicians in general, and GOP incumbents in particular, are desperately afraid of drawing a primary election opponent and so they are loath to break with anything of importance to their party's base voters.[41] Former Republican House member David Jolly, who left Congress and quit the party over his opposition to Trump, summarizes the Republican dilemma: "Anyone who wants to win in this party will have to appease the Trumpist base one way or the other."[42]

As a result, most congressional Republicans refuse to break with Trump often or publicly, for fear of drawing his ire and angering GOP primary voters. During the 115th Congress the typical Republican was a loyal party soldier, at least in public. When journalists ask members about Trump's more egregious scandals or controversial statements, most members respond with support of the president, or some variation of "I don't know enough about that to comment." And when Congress votes, Republican members fall in line. Across all the votes Trump took a public position on, the median Republican senator voted with Trump 92.5 percent of the time, and the median Republican House member voted with him 95.7 percent of the time.[43]

Members who refuse to come around are being culled from the party. One high-profile example is Jeff Flake, one of the Senate skeptics discussed earlier. Of all congressional Republicans, Flake had been Trump's most consistent and often sharpest critic, starting at the beginning of the presidential primary campaign early in 2015. Although Flake usually voted with Trump on legislation and in favor of Trump's appointees, he was not afraid to issue public statements in opposition to Trump's style and rhetoric. During Trump's presidential campaign, Flake criticized Trump's penchant for leading "Lock her up" chants directed at Hillary Clinton and Trump's fact-free questioning of Barak Obama's birthplace. Flake wrote "These jokes and bromides . . . cheapen the very real arguments that need to be made to the broader public."[44] During Trump's presidency, Flake accused Trump of "scapegoating" immigrants and claimed that Trump's erratic behavior would lead other nations to "question whether [the United States is] a reliable partner."[45] Flake even wrote a book, *The Conscience of a Conservative,* the bulk of which is a critique of the direction Trump is leading the Republican Party.

These criticisms cost Flake dearly. In 2017, Flake's approval rating dropped to just 22 percent among Arizona Republicans, disastrously low for a Congress member who would face a primary election within a year.[46] Sure enough, Flake drew a strong primary opponent, state senator Kelly Ward, and early polls showed him trailing Ward by more than twenty points. Flake, who was once a darling of Tea Party conservatives, calculated that in order to win the primary election he would have to fall in line with the rest of the party and stop criticizing Trump. Rather than do that, Flake chose to retire, saying in his speech "There may not be a place for a Republican like me in the current Republican climate or the current Republican Party. . . .The path that I would have to travel to get the Republican nomination is a path I'm not willing to take, and that I can't in good conscience take."[47] Flake's opposition to Trump cost him his political career.

Bob Corker traveled almost the exact same path as Flake. Corker, from Tennessee, was a Senate Republican who was skeptical of Trump, calling for protecting special counsel Robert Mueller from Trump's potential interference, and offering frequent criticism of Trump on issues ranging from tariffs to the Saudi Arabia affair. This opposition earned Trump's wrath, with the president calling Corker "incompetent" and dubbing him "Liddle Bob Corker."[48] Like Flake, Corker retired rather than face a difficult primary challenge from a pro-Trump Republican—in Corker's case current senator Marcia Blackburn—in 2018. When a reporter asked Corker why he decided to retire, Corker was very candid about Trump's role in his decision: "The president is, as you know—you've seen his numbers among the Republican base—it's very strong. It's more than strong, it's tribal in nature. People . . . don't ask about issues anymore. They don't care about issues. They want to know if you're with Trump or not."[49]

A third example is House member Justin Amash (I-MI). For as long as he has been in the House, Amash was a Republican and, as a founding member of the Freedom House Caucus, one of the more conservative members of the party at that. Like Flake though, Amash has never been shy about criticizing President Trump. Amash's criticism escalated when the results of Mueller's investigation indicated that Trump's had likely colluded with Russia during the 2016 election, and later likely committed obstruction of justice. In the wake of the report, Amash was the only Republican who called for Trump to be impeached. Amash faced significant backlash, and almost immediately Jim Lower, a pro-Trump Republican state legislator, announced he would challenge Amash in the 2020 primary. Early polls showed Amash down sixteen points in that context (Welch 2019).[50] In response, Amash resigned from the Republican Party and is now a political independent. Amash, like Flake and Corker, decided against seeking re-election and will oppose Trump from the sidelines after his term ends.

Indeed, this or something like it has been the fate of a great deal of Congress' #NeverTrump Republicans, at least on the House side. Of the thirty-six House members who opposed Trump in 2016, only fourteen remained in office as of mid-2019. Nine of them retired from office voluntarily in 2016 or 2018, choosing the private sector over having to win over pro-Trump Republican primary voters. Eleven more lost races for reelection in 2018, victims of a wave elections in which Democrats gained forty-one House seats. These eleven lost in general elections rather than primaries so it's not clear that their opposition to Trump lead directly contributed to their departures. However, #NeverTrump Republicans disproportionately represented moderate (rather than conservative) districts, which made them the most likely Republican victims of ascendant Democratic candidates. On the Senate side, Flake and Corker retired, while senators Kelly Ayotte (R-NH), Mark Kirk (R-IL), and Dean Heller lost reelection bids, again in the general election. John McCain died in 2018 of brain cancer. Indeed, the knowledge that he would likely not survive to his next reelection date is what gave McCain the freedom to be candid about how he felt about Trump. Eleven of the sixteen original #NeverTrump GOP senators are still in office, though nine of them have not faced a reelection yet. Five are up for reelection in 2020, and that prospect is causing at least a couple of them to abandon their #NeverTrump principles.

#NEVERTRUMPERS' OTHER CHOICE:
CAVING TO TRUMP

Whereas Flake, Corker, and Amash prioritized their principled opposition to Trump at the expense of their political careers, a few #NeverTrump Republicans have chosen a different route: saving their careers by abandoning their opposition to Trump. Ben Sasse, for instance, voted against Trump in 2016 (he compared Trump to David Duke and instead voted for Mike Pence as a write-in candidate) and was a frequent critic of Trump throughout the first year or more of his presidency. Sasse called Trump's tariffs on Chinese products "dumb" and described the Trump administration as a "reality-show, soap opera presidency."[51] Sasse's relationship with Trump and the Republican Party eventually became so bad that he began describing himself as a "independent conservative who caucuses with the Republicans" and admitted that he thought about leaving the party "every morning."[52]

But rather than following Amash's out of the GOP, Sasse changed his tune as his 2020 reelection date drew nearer. Like other Republicans, if Sasse wanted to win reelection he would have to support the president. In 2016, Trump won Nebraska by twenty-five points, and Sasse drew an early pro-Trump opponent in the Republican primary. Party official Matt Innis began running right away on a pro-Trump agenda, saying "You can't find anything [Sasse] has really accomplished other than bashing the President."[53] So, starting in late 2018, Sasse toned down his criticism of the president and the party, staying silent on questions put to him about Trump for months at a time. In September, Sasse helped give Trump a rare legislative win by voting to declare a national emergency, which would allow the president to divert military spending to building the border wall. Months prior, the Nebraska senator had voted against wall spending and sharply criticized efforts the national emergency strategy. Moreover, around the same time as the national emergency vote, Sasse vowed to vote for Trump in the 2020 elections.

The effort worked. Right after Sasse's vote in favor of the national emergency, Trump tweeted, "Senator Ben Sasse has done a wonderful job representing the people of Nebraska. He is great with our Vets, the military, and your very important Second Amendment. Strong on Crime and the Border, Ben has my Complete and Total Endorsement!"[54] With Trump's support, Sasse is a shoe-in in his primary contest, and will almost certainly win reelection in 2020. But Sasse had to completely abandon any opposition to Trump to win that support.

Lindsey Graham (R-SC) has similarly moved from Trump skeptic to Trump supporter. If anything, Graham's swing has been more extreme—he took sharper potshots at Trump than Sasse did initially, and now is one of Trump's most ardent supporters in Congress. Graham was one of Trump's opponents in the 2016 presidential primary and criticized him sharply, calling Trump "crazy" and a "jackass," and stating that "I don't think [Trump] has the temperament or judgement to be commander in chief."[55] Like Sasse, Graham voted against Trump in 2016 continued to oppose him through the first year of Trump's presidency. As discussed above, Graham criticized Trump sharply on Trump's intention to withdraw troops from Syria, and also on the Saudi Arabia affair. Graham also coauthored the bill, mentioned above, which sought to protect special counsel Robert Mueller from being fired by Trump.[56]

But Trump has such a hold on Republican voters in Graham's home state of South Carolina that one of Graham's aides has referred to the state as "Trumpistan."[57] Like Sasse, Graham is facing reelection in 2020. Thus, Graham more recently emerged as one of the fiercest defenders of Trump Supreme Court nominee Brett Kavanaugh, shouting "This is the most unethical sham since I've been in politics!" during Kavanaugh's heated confirmation hearings.[58] Graham defended Trump's controversial call to end birthright citizenship, calling it an "absurd policy," and has become one of Trump's most steadfast allies during the House of Representatives' impeachment effort. Graham has described impeachment as "a political setup. It's all hearsay . . . You can't get a parking ticket based on hearsay . . . .So this is a sham as far as I'm concerned."[59] As of this writing, Trump has not yet endorsed Graham as explicitly as he has Sasse, but it's not clear he'll need to. Graham's embrace of Trump appears to have satisfied South Carolina conservatives, and as of this writing Graham doesn't have a primary opponent—despite having had seven in 2014.

CONCLUSION

Unified control of government has been relatively rare in recent history, but when one party controls all the levers of power in the federal government they can usually translate that power into significant legislative victories. The 115th Congress was an exception to this rule: in 2017–2018, Republicans enjoyed unified control, but the most part they failed to pass bills into law that would enact their most important policy items. This was most true for issues that Donald Trump focused on in his campaign, including immigration reform, lowering domestic spending levels, funding a border wall, and Obamacare repeal. Aside from a single tax reform bill, Republicans failed to enact into law any of Trump's—or the party's—major legislative priorities.

One major reason for this is Donald Trump himself. Trump's controversial history and behavior during the campaign caused a number of Republican Congress members to oppose not just some of his individual statements but his very election—more than fifty of them could not bring themselves to even vote for him. Certainly, this did not represent a majority of Republican Congress members, but it was an unprecedented level of opposition to a presidential nominee from a party's congressional caucus. Republican members' opposition to Trump continued into the 115th Congress. Republican members voted for Trump's bills when those bills were considered on the floor of their respective chambers, and Republican senators consistently voted to confirm Trump-appointed judges. However, in less-public ways, Republicans showed very little enthusiasm for Trump and his policies, and this disconnect prevented Republicans from accomplishing much with their unified control of government.

However, as Trump's hold on Republican primary election voters solidified, Republican Congress members have grown more reluctant to speak out against the president. In July of 2019, Trump posted a series of racist tweets aimed at four minority, female, Democratic House members, urging them to "go back" to the countries they "originally came from"—despite the fact that three of them were born in the United States and all four are United States citizens.[60] (Indeed, being a citizen is a constitutional requirement for serving in Congress.) Pushback from congressional Republicans was more muted than for Trump's previous scandals. The two remaining African Americans in Congress, Sen. Tim Scott (R-SC) and Rep. Will Hurd (R-TX) directly rebuked the tweets as racist, but most others refused to. Many Republican members used words like Rep. John Katko's (R-NY) "wrong" or Rep. Tom Cole's (R-OK) "inappropriate." Others partnered a light condemnation of Trump with a swipe at the four Democrats. Rep. Elise Stefanik gave a typical example, "While I strongly disagree with the tactics, policies, and rhetoric of the far-left socialist [House members], the President's tweets were inappropriate, denigrating, and wrong."[61] Others fully supported Trump, such as Rep. Ralph Abraham (R-LA): "I'll pay for [the four members'] tickets out of this country if they just tell me where they'd rather be," and Sen. Steven Daines (R-MT): "Montanans are sick and tired of listening to anti-American . . . radical Democrats trash our country and our ideals."[62]

Indeed, the future is not bright for #NeverTrumpism in Congress. Three of the Senate's anti-Trump members have already left and five more are up for reelection in 2020; of these five Susan Collins appears to be in real trouble and two more (Sasse and Graham) are now Trump supporters. On the House side, the movement is in even bigger trouble: three-quarters of the original #NeverTrump Republicans have already left. The chances of the Republican Party electing new #NeverTrump members to office are slim-to-none, as loyalty to Donald Trump has become a litmus test among most voting blocs within the Republican electorate. Going forward, congressional #NeverTrumpism will be limited to *former* members speaking out against Trump. Former members hold no formal power, so they can only plead with current members to "please follow the facts," like Slade Gordon; point out the different standards congressional Republicans are holding Trump to as compared to past Democratic presidents, like Bob Inglis; plead with current members to abandon the GOP altogether, like David Jolly; or even challenge Trump in the 2020 presidential primary election like Joe Walsh.[63] Indeed, Jolly reports "I can't tell you how many [current] Republican members of Congress have told me 'I'm just trying to keep my head down and not get noticed.'"[64] However, when it comes to sitting members, electoral dynamics will continue to force them to be strong Trump supporters for as long as he holds the presidency.

This dynamic was in evidence throughout President Trump's impeachment and subsequent trial. All of the votes in both chambers were overwhelmingly partisan. When the House voted to adopt two articles impeachment, not a single Republican voted in favor of impeachment in either vote (although former Republican Amash voted to impeach, and two Republicans abstained). Later, when the Senate voted on whether to remove the president from office all Republicans voted against removal except one. Although fifty-two of fifty-three Republican senators voted against removal, Mitt Romney (R-UT) became the first senator in American history to vote to remove a president of his own party. If there is a future for #NeverTrumpism in the U.S. Congress, Romney will likely be the movement's leader.

Even after Trump is gone, his hold on the party is unlikely to weaken. Former House member Jolly goes on: "I don't think we will see a reversal the day Trump leaves office. I'm curious who follows Trump because the politics aren't going to change so dramatically."[65] Trump's support within the Republican electorate is so strong that a majority of Republican voters say Trump is a greater president than Abraham Lincoln was.[66] This means that, regardless of the outcome of the 2020 elections, Trump will almost certainly remain a dominant influence in Republican politics. If Trump wins, it will be seen as vindication of the new brand of politics he has brought to the fore. This will allow a second-term President Trump to directly dictate the direction of the party. But even if Trump loses, he will retain the support of most Republican voters, which will allow him to influence Republican primary elections for as long as he wants.

The fact that congressional Republicans so quickly and thoroughly gave up any serious attempt to check Trump's behavior reflects a serious flaw in the federal government's constitutional design. The Framers laid out a separation of powers system expecting members of Congress to provide a robust check on the presidency. However, what they didn't foresee was the extent to which political parties would dominate electoral politics. Today, Congress members' electoral fortunes are tied to that of the president—if the president is popular, members of his party do well when they run for reelection.[67] This linked electoral fate helps create national political parties—Democrats and Republicans each operate as unified teams. Congress members have more to gain by working with members of their party in other branches or levels of government than with members of their chamber of the other party.

Going forward, this is not likely to change. Increasing polarization means as the parties grow more and more ideologically cohesive and distinct from one another. Politicians will probably see less and less of a reason to cross party lines. For decades, Congress has been more willing to investigate the executive branch during divided government—that is, when the president is of a different party than the congressional majority.[68] Congressional Republicans' actions during Trump's presidency merely continued that trend.

NOTES

1. Ryan Lizza, "John McCain Has a Few Things to Say About Donald Trump," *The New Yorker*, July 16, 2015, https://www.newyorker.com/news/news-desk/john -mccain-has-a-few-things-to-say-about-donald-trump.

2. Ben Schreckinger, "Trump Attacks McCain: I Like People Who Weren't Captured," *Politico*, July 18, 2015, https://www.politico.com/story/2015/07/trump-attacks-mccain-i-like-people-who-werent-captured-120317.

3. The more complicated truth is that McCain had several reasons to oppose the bill. There was bad blood between McCain and Senate majority leader Mitch McConnell, stemming from McConnell filing—and winning—a lawsuit to overturn a campaign finance reform law McCain had sponsored, which McCain considered to be one of his signature career achievements. McCain also stated publicly that he opposed the particular form the repeal bill took, preferring "repeal and replace" to "skinny repeal." Finally, McCain also stated publicly that he opposed the legislative process used to produce the bill, although procedural objections rarely produce opposition to a bill a Congress member otherwise prefers.

4. Karen Yourish, Larry Buchanan, and Alicia Parlapiano, "More Than 160 Republican Leaders Don't Support Donald Trump, Here's When They Reached Their Breaking Point," *The New York Times*, October 9, 2016, https://www.nytimes.com/interactive/2016/08/29/us/politics/at-least-110-republican-leaders-wont-vote-for-donald-trump-heres-when-they-reached-their-breaking-point.html.

5. John Sides, Michael Tesler, and Lynn Vavreck, *Identity Crisis: The 2016 Presidential Campaign and the Battle for the Meaning of America* (Princeton: Princeton University Press, 2019).

6. Michael X. Delli Carpini, and Scott Keeter, *What Americans Know About Politics and Why It Matters* (New Haven: Yale University Press 1996).

7. Gary C. Jacobson, Samuel Kernell, and Jeffrey Lazarus, "Assessing the President's Role as Party Agent in Congressional Elections: The Case of Bill Clinton in 2000," *Legislative Studies Quarterly*, 29, no. 1 (May 2004): 159–84.

8. Yourish, Buchanan, Parlapiano, "More Than."

9. Jake Sherman and Anna Palmer, *The Hill to Die On: The Battle for Congress and the Future of Trump's America* (Phoenix: Crown Publishing Group, 2019).

10. Yourish, Buchanan, Parlapiano, "More Than."

11. Frances E. Lee, *Insecure Majorities: Congress and the Perpetual Campaign* (Chicago: University of Chicago Press, 2016).

12. Tom Brune, "Reps Peter King, Lee Zeldin Endorse Donald Trump for President," *New York Newsday*, May 4, 2016, https://www.newsday.com/long-island/politics/spin-cycle/reps-peter-king-lee-zeldin-endorse-donald-trump-for-president-1.11762295.

13. Brune, 1 "Reps Peter King."

14. Hanna Trudo, "Mitch McConnell Issues Tepid Endorsement of Donald Trump," *Politico*, May 4, 2016, https://www.politico.com/story/2016/05/mitch-mcconnell-donald-trump-222826.

15. David Mayhew, *Congress: The Electoral Connection* (New Haven: Yale University Press, 1974); R. Douglas Arnold, *The Logic of Congressional Action* (New Haven: Yale University Press, 1991).

16. Gallup Organization, "Presidential Approval Ratings—Donald Trump," https://news.gallup.com/poll/203198/presidential-approval-ratings-donald-trump.aspx.

17. Sarah Binder, "Polarized We Govern?" *Center for Effective Public Management, Brookings Institute*, May 27, 2014, https://www.brookings.edu/wp-c ontent/uploads/2016/06/BrookingsCEPM_Polarized_ figReplacedTextRevTableRe v.pdf. For example Democrats enjoyed unified control in 2009–2010 and passed Obamacare and a massive economic stimulus package, and created the Consumer Finance Protection Bureau, among other achievements. In 2002–2006, Republicans passed Medicare Part D, No Child Left Behind, and the Patriot Act, among others.

18. This does not include the many executive orders Trump signed without Congress' input, nor the many Trump-nominated judges the Senate confirmed.

19. Barbara Sinclair, *Party Wars: Polarization and the Politics of National Policy Making* (Norman: University of Oklahoma Press, 2006); Jim Curry and Frances Lee, "Non-Party Government: Bipartisan Lawmaking and Party Power in Congress," *Perspectives on Politics*, 17, no. 1 (March 2019): 47–65.

20. George C. Edwards, and B. Dan Wood, "Who Influences Whom? The President, Congress, and The Media," *American Political Science Review*, 93, no. 2 (June 1999): 327, 344; Samuel Kernell, *Going Public: New Strategies of Presidential Leadership* (Washington, DC: CQ Press, 2006); George C. Edwards, *At the Margins: Presidential Leadership of Congress* (New Haven: Yale University Press, 1990); Richard Neustadt, *Presidential Power and the Modern Presidents* (Washington, DC: American Enterprise Institute, 1991).

21. Julie Hirschfeld Davis, Sheryl Gay Stolberg and Thomas Kaplan, "Trump Alarms Lawmakers with Disparaging Words for Haiti and Africa," *The New York Times*, January 11, 2018, https://www.nytimes.com/2018/01/11/us/politics/trump-sh ithole-countries.html.

22. Mark Landler, Helene Cooper and Eric Schmitt, "Trump to Withdraw U.S. Forces from Syria, Declaring 'We Have Won Against ISIS," *New York Times*, December 19, 2018, https://www.nytimes.com/2018/12/19/us/politics/trump-syria-t urkey-troop-withdrawal.html.

23. Haley Byrd, "Sanford: Tariffs Are an 'Experiment with Stupidity,'" *The Weekly Standard*, March 6, 2018, https://wwwwashingtonexaminer.com/weekly-stan dard/sanford-tariffs-are-an-experiment-with-stupidity.

24. Deb Reichmann, "Trump's Embrace of Saudi Arabia Causes GOP Rift," *Associated Press*, November 21, 2018, https://apnews.com/b5b88f75cc8c450c906f4 959744757c7.

25. Keith Krehbiel, *Pivotal Politics: A Theory of U.S. Lawmaking* (Chicago: University of Chicago Press, 1999).

26. Steve Mistler, "Susan Collins Reiterates Support for Mueller's Investigation," *Bangor Daily News*, March 20, 2018, https://bangordailynews.com/2018/03/20/politi cs/susan-collins-reiterates-support-for-muellers-investigation/.

27. Dave Boucher, "Corker: Firing Mueller Would Cause 'Total Upheaval,'" *Tennessean*, March 19, 2018, https://www.tennessean.com/story/news/politics/2018 /03/19/bob-corker-trump-mueller-upheaval-senate/440134002/.

28. Caroline Kelly, "Sen Jeff Flake: 'Worth Using a Little Leverage' to Get Mueller Bill Passed," *CNN*, November 30, 2018, https://www.cnn.com/2018/11/18/ politics/flake-mueller-judges-sotu-cnntv/index.html.

29. Emmarie Huetteman, "The Rocky Relationship of Donald Trump and Paul Ryan, a History," *The New York Times*, August 3, 2016, https://www.nytimes.com/2016/08/04/us/politics/paul-ryan-donald-trump.html.

30. Dierdre Walsh and Manu Raju, "Paul Ryan Rips Donald Trump Remarks as 'Textbook Definition of a Racist Comment,'" *CNN*, June 7, 2016, https://www.cnn.com/2016/06/07/politics/paul-ryan-donald-trump-racist-comment/index.html.

31. Justin Wise, "Paul Ryan Told GOP Lawmakers He Wouldn't 'Defend' Trump After 'Access Hollywood' Tape: Book," *The Hill*, April 7, 2019, https://thehill.com/homenews/administration/437763-paul-ryan-told-gop-lawmakers-he-wouldnt-ever-defend-trump-after.

32. Tim Alberta, "Inside Trump's Feud with Paul Ryan: It Was a Struggle for the Soul of the Republican Party, Trump Won," *Politico*, July 16, 2019, https://www.politico.com/magazine/story/2019/07/16/donald-trump-paul-ryan-feud-227360.

33. Alberta, "Inside Trump's Feud."

34. Wise, "Paul Ryan Told."

35. Alberta, "Inside Trump's Feud."

36. Christal Hayes, "Paul Ryan Clarifies Comments to Say Trump, Not Democrats, Will Win in 2020," *USA Today*, March 13, 2019, https://www.usatoday.com/story/news/politics/2019/03/13/paul-ryan-clarifies-say-trump-not-democrats-win-2020/3150508002/.

37. Gallup Organization, "Presidential Approval Ratings—Donald Trump," https://news.gallup.com/poll/203198/presidential-approval-ratings-donald-trump.aspx (accessed November 30, 2019).

38. Quinnipac, "Biden Retakes Lead as Warren Plunges," November 26, 2019, https://poll.qu.edu/national/release-detail?ReleaseID=3650.

39. Pew Research Center, "Most Border Wall Opponents, Supporters Say Shutdown Concessions are Unacceptable," *Pew Research Center*, January 16, 2019, https://www.people-press.org/2019/01/16/most-border-wall-opponents-supporters-say-shutdown-concessions-are-unacceptable/.

40. Gary C. Jacobson, "Extreme Referendum: Donald Trump and the 2018 Midterm Elections," *Political Science Quarterly*, 123, no. 1 (Spring 2019) 185–99.

41. This lesson was driven home in 2014 by Majority Leader Eric Cantor's (R-VA) shocking primary loss. That year Cantor was the second-ranking House Republican, reliably conservative and a fourteen-year House member. However, he also made some public statements indicating that he'd be open to compromising with Democrats to pass a bill on immigration reform. Suddenly, conservative media branded Cantor an "establishment Republican" (an epithet in the conservative media) and threw their weight behind Cantor's 2014 primary election opponent, political novice David Brat. Brat defeated Cantor despite Cantor's 40-1 edge in spending in one of the biggest political upsets in American history. For more on this, see Seth Masket, *No Middle Ground: How Informal Party Organizations Control Nominations and Polarize Legislatures* (Ann Arbor: University of Michigan Press, 2009) and Hans Hassell, "Party Control of Party Primaries: Party Influence in Nominations for the US Senate," *Journal of Politics*, 78, no. 1 (January 2016): 75–87.

42. Sean Illing, "A Former Republican Congress Member Explains What Happened to His Party," *Vox*, December 6, 2019, https://www.vox.com/policy-and-politics/2019/12/6/20993403/impeachment-hearing-trump-congress-david-jolly.

43. This does not mean Republican members were always in lock-step support behind Trump: it is possible to register opposition in less-public ways so that the media or the voters in your district do not find out. GOP members might undermine bills in committee, express doubts to confidants behind closed doors, or focus their less-public legislative efforts on conservative causes not championed by Trump; these behind-the-scenes strategies are how congressional Republicans in the 115th Congress frustrated Trump on most of the issues discussed above. But when the lights were on and people were paying attention, Republican members largely fell in line to protect their own political careers.

44. Jeff Flake, "Some Thoughts on This Election," *Medium*, July 20, 2016, https://medium.com/@JeffFlake/as-a-conservative-republican-i-believe-that-hillary-clinton-needs-to-be-defeated-in-november-6cb9a70686c3.

45. Burgess Everett, "Flake Takes on Trump—and Risks It All," *Politico*, October 19, 2017, https://www.politico.com/story/2017/10/19/jeff-flake-trump-arizona-243925.

46. Public Policy Polling, "Arizona Survey Results," *Public Policy Polling*, July 31–August 1, 2017, https://ourlivesontheline.org/wp-content/uploads/2017/08/PPP-Poll-Arizona.pdf.

47. Andrew Prokop, "Sen Jeff Flake vs. Donald Trump, Explained," *Vox*, October 24, 2017, https://www.vox.com/policy-and-politics/2017/8/9/16079244/jeff-flake-retires-trump.

48. Burgess Everett, "Corker Decides Against Reelection Bid, Sticks with Retirement," *Politico*, February 27, 2018, https://www.politico.com/story/2018/02/27/corker-tennessee-senate-retirement-midterms-423573.

49. David M. Drucker, "Congressional Republicans Hesitant to Antagonize Trump over Russia Probe," *Washington Examiner*, March 21, 2018, https://www.washingtonpost.com/politics/sen-ben-sasse-said-he-thinks-about-leaving-the-gop-every-morning/2018/09/09/8c131758-b439-11e8-a2c5-3187f427e253_story.html.

50. Matt Welch, "Shock Poll: Amash Down 16 Points in Republican Primary," *Reason*, June 12, 2019, https://reason.com/2019/06/12/shock-poll-amash-down-16-points-in-republican-primary/.

51. James Hohmann, "Ben Sasse Scores Trump Endorsement after Biting His Tongue and Keeping His Head Down," *The Washington Post*, September 11, 2019, https://www.washingtonpost.com/news/powerpost/paloma/daily-202/2019/09/11/daily-202-ben-sasse-scores-trump-endorsement-after-biting-his-tongue-and-keeping-his-head-down/5d78942588e0fa7bb93a8a94/; Christian Davenport, "Sen. Ben Sasse Said He Thinks About Leaving the GOP 'Every Morning,'" *The Washington Post*, September 9, 2018, https://www.washingtonpost.com/politics/sen-ben-sasse-said-he-thinks-about-leaving-the-gop-every-morning/2018/09/09/8c131758-b439-11e8-a2c5-3187f427e253_story.html.

52. Davenport, "Sen. Ben Sasse."

53. Hohmann, "Ben Sasse Scores."

54. Donald Trump, @realDonaldTrump, 2019, September 10, 2019, 9:23 p.m., https://twitter.com/realDonaldTrump/status/1171595113673347072?s=20.

55. Ted Barrett and Clare Foran, "How Lindsey Graham's Support for Trump—A Man He Once Called 'Jackass'—Has Evolved," *CNN*, October 1, 2019, https://www.cnn.com/2019/10/01/politics/lindsey-graham-defends-trump-whistleblower/index.html.

56. Jeremy Herb, "Senate Panel Approves Bill to Protect Special Counsel," *CNN*, April 26, 2018, https://www.cnn.com/2018/04/26/politics/special-counsel-protection-bill-passes-senate-committee/index.html.

57. Dana Bash, "Trump and Lindsey Graham: It's Complicated," *CNN*, October 17, 2019, https://www.cnn.com/2019/10/17/politics/lindsey-graham-donald-trump-complicated/index.html.

58. Manu Raju, "Hill Republicans Revolt Over Trump's Plans to Build Border Wall," *CNN*, February 6, 2017, https://www.cnn.com/2017/02/03/politics/border-wall-republicans/index.html.

59. Barrett and Foran, "How Lindsey."

60. Reuters, "Trump Accuses Democratic Congresswomen of Hating America, Says They Can Leave," *Reuters*, July 15, 2019, https://www.reuters.com/article/us-usa-trump-democrats-whitehouse/trump-accuses-democratic-congresswomen-of-hating-america-says-they-can-leave-idUSKCN1UA1Y7.

61. *CNN*, "Which GOP Lawmakers Have Condemned Trump's Tweet," *CNN*, July 15, 2019, https://www.cnn.com/2019/07/15/politics/republican-members-of-congress-trump-tweets/index.html.

62. Ralph Abraham, @RepAbraham. July 15, 2019, 3:59 p.m., https://twitter.com/repabraham/status/1150857471461855232?lang=en; Steve Daines @SteveDaines. July 15, 2019. 4:05 p.m., https://twitter.com/stevedaines/status/1150859069084905472?lang=en

63. Slade Gordon, "My Fellow Republicans, Please Follow the Facts," *The New York Times*, November 25, 2019, https://www.nytimes.com/2019/11/25/opinion/my-fellow-republicans-please-follow-the-facts.html; Joseph Bustos, "Obama Would Have Been Impeached for Trump's Alleged Actions, ex-SC GOP Congressman Says," *The State*, November 22, 2019, https://www.thestate.com/news/politics-government/article237665149.html; David Jolly, "You Can't Be Never-Trump and Be a Republican: Why This Congressman Left the GOP," *NBC News*, October 27, 2018, https://www.nbcnews.com/think/opinion/you-can-t-be-never-trump-be-republican-why-former-ncna922966; Grace Panetta, "Trump Will Likely Survive His Primary Challenge from Joe Walsh—But History Suggests That It Could Hurt Him in the General Election," *Business Insider*, September 23, 2019, https://www.businessinsider.com/joe-walsh-gop-primary-challenge-could-hurt-trump-2020-election-2019-8.

64. Illing, "A Former Republican."

65. Illing, "A Former Republican."

66. Deanna Paul, "Trump Greater than Lincoln? Republicans Polled Said Yes in a Party Lincoln Wouldn't Recognize," *The Washington Post*, December 5, 2019, https://www.washingtonpost.com/history/2019/12/03/republicans-prefer-trump-lincoln-poll-shows-todays-gop-couldnt-be-more-different/.

67. Gary Jacobson, "Strategic Politicians and the Dynamics of US House Elections," *American Political Science Review*, 83, no. 3 (September 1989): 773–93.

68. David C. W. Parker and Matthew Dull, "Divided We Quarrel: The Politics of Congressional Investigations, 1947-2004," *Legislative Studies Quarterly*, 34, no. 3 (August 2009): 319–345.

Chapter 3

Laboratories of Resistance?

#NeverTrumpers and the Opportunities and Limits of State and Local Autonomy in a Polarized Era

Anthony Sparacino[1]

A hallmark of federalism is diversity across jurisdictions within the larger polity. Daniel Elazar notes distinctions among states and localities in terms of overarching political cultures or, "the particular pattern[s] or orientation[s] to political action in which each political system is imbedded."[2] State and municipal populations can vary in terms of general partisan and ideological orientations, attitudes toward government, and, as a result of these, general voting patterns. States and localities also vary on a range of public policies from speed limits to voter registration requirements to the legality of recreational and medical marijuana. This chapter explores the importance of diversity of political cultures and policies across the states to the development and continuance of the #NeverTrump movement.

In today's polarized political climate, the result of this diversity across the states is often conflict between the national government and the state and/or local governments. This conflict often aligns along national partisan divisions. Indeed, a host of scholarship, including recent work by David Hopkins, underscores the importance of geography and state-based electoral rules for the shape and scope of contemporary partisan polarization.[3] In terms of policy, Democratic governors, attorneys general, state legislators, mayors, and other municipal officials have, not surprisingly, been critical agents in challenging President Trump's rhetoric and policy initiatives. In 2018, for instance, California passed a series of "sanctuary state" laws that restricted local law enforcement from cooperating with federal immigration officials, encouraged the state's attorney general to visit federal immigration detention centers, and instituted penalties on businesses that voluntarily allowed federal officials to inspect their worksites.[4] Such efforts reflect the United States' federal governing structure, which offers interests based in states and localities means of challenging national policies.

Yet, the focus on the use of the powers of the states by one party to challenge the program of the other party, what some scholars have labeled partisan federalism, misses the ways in which the American party system structures *intraparty* contestation.[5] Political parties are not monoliths, even in today's polarized political climate. Rather, federalism allows for diversity *within* political parties and this institutional arrangement has allowed for resistance to President Trump from within his own party. Republicans elected to state and local offices, especially, though not exclusively, those in "blue" and "purple" states and municipalities, have often voiced concerns over, and sometimes opposition to, President Trump and the national party's governing agenda.

State and local #NeverTrumpers' resistance to the president is rooted in two basic sets of concerns. The first set relates to electoral motivations. Put simply, in a political environment in which the presidency is so central to the public's understanding of partisanship and, in the case of President Trump, so much attention is paid to the president's personality, state and local Republican officials must be wary of how voters are responding to Trump and his agenda within their jurisdictions. Being a member of the president's party has consequences. Blue-state Republicans are particularly vulnerable to antipathy toward the president in that they are already operating in hostile electoral environments. The same can be said for red state Republicans operating in blue counties, especially in urban areas with large numbers of minority voters as well as suburban areas that have been trending purple or even blue in recent electoral cycles.

A second set of concerns regards the president's policy agenda. Of course, Republicans in state and local office must be conscious of how the president's policies are being viewed by voters in connection with electoral outcomes. However, policies coming out of Washington can also have tangible effects on state and local governments and their constituents, such as the amount of federal money going to states and localities toward education, healthcare, and transportation initiatives; the number and invasiveness of federal regulations imposed on state-run programs; and even the level of coordination among law enforcement agencies across levels of government, such as the ability to share information on immigrants subject to criminal investigations. In sum, federal policymaking affects the resources available to state and local governments and the discretion they have in developing and executing public policy within their jurisdictions. Thus, the policies emerging from Washington affect the abilities of GOP officials in the states to govern.

In this chapter, I illustrate how a number of state and local Republicans have engaged in resistance to candidate and now President Trump and how these two sets of motivations—electoral concerns and policy differences—manifested within this resistance. I first discuss state and local resistance to Trump within the context of elections, including the 2016 nomination contest and general election and elections since President Trump took office, emphasizing the electoral concerns of these actors. I then discuss resistance to Trump while in office, emphasizing policy-based disagreement across levels of government among members of the Republican Party. I conclude with reflections or "lessons learned" from the case of state and local #NeverTrumpers in order to better understand the role federalism plays in political party development.

STATE AND LOCAL #NEVERTRUMPERS IN THE 2016 ELECTION

During the 2016 Republican nomination contest, state and local #NeverTrumpers emphasized the Trump candidacy's implications for the collective image of the Republican Party, especially its impact on down-ballot races. Numerous state and local officials reacted to Trump's initial announcement of his candidacy in the same way many national party officials responded: they did not believe he could win the nomination or the general election; he was an extreme voice that did not represent the party's base; and he may have been using the announcement as a publicity stunt that could be detrimental to the party's collective reputation. For instance, Texas Governor Rick Perry, a presidential candidate who later became Trump's Secretary of Energy, called Trump a "cancer to conservatism" and a "toxic mix of demagoguery, mean-spiritedness and nonsense."[6] Trump's unique style, celebrity status, and lack of traditional qualifications for elected office, prior service as an elected official for instance, raised concerns among many party elites about the potential implications of a Trump candidacy on the collective image of the Republican Party.

State-level politicians, especially governors, when running for national office, especially the presidency, have often run as outsiders. Theodore Roosevelt, Woodrow Wilson, Franklin Roosevelt, Jimmy Carter, Ronald Reagan, Bill Clinton, and George W. Bush all served as governor before entering the White House and, in various ways and to varying degrees, challenged the orthodoxy of the party to which they belonged.[7] Carter, the "peanut farmer" and engineer from Georgia, ran a personal, candidate-centered, campaign in 1976 and was not the favorite of the national party establishment. Reagan, in 1976, ran a strong insurgent campaign against President Gerald Ford. Yet, governors have run for the White House based on their records in the states, in terms of both policy accomplishments and electoral victories. That is, they have run as *Washington* outsiders. Trump ran a very different type of outsider campaign. He not only had never served in office in Washington but had never held elected office at any level. He never served in a federal agency (in contrast to Herbert Hoover) or in the military (in contrast to Dwight Eisenhower).

The 2016 GOP presidential primary field included nine then current and former GOP governors, each with their own stories to tell. For instance, Ohio Governor John Kasich began his own presidential bid touting his electability, noting his strong showing among women, moderates, and African Americans in his 2014 reelection in the all-important swing state, voters that many Republicans felt they needed to do a better job of courting and who Trump seemed to be isolating. According to exit polls, Kasich carried over 25 percent of African American voters and 51 percent of urban voters in his 2014 gubernatorial race.[8] Significantly, Kasich won Cuyahoga County, a Democratic stronghold that includes the city of Cleveland, by 7 percentage points. Trump, who carried Ohio by eight points two years later, lost the county by 35 percentage points.[9] In this way, Kasich's electoral story reflected the calls for the GOP to expand its base made in the Growth and Opportunity Project Report (GOPR), put together by the Republican National Committee in the aftermath of the 2012 election.[10]

Other Republican governors seeking the nomination made similar types of arguments regarding their electoral viability in a post-Obama era. Jeb Bush boasted of two convincing electoral victories in the critical state of Florida. In particular, Bush had a strong showing among Hispanic voters in his 2002 reelection campaign.[11] Scott Walker of Wisconsin could boast winning a "blue wall" state not once but three times, including surviving a high-profile recall election.

After two consecutive losses in presidential elections, especially with the party receiving diminished support from Hispanics, Asian Americans, and women, these types of electability arguments from those not serving in Washington seemed to resonate with many within and outside of the party. The stage seemed set for a Washington outsider with a record of broad-based electoral coalition building to obtain the GOP nomination. The fact that this did not happen surprised many. For instance, Dan Balz, long-time and well-respected reporter for the *Washington Post*, commenting on the governors' inability to overcome the Trump phenomenon, noted,

> In the 2014 campaign, RGA [Republican Governors Association] leaders had touted their members as leading the party and, more subtly, as the grown-ups of the GOP. Governors, they noted, were providing models of successful conservative governance that could be sold in 2016 as a contrast to the record of

President Obama's administration . . . [but] That kind of experience has been a tough sell in this campaign.[12]

Put simply, Donald Trump's outsider status exceeded that of the governors running in the race. Trump ran as a different type of outsider, one who challenged the party's ideological orthodoxy. This perspective was also a mainstream view, embraced by many #NeverTrumpers. From this perspective, GOP candidates needed to de-emphasize cultural and racial issues in order to win elections in a changing, diversifying, electoral landscape.

This view of the GOP's path back to electoral success was not limited to his rivals for the nomination. Blue and swing state Republicans especially voiced concerns over what Trump's rhetoric meant for the national party brand. Massachusetts State Representative Keiko Orrall, for instance, noted that "I take great offense to the things he's said about women and minorities, and it is a very unfortunate position that he's put us in. I find it unbelievable that he is out in front because he is saying things that are not Republican; they're not Republican values."[13] Embattled Illinois Governor Bruce Rauner, who like Trump came to executive office with a business as opposed to a political background, notably avoided a Trump campaign rally in his state in November 2015. For blue-state Republicans, association with Trump was seen as imperiling their ability to win much needed minority and women voters. An unpopular candidate at the top of the ticket risked undermining the campaigns of Republicans down-ballot, including governors and state legislators.

Concerns over Trump's viability as the Republican nominee and subsequent effects on party candidates down-ballot continued even as Trump proved to be able to win state primaries and not just lead public opinion polls. At an RGA meeting in late February, Karl Rove participated in a session in which governors and other party elites sought to find a way to block Trump.[14] Governor Susana Martinez of New Mexico, the first female Latin American elected governor and then chairwoman of the RGA, refused to say whether or not she would support Trump in the general election if he became the nominee. Massachusetts Governor Charlie Baker, along with a slew of other governors from blue, swing, and even deeply red states voiced concern over Trump's potential influence on down-ballot races. Even the notably divisive Maine Governor Paul LePage called for the RGA to issue a letter on behalf of the party's governors disavowing Trump's candidacy, citing Trump's divisiveness. This move was not taken.[15]

LePage's initial opposition to Trump is often seen as surprising given that the former governor said, in endorsing the real estate mogul a short while later, that "I was Trump before Donald Trump became popular. So I think I should support him since we're one of the same cloth."[16] LePage initially supported New Jersey Governor Chris Christie's short-lived bid. Christie, a former RGA chairman, could boast having won two elections in a blue state, and in his reelection bid, had received a slew of endorsements from state and locally elected Democrats.[17] Christie and LePage announced their support for Trump on the same day. Yet, neither of these governors have run for elected office since 2016. Other governors who had initially endorsed Christie, including Baker and Maryland Governor Larry Hogan, would be up for reelection in 2016 or 2018. These governors did not move to support Trump early on and have been among Trump's staunchest critics from within the party. Again, electoral incentives seem to have, at least in part, motivated resistance to Trump's candidacy.

By the time of Christie's endorsement, Trump had won three of four primaries and caucuses, including South Carolina's winner-take-all primary. At around the same time, Florida senator Marco Rubio seemed to be emerging as the favored "establishment" candidate, picking up several endorsements from sitting governors, including Martinez. Bush, the one-time frontrunner, exited the race after the February 20 South Carolina primary, leaving only Kasich as an alternative for the "establishment GOP" vote to Rubio. Trump, however, picked up the endorsement of former candidate Christie, an endorsement that received ample media attention, overshadowing the litany of endorsements received by Rubio. Trump continued to amass victories in the primaries in March as the GOP field winnowed. On March 1, "Super Tuesday," Trump won seven of the eleven contests held, yet he continued to win with only 30–40 percent of the vote in most of those races.

As Trump's nomination became more and more likely, opposition to Trump among state and local officials softened, though concerns over his divisive rhetoric and policy proposals endured. Governor Martinez continued to refuse to say whether she would support Trump in the general election. She did, however, voice opposition to Trump's proposal to build a wall along the southern border, noting that "we [in New Mexico] have a lot of exports that go to Mexico, South America and Central America, and we want to maintain those relationships."[18] Trump responded to Martinez's lack of support by unleashing "a blistering assault on the governor" at a campaign rally in New Mexico in late May. Trump blamed the governor for allowing Syrian refugees into the state (a false claim), the state's high unemployment numbers, and elevated levels of New Mexico residents receiving food stamps.[19] In this way, Trump made an example of Martinez, despite her status as the only Hispanic female Republican governor. It was becoming increasingly clear that criticism of Trump resulted in isolation from the national party and from the Republican base.

Martinez ultimately attended the GOP convention, leading her state's delegation and casting her ballot for Trump. Other governors, including

Kasich, Baker, Hogan, Rauner, Brian Sandoval of Nevada, and Rick Snyder of Michigan refused to attend the convention. A spokesperson for Snyder, the governor of a state Trump would barely win that November, noted that "Michigan has some pressing challenges right now and state issues are his [Snyder's] foremost priority."[20]

Even before Trump's general election victory, other state leaders began to make overtures to Trump. Arizona Governor Doug Ducey led his state's delegation at the convention and was noted for his steadfastness in his desire to keep Arizona red in 2016.[21] Former Mississippi governor and RNC chairman Haley Barbour reportedly urged GOP governors to rally to Trump at an RGA meeting in Aspen a few weeks after the convention, arguing that maintaining party unity was key to the party's success in November.[22] On the other hand, significant weakness at the top of the ticket could be detrimental down-ballot. For instance, though Arizona is trending blue, party unity and maintaining high levels of turnout among the party base rather than reaching out to independent voters, was seen as important in terms of the party's performance down-ballot.

Leading into the general election, especially after the release of the Access Hollywood tapes, state and local politicians including Martinez, like many national Republican officials, pulled back their endorsements of Trump. Ultimately, eleven sitting Republican governors refused to publicly support Trump in the general election. Fred Malek noted at the time that "you have an unheard-of number looking to their own election prospects and feeling they are better served by not supporting him [Trump]."[23]

The results of the 2016 general election were just as surprising, if not more so, than that of the GOP nomination contest. Republicans found themselves in control of not just the White House and both chambers of Congress but thirty-three governorships and sixty-eight of ninety-nine state legislative chambers. Straight ticket voting between presidential and senatorial races hit an all-time high in 2016. Levels of straight ticket voting between presidential and gubernatorial races, however, dipped somewhat from that seen in 2012.[24] Ultimately, the results of the election demonstrated the strength of partisanship in voting behavior even with a nonconventional candidate at the top of the Republican ticket.

ELECTORAL CONCERNS IN 2017, THE MIDTERMS, AND 2019

Off year elections in the Trump era suggest that many state and local races have been nationalized, with evaluations of the president increasingly on the minds of voters even in balloting for state and local elections. In 2017, for instance, Virginia's gubernatorial race featured an establishment Republican, Ed Gillespie, who had chaired the RNC and came incredibly close to defeating popular Democratic senator Mark Warner in 2014, against Democrat Ralph Northam. Gillespie survived a close primary contest against Corey Stewart, who had embraced Trump. He also made MS-13, a gang frequently mentioned by the president, a focus of his general election campaign. Jim Geraghty of the *National Review* noted,

> If Gillespie loses, some Trump-friendly Republicans will no doubt conclude that northern Virginia's increasing ethnic diversity and social progressivism have made the state unwinnable for Republicans and that, with nothing to lose, GOP candidates ought to let their angry, populist freak flag fly. But if Gillespie wins, it will show that traditional pre-Trump Republicanism can still prevail in a purple state. And in some future cycle, Gillespie will be able to sit in the back seat of another car, telling some other future GOP gubernatorial candidate how to drive.[25]

Gillespie lost that race, due in part to the drift of suburban voters in northern Virginia and the Virginia Beach area to the Democratic party. For instance, Trump narrowly won Virginia Beach and Chesapeake counties in Southeastern Virginia. Gillespie narrowly lost both counties.[26]

The 2018 midterm elections only reinforced several of the concerns state and local officials raised regarding the effects of Trump's presidency on down-ballot elections. Despite Trump not being on the ticket, the results of the midterms have been painted as a referendum on Trump's presidency. Gary Jacobson, for instance, notes that "Trump's embrace of the election as a referendum on his presidency, while a reflexive appropriation of center stage, also acknowledged a reality that his person and conduct had created. From the beginning of his campaign for the White House and throughout his first two years in office, Trump's words and actions provoked the most intense and divergent responses to a president yet measured."[27] Moreover, "if asked to choose, most Republicans put Trump ahead of his party."[28] The unmistakable truth is that the Grand Old Party has become Trump's party.

While Republicans benefited greatly from political geography in expanding their majority in the Senate, they lost control of the House of Representatives. More importantly for our purposes are the results of elections for state offices. Thirty-six gubernatorial elections were held in 2018. Republicans had a net loss of six seats, dropping from control of thirty-three governorships to twenty-seven. Democrats also gained ground in state legislatures, picking up control of six legislative chambers, from thirty-one to thirty-seven out of ninety-eight. Included in these gains were control over the Colorado State Senate and both house of the New Hampshire legislature.[29]

Several of these races were notable in terms of the implications for the #NeverTrump movement. Three Republican governors who had been critical of the president—Hogan, Baker, and Phil Scott of Vermont—handily won their reelection bids in deeply blue states. These victories ensured that several high-profile governors that had been critical of the president would have continued opportunities to engage in discussions over the direction of the national party, and have successful electoral campaigns to use as examples of how to build winning coalitions. Baker's victory was particularly impressive, winning over two-thirds of the vote and carrying every congressional district in the state, all of which elected Democratic members of Congress. Baker, at an RGA meeting after the midterms, drew an implicit but obvious contrast with the president said that he "relished being 'called the most boring governor in the history of Massachusetts.'"[30] Hogan, who became only the second Republican governor in Maryland's history to win reelection, argued that the president's lack of popularity hurt Maryland Republicans down-ballot, including losses in county executive races that the party had won in 2014.[31]

Other state results showed that the Republican Party's inability to win over minority voters could cost them leading into 2020. In Nevada, a swing state with a burgeoning Hispanic voting bloc, Republican gubernatorial candidate Adam Laxalt, the former state attorney general, lost to Democrat Steve Sisolak. Laxalt received an endorsement from the president but not from the sitting GOP Governor Sandoval. In Texas, Republicans lost twelve seats in the state House of Representatives. Governor Greg Abbott, while winning by a respectable margin, underperformed relative to his 2014 election. He received 42 percent of the Hispanic vote, according to exit polls, higher than many other GOP officials nationwide (Abbott won 44 percent of Hispanic voters in 2014), thanks in part to a substantial outreach effort. However, even here he slightly underperformed relative to 2014, and Hispanics made up a larger share of the Texas electorate.[32]

Other state-level elections showed that association with the president limited the extent to which Republican candidates could build support among non-Republican voters. In Wisconsin, which barely and surprisingly went for Trump in 2016, Walker narrowly lost a bid for a full third term. According to exit polls, attitudes toward President Trump were strong predictors of support in the gubernatorial race. Eighty-eight percent of those who disapproved of the president supported Democrat Tony Evers, while 87 percent of those who approved of the president backed Walker.[33] Unfortunately for Walker, more voters disapproved than approved of the president.[34]

In ruby-red Kansas, Republican secretary of state Kris Kobach, who took hardline positions on immigration and echoed the president's claims regarding voter fraud in 2016, lost the gubernatorial race to Democrat Laura Kelly. Particularly noteworthy in this campaign was the number of Republican officials who broke ranks to support Kelly even after the president backed the controversial Kobach. Among the Republicans to back Kelly were former governors Bill Graves and Mike Hayden. While third party candidate Greg Orman won 6 percent of the vote, Kobach polled over thirteen points behind Trump's 2016 vote share. Kobach's loss is partly attributable to falling support for Republicans in affluent suburban areas that were once a bedrock of support for the GOP. In Johnson County, which is part of the Kansas City metropolitan area, for instance, Kobach underperformed Trump by over 8 percentage points. In Shawnee County, which includes Topeka, Kobach underperformed Trump by over 12 points.[35]

Suburban losses for the GOP continued in 2019. In a hotly contested gubernatorial race in Kentucky, Matt Bevin lost his reelection bid to Democratic Attorney General Andy Beshear in a strongly Republican state, initially refusing to concede the race because of claims of "voting irregularities."[36] In Virginia, Democrats seized control of both chambers of the state legislature for the first time in decades, building in particular on gains made in the DC suburbs.

#NEVERTRUMPERS AND INTERGOVERNMENTAL RELATIONS: POLICY DIFFERENCES IN A NATIONALLY POLARIZED AND PRESIDENCY-CENTERED ERA

The Republican Party has long championed state autonomy, often as a means of limiting the size and scope of national governing authority. Richard Nixon and Ronald Reagan both proposed their own versions of "New Federalism," seeking to devolve authority back to the states.[37] The 2016 Republican platform echoed this sentiment: "Every violation of state sovereignty by federal officials is not merely a transgression of one unit of government against another; it is an assault on the liberties of individual Americans."[38] In a statement put out by the RGA after the inauguration, Republican governors noted that "With a Republican presidency, a strong majority of Republican governors in our state capitals, and a Republican Congress, the new possibilities and opportunities are endless as we empower Americans and restore the balance between states and the federal government."[39]

Trump and the Republican Congress's approach to intergovernmental relations has been exceptionally partisan and has had significant implications for Republicans, especially in blue states. For one, early attempts to replace the Affordable Care Act caused concern among GOP governors and state legislators in states that had expanded Medicaid and established health insurance exchanges, which included Ohio and New Mexico. An outright repeal of the law, a hallmark of national GOP messaging since the law's passage, had the potential to result in significant cuts in federal aid as well as jumps in the levels of the uninsured in these jurisdictions.

State governors, as Jennifer Jensen has argued, must often weigh the interests of their states against those of the national party.[40] This tension was on display during the Obamacare repeal and replace effort. While this effort failed, the effects of the intergovernmental lobby, including Republican governors, have been found to be modest. Thompson, Gusmano, and Shinohara, for instance, argue that "most Republican governors behaved more as members of a vertical partisan coalition than as defenders of insurance coverage in their states."[41] Republican governors called for reforms allowing for more state flexibility in implementing healthcare policy and some, including Walker, voiced support for new requirements for Medicaid recipients such as drug screening and work requirements.[42] Walker, who refused to expand Medicaid under the ACA, noted that he "thought Medicaid is for people living in poverty."[43]

Nevertheless, there were *some* meaningful and high-profile critiques of the various iterations of repeal and replace legislation by Republican governors, and these critiques were often based on state interests. Christie, for instance, noted that a proposal put forward by Senators Lindsey Graham and Bill Cassidy would cost his state $4 billion.[44] Kasich and Sandoval were particularly vocal in their opposition to any legislation that would increase the percentage of the population without coverage. Kasich, who had expanded Medicaid as governor, noted that "I think there are some very conservative Republicans in the House who are going to say, 'just get rid of the whole thing'. . . and that's not acceptable when you have 20 million people, or 700,000 people in my state, because where do the mentally ill go? Where do the drug addicted go?"[45]

Kasich, along with fellow governors Asa Hutchison of Arkansas, Rick Snyder of Michigan, and Sandoval sent a letter to Senate Majority Leader Mitch McConnell, in which they argued that the states should be granted more flexibility on issues relating to the scope of benefits covered under state Medicaid programs. Flexibility served two purposes. One the one hand, the national party could obtain a victory by passing an Obamacare replacement. On the other hand, state-level officials could offset potential cuts in federal aid to the states. In sum, though the GOP governors' calls for flexibility offered a means for the national party to strike down Obamacare while preserving a commitment to state autonomy, the repeal and replace effort ultimately failed.

The passage of the 2017 tax law also demonstrated the extent to which intergovernmental relations has become partisan. Changes to provisions relating to state and local tax deductions (SALT) adversely affected high-income residents in high tax states, particularly those on the West Coast and in the Northeast, while benefiting lower income property owners in the rest of the country.[46] As John Kincaid notes, "Elimination [of SALT deductions] would also produce substantial downward political pressure on state and local taxes," thus affecting state budgets.[47] Again, while these changes mainly adversely affected states controlled by Democrats, such policies also hurt several states controlled by Republican governors. Additionally, within states, the tax law disproportionately hurt residents in relatively affluent suburbs, areas where Republicans have proven to be increasingly vulnerable in the Trump era.[48]

Trump also deployed state and local actors in his efforts to sell his immigration and crime policies. For instance, in a series of roundtable meetings Trump hosted, broadcast by Fox News, these officials largely touted the president's actions. At a roundtable in Bethpage, New York, Nassau County Commissioner Patrick Ryder, for instance, noted the deaths of six teenagers at the hands of MS-13 gang members in his county and touted local law enforcement's partnership with ICE and federal officials. Trump, on several occasions, noted that Democrats were inhibiting efforts to handle the issue.[49] In this way, Trump has not only used the formal authorities of the presidency to attempt to bring the states and localities in line but has included allied state and local officials in the political messaging coming from the White House.

The president has also engaged with state and local officials in using the federal executive branch's investigatory powers on the issue of voter fraud and election law. States vary on a number of procedural elements of elections, from deadlines for voter registration to the number of hours polls are open on Election Day to the design of the ballots themselves. In May of 2017, President Trump signed Executive Order 13799, establishing the Presidential Advisory Commission on Election Integrity (PEIC) with Vice President Pence serving as the Commission's chair and Kobach serving as the group's vice-chairman. Unlike previous federal efforts to investigate voter irregularities, such as that chaired by former President Jimmy Carter and Secretary of State James Baker in the mid-2000s, the PEIC's membership did not have a balance of Democrats and Republicans. The Executive Order gave the president sole authority to appoint members "who shall include individuals with knowledge and experience in elections, election management, election fraud detection, and voter integrity efforts, and any other individuals with knowledge or experience that the president determines to be of value to the Commission."[50]

Responses by a number of states to the Commission's request for information varied but generally did not satisfy the desires of the administration. California Secretary of State Alex Padilla was quoted as saying that his state's "participation would only serve to legitimize the false and already debunked claims of massive voter fraud made by the president, the Vice President and Mr. Kobach."[51] Other states, including those with Republican Secretaries of State cited state law restrictions on sharing personal election data based on privacy grounds. Indiana secretary of state Connie Lawson pointed out, for example, that "Indiana law doesn't permit the Secretary of State to provide personal information requested by Secretary Kobach."[52] Even Republican controlled states were willing to only submit data to the Commission that was already publicly available.

Despite Trump's partisan approach to intergovernmental relations, some GOP leaders within the states have used their positions to voice opposition to the Trump agenda. In terms of immigration, for instance, Illinois Gov. Rauner signed legislation preventing state and local law enforcement activities based solely on federal detainers. Hogan joined a bipartisan group of Maryland elected officials in voicing opposition to Trump's decision to rescind DACA.[53] A press release issued by the governor's office argued that "focusing immigration efforts on children and young people, many of whom have never known another home and came to this country by no fault of their own, should not be where enforcement efforts are concentrated. Instead of targeting innocent kids, we should be targeting criminals."[54]

On environmental policy, Hogan, Baker, and Phil Scott became the only three Republican governors to join with nineteen states controlled by Democrats in the U.S. Climate Alliance, a group formed after Trump withdrew the United States from the Paris Agreement on climate change. These efforts are consequential from a policy standpoint. Hogan and Baker have both worked with Democratic state legislatures on environmental issues such as waste management. Baker, for his part, has called for a comprehensive statewide plan to deal with the effects of climate change. While the Trump administration, through executive action, has worked to reduce federal environmental regulations, some Republican governors and state legislators have worked to reduce greenhouse gas emissions in their jurisdictions.

In summary, the Trump administration's approach to intergovernmental relations has created a number of challenges for Republicans at the state level, especially those attempting to govern blue states. Changes to the healthcare law, the federal tax code, and environmental regulations, among other policy changes, have effects on state and municipal budgets and governing capacities. Republican officials at the state and local levels must grapple with these effects, which can highlight the inherent tensions between the interests of specific state and/or local jurisdictions and those of the national party.

CONCLUSION: LESSONS LEARNED FOR A POST-TRUMP REPUBLICAN PARTY

As of this writing, the likelihood of #NeverTrumpers blocking Trump's nomination in 2020 appears miniscule. #NeverTrumpers currently have alternatives to Trump in the primary in former Massachusetts Governor William Weld and former Illinois Congressman Joe Walsh. However, it is exceptionally difficult to oust a sitting president, especially one who now has a strong approval rating among Republican voters nationally. Beyond the plebiscitary nature of the current presidential nominating system, the Trump reelection campaign has initiated efforts to ensure that "the 2020 GOP convention is free of any anti-Trump mayhem."[55] The Trump campaign is attempting to manage delegate selection in the states, demonstrating that a president's control of a party often includes tight supervision over the party as organization in addition to strong ties to voters provided by rhetorical leadership.[56] This has included a number of states cancelling their primaries, a move that is not unprecedented—a number of states did so in 2004 when George W. Bush was in office—but somewhat surprising given that there are announced challengers to the president in the nomination contest.

Unlike the pre-McGovern-Fraser era when the likes of New York Governor Thomas Dewey and other moderate GOP governors were able to control state delegations to block the nomination of conservative stalwart Robert Taft and throw the nomination to Dwight Eisenhower, today's state and local officials only have indirect means of contributing to the outcomes of presidential nomination contests. Indeed, the emergence of a party system more centered on presidential leadership than in the past has provided numerous challenges for #NeverTrump Republicans, even those at the state and local levels.

Nevertheless, the decentralized nature of America's federal system continues to provide a degree of autonomy for #NeverTrumpers to develop alternatives to the national Republican program within their jurisdictions. Moreover, the nature of American federalism will continue to provide incentives for state and local party officials to present competing public policy visions with those of national party leaders, even those bolstered by the "bully pulpit" of a strong president with high approvals among the base of the party.

The case of #NeverTrumpers situated within the states suggests a few key lessons concerning the nature of the contemporary American party system. First, *Trump's impact on the national Republican Party's brand is having effects on the outcomes of elections down-ballot, which sometimes incentivizes state and local GOP elected officials to resist the president, especially in blue and purple states and localities.* Elected officials across levels share a common label and are often associated with a particular party reputation or "brand." Party brands provide, as Heersink notes, "an understanding among voters as to what the party's positions are at a given moment in time. Such brands, or party images, are important to parties and candidates because they provide voters with information that lowers the cost of becoming informed about individual candidates."[57]

That the Republican brand is reflective of the president is true not just in elections for national office but for state and local offices as well. In the case of Trump and the GOP, the president's approval rating consistently being below 50 percent, especially in blue states, coupled with the emergence of a presidency-centered party system, has created incentives for #NeverTrumpers to be active in critiquing the president. Polling data from the *Morning Consult* indicates that the president's net approval rating as of June 2019 was negative in twenty-nine states, including eight that he carried in 2016.[58] State and local #NeverTrumpers must therefore navigate difficult terrain running as Republicans, especially in states and localities with significant numbers of minority, urban, and liberal voters. A lack of popularity at the top of the ticket could have significant implications down-ballot, especially in jurisdictions already prone to electing Democrats.

In certain cases, state and local Republican officials have gone beyond simply critiquing the president. For instance, Georgia Governor Brian Kemp resisted pressure from the White House in filling a senate seat vacated by retiring senator Johnny Isakson. Kemp appointed Kelly Loeffler, a Georgia businesswoman over Congressman Doug Collins, an ally of the president. Again, competing views on how the GOP could succeed in 2020 and beyond were pitted against each other. As Nadler and Miller note:

> The tension between Republicans underscores a divide within the party on how the GOP can best position itself for success in 2020: by firing up and turning out Trump conservatives or pivoting to try to win back suburban woman and moderates who have fled the party since Trump's election. Kemp's selection of Loeffler, and the support she's received from Senate leadership, signals that party leaders recognize the perils of catering to the right and hitching every wagon to the president.[59]

Still other state and local Republicans, especially those representing suburban districts that have been trending away from the GOP in recent election cycles, have taken the dramatic step of switching parties. New Jersey state senator Dawn Marie Addiego, for instance, in taking this step, noted that the "core values that originally drew me to the Republican Party have not changed, but the party which once echoed the vision of Ronald Reagan no longer exists."[60] As political scientist Antoine Yoshinaka has noted, "We can't underestimate the effect of the president on the party brand and what it means to be a Republican or a Democrat," including at the state and local levels.[61]

Yet, we must recognize that #NeverTrumpers must be cautious in their resistance to the president. Party switchers, as Yoshinaka notes, "do get punished by voters who aren't particularly fond of politicians who switch sides. As an act of self-preservation, it's not always the most effective one."[62]

While party switchers may be wooed with favorable committee assignments or campaign resources, these officials are entering a party with a vastly different electoral base and a group of colleagues who they may have, until very recently, been working against on a regular basis.

Moreover, Trump's approach to engaging with other elites within the party (including #NeverTrumpers who stayed in the party) has been exceptional in that he appears willing to call out members of his own party who do not support his positions, as the case of Governor Martinez above illustrates. All presidents must grapple with diversity within their party's coalition and recent Republican presidents, including George W. Bush, have sought to use their influence over the party organizations to shape the party in ways that make the coalition more amenable to the desires of the president. Trump has taken this element of the president's relationship with his party including its members in the states, directly to Twitter, elevating the centrality of the president to the party in the mind of the public.

Second, *the governing agenda emerging from the Trump White House and the national GOP regarding intergovernmental relations has forced state and local Republican officials to weigh the interests of the national party against state and local interests.* Ultimately, "The Trump administration is finding, much as the Obama administration found, that its efforts to reassert leadership provoke sustained resistance from emboldened state and local stakeholders, who counter with both legal and de facto challenges to executive actions, even in domains where the federal government's plenary authority remains intact."[63] As illustrated above, changes to national policies concerning healthcare, taxation, and even immigration have consequences for state governments. Although governors, state legislators, attorneys general, and even mayors derive their governing authority from elections and state constitutions, their abilities to govern are not independent from decisions made in Washington.

Still, #NeverTrumpers at the state and local level can also deploy their unique governing prerogatives to contest the implementation of President Trump's agenda. While the bulk of legal resistance to these actions has come from Democrats, #NeverTrump Republicans, particularly those in blue states, have voiced their own concerns over Trump's policies and have sometimes acted in ways that have cut against the Trump agenda. Refusing to implement a policy backed by the president, or pressing forward with a policy opposed by the president, does more than change policy on the ground within a particular jurisdiction—it offers an alternative that can be considered at the national level or in other jurisdictions by members of the party. The interests of individual states and localities, therefore, can come into conflict with the interests of the national party and, in some cases, *can be brought to bear on the interests of the national party.*

Finally, and relatedly, *the decentralization of American party politics offers pathways for change within the party.* As noted above, governors have often been contenders for the parties' presidential nominations. They have often run as outsiders to Washington with distinctive governing records within their states, taking records cultivated at the state level and adapting them to national political campaigns and, potentially, toward developing national governing agendas.[64] In sum, states and localities remain important spaces for American political development both because they can be important sites of national partisan contestation and because they can provide models for future national political developments. As such, state and local political arenas will likely be important spaces for #NeverTrump conservatives to develop feasible alternatives to the president's political coalition and policy agenda going forward if the movement is to have an effect on the national Republican Party in the post-Trump era.

NOTES

1. The author would like to thank several colleagues for their feedback on early iterations of this chapter including Richard Burke, B. Kal Munis, Rachel Smilan-Goldstein, Tyler Syck, Nicholas Jacobs, and Dan Palazzolo.

2. Daniel J. Elazar, *American Federalism: A View from the States* (New York: Thomas Y. Crowell, 1966), 84–88.

3. David A. Hopkins, *Red Fighting Blue: How Geography and Electoral Rules Polarize American Politics* (New York: Cambridge University Press, 2017).

4. John Myers, "Federal Judge Denies Trump Administration Effort to Block California 'sanctuary' Law," *Los Angeles Times*, July 5, 2018, https://www.latimes.com/politics/la-pol-ca-sanctuary-law-ruling-20180705-story.html#.

5. See, for instance, Jessica Bulman-Pozen, "Partisan Federalism," *Harvard Law Review*, 127, no. 4 (February 2014): 1078–146.

6. Maggie Haberman and Jonathan Martin, "Blustery Poll Leader Vexes G.O.P. Rivals," *The New York Times*, July 23, 2015, A19.

7. See Saladin M. Ambar, *How Governors Built the Modern American Presidency* (Philadelphia: University of Pennsylvania Press, 2012); Saladin M. Ambar, "The Rise of Sunbelt Governors: Conservative Outsiders in the White House," *Presidential Studies Quarterly*, 44, no. 1 (March 2014): 72–94.

8. Decision 2014. *NBC News.* https://www.nbcnews.com/politics/elections/2014/OH/governor/exitpoll.

9. Kasich also noted that unauthorized immigrants in Ohio could obtain drivers' licenses, underscoring how immigration had state and local, and not just national, policy implications.

10. See the Republican National Committee, *Growth and Opportunity Project*, Washington DC (2013).

11. Joshua Gillin, "Jeb Bush SaysHhe Won 60% of the Hispanic Vote in 2002 Election," *Politifact*, July 31, 2015, https://www.politifact.com/florida/statements /2015/jul/31/jeb-bush/jeb-bush-says-he-won-60-hispanic-vote-2002-electio/.

12. Dan Balz, "In a year of Trump and Carson, GOP governors struggle in presidential race: Executive experience in state capitals has not translated into success so far in the GOP nomination contest," *The Washington Post*, November 18, 2015, A4.

13. Matt Murphy and Colin A. Young, "Mass. GOP Looking Beyond Trump," *Lowell Sun*, April 14, 2015, https://www.lowellsun.com/2015/08/14/mass-gop-look ing-beyond-trump/.

14. Alexander Burns, Maggie Haberman, and Jonathan Martin, "Frantic Efforts to Halt Trump Fail for G.O.P.," *The New York Times*, February 28, 2016, A1.

15. Burns, Haberman, and Martin, "Frantic Efforts," A1.

16. Ashley Young, "Maine Gov. Paul LePage Endorses Trump for President," *CNN*, February 26, 2016, https://www.cnn.com/2016/02/26/politics/paul-lepage-don ald-trump-endorsement/index.html.

17. Steve Benen, "Republican Governors Association Exploits its Pawn in Maine," *MSNBC*, October 28, 2014, http://www.msnbc.com/rachel-maddow-show/ republican-governors-association-exploits-its-pawn-maine.

18. Russell Contreras and Morgan Lee, "New Mexico Governor Rebukes Trump on Border-Fence Plan," *The Washington Times*, April 19, 2016, https://www.was hingtontimes.com/news/2016/apr/19/new-mexico-governor-rebukes-trump-on-bord er-fence-/.

19. Ashley Parker and Jonathan Martin, "Trump Takes a Female, Hispanic Governor to Task," *The New York Times*, May 26, 2016, A15.

20. Jeremy W. Peters, "Notable Republicans to Skip Convention," *International New York Times*, June 3, 2016, 5.

21. Jeremy Duda, "Ducey Tells Trump He's Committed to Keeping Arizona in GOP Column," *The Arizona Capitol Times*, June 14, 2016.

22. Jonathan Martin, "Republicans Worry a Falling Donald Trump Tide Will Lower All Boats," *The New York Times*, August 18, 2016, A14.

23. Paul Singer, "Republican Revolt Engulfs Party," *Dayton Daily News*, October 12, 2016, Z1.

24. See Geoffrey Skelley, "Straight Tickets for Senate, Split Tickets for Governor: The 2016 Senate and Gubernatorial Elections," in *Trumped: The 2016 Election that Broke All the Rules*, eds. Larry J. Sabato, Kyle Kondik, and Geoffrey Skelley (Lanham: Rowman & Littlefield, 2017), 52–69.

25. Jim Geraghty, "The Normal One," *National Review*, October 16, 2017, https:/ /www.nationalreview.com/magazine/2017/10/16/normal-one/.

26. Mathew Bloch, Nate Cohn, Josh Katz, Jasmine Lee, and Kevin Quealy, "Northam Defeats Gillespie in Governor Race," *The New York Times*, December 20, 2017, https://www.nytimes.com/elections/results/virginia-governor-election-gillespie -northam; "Presidential Election Results: Donald J. Trump Wins," *The New York Times*, August 9, 2017, https://www.nytimes.com/elections/2016/results/president.

27. Gary C. Jacobson, "Extreme Referendum: Donald Trump and the 2018 Midterms," *Political Science Quarterly*, 134, no. 1 (2019): 13.

28. Jacobson, "Extreme Referendum," 15.

29. NCSL StateVote, *National Conference of State Legislatures*, http://www.ncsl .org/research/elections-and-campaigns/statevote-2018-state-legislative-races-and -ballot-measures.aspx, accessed July 30, 2019.

30. NCSL StateVote.

31. Rachel Chason, "Larry Hogan Blames President Trump for Downballot GOP Losses in Maryland," *The Washington Post*, November 7, 2018, https://www.was hingtonpost.com/local/md-politics/larry-hogan-blames-president-trump-for-downbal lot-gop-losses-in-maryland/2018/11/07/82a5bf88-e2a4-11e8-8f5f-a55347f48762_ story.html?noredirect=on&utm_term=.6582248a8bc8.

32. CNN Politics Election Center, Exit Polls, *CNN*, https://www.cnn.com/elect ion/2018/exit-polls/texas/governor, accessed March 30, 2019; CNN Politics Election Center, Exit Polls, CNN, http://www.cnn.com/election/2014/results/state/TX/gover nor/, accessed December 10, 2019.

33. Wisconsin Exit Polls 2018, *CNN*, https://www.cnn.com/election/2018/exit-p olls/wisconsin, accessed July 30, 2019.

34. Because of the closeness of the race, Walker may also have been hurt by a drop-off in turnout among Trump supporters. For instance, Walker underperformed Trump's vote share in a number of lightly populated counties in the southeastern part of the state that went for Trump in 2016 but for Walker's Democratic opponent Tony Evers in 2018.

35. "Kansas Election Results," *The New York Times*, November 6, 2018, https://www.nytimes.com/elections/results/kansas-governor; "Kansas Results," *The New York Times*, August 1, 2017, https://www.nytimes.com/elections/2016/results/ kansas.

36. Daniel Desrochers, "Republicans Urge Bevin to Provide Proof of Election Fraud or 'Let It Go' and Concede," *Lexington Herald Leader*, November 7, 2019, https://www.kentucky.com/news/politics-government/article237113614.html.

37. Timothy Conlan, *New Federalism: Intergovernmental Reform from Nixon to Reagan* (Washington, DC.: The Brookings Institution, 1988).

38. The Republican National Committee, *The Republican Party Platform*, 2016, Washington, DC., 15.

39. "RGA Chairman Scott Walker: Our New Possibilities, Opportunities Are Endless," *Targeted News Service*, Obtained on March 27, 2019, Lexis Nexis.

40. Jennifer M. Jensen, *The Governors' Lobbyists: Federal-State Relations and Governors Associations in Washington* (Ann Arbor: University of Michigan Press, 2016).

41. Frank J. Thompson, Michael K. Gusmano, and Shugo Shinohara, "Trump and the Affordable Care Act: Congressional Repeal Efforts, Executive Federalism, and Program Durability," *Publius: The Journal of Federalism* 48, no. 3 (Summer 2018): 397.

42. Amy Goldstein and Juliet Eilperin, "Medicaid with Strings: Time Limits, Drug Tests," *The Washington Post*, May 26, 2017, A1.

43. Amy Goldstein and Juliet Eilperin, "ACA Replacement Effort Tries to Placate GOP Governors," *The Washington Post*, February 26, 2017, A3.

44. Matt Arco and Jonathan D. Salant, "Christie Opposes New GOP Health Bill," *The Star Ledger*, September 21, 2017, 1.

45. Emily Schultheis, "Ohio Gov. Kasich Says House Conservatives May Cause 'problem' Passing Obamacare Replacement," *CBS News*, February 26, 2017, https:// www.cbsnews.com/news/ohio-governor-john-kasich-says-house-conservatives-will-be-a-problem-obamacare/.

46. Alexander Burns, "Tax Plan Carries Political Peril for Republicans in Blue States," *The New York Times*, November 6, 2017, A1–A15.

47. John Kincaid, "Introduction: The Trump Interlude and the State of American Federalism," *State and Local Government Review*, 49, no. 3 (September 2017): 157.

48. Ronald Brownstein, "GOP Tax Plans Could Fuel the Suburban Revolt Against Trump," *CNN*, November 15, 2017, https://www.cnn.com/2017/11/14/politics/gop-t ax-plans-could-fuel-the-suburban-revolt-against-trump/index.html.

49. "Remarks by President Trump at a Roundtable Discussion on Immigration, Bethpage, NY," May 23, 2018, https://www.whitehouse.gov/briefings-statements/re marks-president-trump-roundtable-discussion-immigration-bethpage-ny/.

50. Executive Order 13799—Establishment of Presidential Advisory Commission on Election Integrity, May 11, 2017, https://www.govinfo.gov/content/pkg/DCPD -201700326/pdf/DCPD-201700326.pdf.

51. Erica R. Hendry, "A Trump Commission Requested Voter Data. Here's What Every State is Saying," PBS Thirteen, June 30, 2017, https://www.pbs.org/newshour /politics/trump-commission-requested-voter-data-heres-every-state-saying.

52. Hendry, "Trump Commission."

53. Saliqa A. Khan, "Maryland Leaders Weigh in on Decision to Rescind DACA," *WBAL-TV*, September 5, 2017, https://www.wbaltv.com/article/marylands-congressi onal-delegation-weighs-in-on-decision-to-rescind-daca/12173906.

54. Khan, "Maryland Leaders."

55. Alex Isenstadt, "New Trump Campaign Hires to Focus on Convention Delegates, Party Organization," *Politico*, January 18, 2019, https://www.politico .com/story/2019/01/18/trump-campaign-aides-2020-rnc-1110672.

56. See, for instance, Daniel J. Galvin, *Presidential Party Building: Dwight D. Eisenhower to George W. Bush* (Princeton: Princeton University Press, 2010); Sidney M. Milkis, *The President and the Parties: The Transformation of the American Party System Since the New Deal* (New York: Oxford University Press, 1993).

57. Boris Heersink, "Party Brands and the Democratic and Republican National Committees, 1952-1976," *Studies in American Political Development*, 32, no. 1 (April 2018): 80; See also John H. Aldrich, *Why Parties? A Second Look* (Chicago: University of Chicago Press, 2011): 47–50.

58. "Tracking Trump: The President's Standing Across America," *The Morning Consult*, https://morningconsult.com/tracking-trump/, accessed July 30, 2019.

59. Ben Nadler and Zeke Miller, "Gov. Kemp Picks Political Newcomer for U.S. Senate," *The Augusta Chronicle*, December 4, 2019, https://www.augustachronicle.c om/news/20191204/gov-kemp-picks-political-newcomer-for-us-senate.

60. Quoted in Alan Greenblatt, "Some Suburban State Lawmakers Are Leaving the GOP: Since the Midterm Elections, Republican Legislators in California, Kansas

and New Jersey Have Switched to the Democratic Party," *Governing*, January 29, 2019, https://www.governing.com/topics/politics/gov-california-kansas-party-switch -lawmaker.html.

61. Greenblatt, "Some Suburban State Lawmakers."

62. Greenblatt, "Some Suburban State Lawmakers."

63. Gary Reich, "Hitting a Wall? The Trump Administration Meets Immigration Federalism," *Publius: The Journal of Federalism* 48 no. 3 (Summer 2018): 373.

64. See Ambar, *How Governors Built the Modern American Presidency*; Ambar, "The Rise of Sunbelt Governors."

Chapter 4

#NeverTrump and the Fourth Estate

April A. Johnson and Karyn A. Amira

News media are the marrow of political campaigns. They are responsible for the portrayal of a candidate's competence, integrity, and issue positions to prospective voters.[1] Because media wield the enormous powers of gatekeeping, agenda setting, and framing (i.e., "spin"), the mass media system has rightfully earned its title as the "fourth branch" of American government. This chapter catalogues how Donald Trump's bid for the GOP nomination in 2015 and 2016 and his subsequent term as president have uprooted this fourth branch. Unsurprisingly, and in line with Republican presidential hopefuls before him, Trump's campaign faced criticism from more left-leaning media outlets, such as MSNBC and the Huffington Post. However, it was a wave of anti-Trump sentiment voiced among conservative media that illuminated the uniquely controversial nature of Donald Trump's candidacy and presidency.

CONSERVATIVE NEWS LANDSCAPE

Conservative media have long provided insights into the news of the day from a perspective that typically emphasizes personal liberty, traditional moral value structures, national security, and laissez faire economics. For some on the American right and in the Republican Party, these outlets serve as places of refuge in what they perceive to be a liberally biased information industry. That which we presently identify as "conservative news media" represent outlets that *explicitly* cater to a right-wing political demographic. Although some consumers may identify otherwise, those who possess conservative ideological orientations are the target audience for this particular "brand" of media, an audience that has proven both sizable and profitable within the U.S. electorate.

Coming to prominence with FoxNews's rollout during the mid-1990s, conservative media exists across all media sectors.[2] However, there are noticeable divisions between print and broadcast media (both radio and television) when it comes to substance and style. Like conservatism itself, conservative media is not a monolith. Traditional, intellectual conservative thought tends to find a home in print newspapers and magazines, such as the *National Review* and the now defunct *The Weekly Standard*. Importantly, some of these perspectives are embedded in more mainstream, non-conservative, outlets. For example, the *New York Times* editorial page features a small handful of center-right columnists, such as Ross Douthat and David Brooks. The same can be said for the *Washington Post*. In contrast, more entertainment-oriented, affectively charged, culture-war-type commentary tends to be featured on conservative talk-radio programs such as The Rush Limbaugh Show and in cable television programming such as FoxNews's Hannity and The Ingraham Angle. Thus, the tenor of print and broadcast media tends to attract different types of conservative audiences. Despite these distinctions, conservative media more generally find common ground in preferences for decentralized government, economic liberty, broad support for the Republican Party, and opposition to the Democratic Party. In the consistent promotion and maintenance of these values, conservative media possessed a partisan unity that had, until the 2016 election, served the GOP well.

ORIGINS OF #NEVERTRUMPISM
WITHIN CONSERVATIVE MEDIA

The launch of Donald Trump's presidential campaign was met with eye rolls and skepticism from many conservative writers. One prominent concern commonly expressed was that Trump showed all the signs of an attention-seeking, ex-reality TV star engaging in a vanity campaign. He had a history of critiquing political officials in order to get media attention and often boasted about running for president himself, though never following through. *The Wall Street Journal*'s editorial page has a history of being economically conservative.[3] It penned an article in July of 2015 about Trump's seemingly absurd campaign, questioning "how long his political and media apologists will keep pretending he's a serious candidate?"[4] Many observers who watched the spectacle unfold from the moment Trump descended down the gilded escalator in Trump Tower reacted similarly to Daniel McCarthy of *The American Conservative*, who in July 2015 called Trump's rise a "popularity blip."[5]

Besides scoffs about the seriousness of his candidacy, another early concern was that Trump, a coastal elite from Manhattan, did not embody the values of conservatism. In July of 2015, the *National Review*, a leading conservative magazine, expressed skepticism over Trump's Republican credentials by listing his past issue stances on abortion, healthcare, trade, taxes, social security and property rights in a piece entitled "Donald Trump's Surprisingly Progressive Past."[6] Although his early campaign efforts sought to clarify his apparently evolving perspectives on these issues, Trump's reputation as businessman, rather than political leader, implied to some that his political allegiances and policy positions were opportunistic and ephemeral. In August of that year, Noah Rothman of the conservative *Commentary* magazine provided a similarly critical assessment of Trump's positions and "lack of principle," admonishing that "it is nevertheless critical to remind those conservatives who maintain some lingering attachment to the principles of conservatism that the GOP's 2016 frontrunner is not one of them."[7]

Of course, criticism and negativity on the campaign trail are hardly novel in American politics. During the early competitive months of the primary season, critiques of prospective candidates' policies and personal qualities (and possible deficiencies) are commonplace and expected among opinion leaders and from media "watchdogs."[8] Yet, in this case, a bigger than life "outsider" candidate who often controlled his own storylines via direct tweets to the public and free press coverage meant that conservative news outlets faced editorial challenges in terms of the gatekeeping function and framing of Trump-related events. At the same time, many within the GOP establishment made their contempt of Trump well known in the early primary season.[9] A unified narrative was slipping from conservative media's hands. The accumulation of negative commentary toward Trump, whose views increasingly resonated with a large portion of rank-and-file Republicans, suggested a forthcoming threat to readership and profit margins. Would the GOP base, 50 percent of whom now expressed pro-Trump sentiment in early April of 2016, shun those outlets critical of their presidential selection?[10] If so, how would conservative news organizations respond? There seemed to be an increasingly obvious disconnect between conservatives in the mass public and those conservative journalists who had been "speaking" to them as an audience for a number of years.

CRACKS BECOME CHASMS

As Trump's candidacy pressed on, concerns from conservative media were no longer limited to the seriousness of his campaign and his apparently dubious conservative credentials. Instead, there was a greater preoccupation with his ability to win a general election and claims that his dangerous rhetoric could harm both the Republican Party and the fabric of American society as a whole. Concerns about the latter were not unfounded. Donald Trump's primary campaign was increasingly characterized by right-wing populism, including anti-establishment rhetoric and anti-immigrant sentiment, which aroused support among white nationalists.[11] In addition, Trump's personalized attacks on fellow Republicans Marco Rubio, Jeb Bush, and Ted Cruz, his admiration of authoritarian leaders, and his positions on trade policy all ran antithetical to traditional conservative principles and bedrock American values. Moreover, in portraying himself as a political outsider, Trump took great pride in building and promoting a political brand based on his propensity for norm-breaking.[12] He also broke from traditional reliance on mainstream news media and instead sharpened his ability to skirt the press by directly communicating with prospective voters via his platform on Twitter.

These efforts did much to deflect attention away from a growing number of serious warnings from right-wing journalists, bloggers and other mainstream establishment figures. In a March 2016 column entitled "No, Not Trump, Not Ever," conservative *New York Times* columnist David Brooks admonished that "Republicans who coalesce around Trump are making a political error. They are selling their integrity for a candidate who will probably lose. . . . As the founders would have understood, he is a threat to the long and glorious experiment of American self-government. He is precisely the kind of scapegoating, promise-making, fear driving and deceiving demagogue they feared."[13] Nevertheless, concerns over the candidate's nationalist infused brand of populism were largely dismissed by Republican voters and he continued to garner even more mass enthusiasm among the Republican electorate.

Trump's unyielding support from the public during the latter half of the primary was demonstrated most starkly by two events. In January 2016, he boldly claimed, "I could stand in the middle of Fifth Avenue and shoot somebody and I wouldn't lose any voters."[14] In other instances, during campaign stops he led crowds to raise their hands and "solemnly swear" to vote for him in the Republican primary.[15] These moments served as blatant signposts of the ever-growing personal loyalty voters felt for the presidential candidate. His base now resembled that of a dedicated consumer market, regardless of elite dissent from certain conservative media outlets.

In order to illustrate the unfolding campaign dynamics, the timeline in table 4.1 catalogues several (though certainly not all) notable moments in the evolution of the #NeverTrump movement among conservative news media. Many of these events were not held in isolation but instead created ripple effects among journalists. For example, after Trump sparred with FoxNews journalist and Republican debate moderator Megyn Kelly, Erik Erickson of Red State, a well-known conservative website, disinvited Trump to his outlet's gathering. Similarly, on December 3, Ross Douthat, a conservative

Table 4.1 Significant Media Moments within Donald Trump's 2016 Campaign

Date	Event
May 30, 2015	*New York Post* publishes article titled "Stop pretending—Donald Trump is not running for president"
June 16, 2015	**Trump officially announces candidacy**
July 19, 2015	Editorial from the *Wall Street Journal* questions Trump as a conservative leader, argues conservative media who applaud Trump "are hurting the cause"
July 20, 2015	*Des Moines Register* publishes editorial calling for Trump to end his presidential bid after Trump stated John McCain is "not a war hero"
August 6, 2015	Trump insults *Fox News* anchor Meaghan Kelly during primary debate
August 7, 2015	Erik Erickson (*RedState*) disinvites Trump to RedState gathering
August 25, 2015	*The Washington Post* publishes article highlighting Trump's continued harassment of *Fox News*'s Meaghan Kelly via Twitter
August 27, 2015	Noah Rothman (*Commentary*) publishes "Donald Trump is making fools of his fans" and questions his conservatism
November 24, 2015	Trump mocks disabled *New York Times* reporter
December 3, 2015	Ross Douthat (*New York Times*) associates Trump with "proto-fascism"
December 7, 2015	*Rolling Stone* publishes "2015: The Year Donald Trump Tyrannized the Presidential Race"
December 7, 2015	Trump publishes "Statement on Preventing Muslim Immigration" on Twitter
December 8, 2015	*CNN* reporter Nia-Malika Henderson questions whether GOP is ready to unite against Trump after proposed Muslim ban
January 15, 2016	*Wall Street Journal* reduces critiques of Trump, publishes "Trump's New York Advantage" which argues the popularity of his candidacy
January 22, 2016	Editors of *National Review* publish "Against Trump" issue, media outlet is swiftly disinvited to GOP debates
January 23, 2016	Trump states at an Iowa rally: "I could stand in the middle of 5th Ave. and shoot somebody and I wouldn't lose any voters," radio host Glenn Beck condemns remarks and expresses support for presidential hopeful Ted Cruz
March 4, 2016	Ben Shapiro (*Daily Wire*) publishes "I Will Never Vote for Donald Trump. Here's Why"
March 6, 2016	Glenn Beck (*The Blaze; Glenn Beck Radio Program*) compares Trump to Hitler on ABC This Week
March 28, 2016	Charlie Sykes (*WTMJ Wisconsin*) tells Trump he's #NeverTrump on his show, questions his character, says he was a "liberal democrat"
May 6, 2016	Bill Kristol (*The Weekly Standard*) publishes "Neither Clinton nor Trump," suggests an Independent candidate

(Continued)

Table 4.1 Significant Media Moments within Donald Trump's 2016 Campaign (*Continued*)

Date	Event
May 26, 2016	**Trump clinches GOP Nomination**
June 24, 2016	Conservative journalist George Will (*Washington Post*, Fox News contributor) leaves Republican Party, cites disdain of Trump
July 18, 2016	**Republican National Convention—Trump officially nominated**
August 7, 2016	David Fahrenthold (*Washington Post*) makes public Trump's 2005 "Access Hollywood" footage, Trump issues video of apology via Twitter
Spetember 7, 2016	Trump spokesperson confirms end of blacklist for certain media outlets (*Washington Post*, Politico, Huffington Post, Daily Beast, BuzzFeed) from his news conferences and campaign events
Spetember 14, 2016	Ross Douthat (*New York Times*) publishes "How Trump Might Win"
November 8, 2016	**Trump wins General Election**
November 11, 2016	Maggie Gallagher (*National Review*) publishes "It's time to disband Never Trump"
December 5, 2016	Republican presidential elector, Christopher Suprun, publishes a *New York Times* op-ed titled "Why I Will Not Cast My Electoral Vote for Donald Trump"
December 20, 2016	Laura Ingraham (Fox News) writes op-ed entitled "The NeverTrump crowd is still a nuisance, and still wrong"
May 30, 2017	Dennis Prager (*National Review*) declares "The Never Trump conservative argument that Trump is not a conservative—one that I, too, made repeatedly during the Republican primaries—is not only no longer relevant, it is no longer true."
December 21, 2017	Charlie Sykes featured on *Frontline* regarding new book "How the Right Lost Its Mind"
December 27, 2017	*The Atlantic* publishes "'Never Trump' Will Be the Only Faction Still Standing When He's Gone," calls on #NeverTrumpers to rebuild the Republican Party
Spetember 5, 2018	Rick Wilson, a #NeverTrump Republican consultant, publishes "#NeverTrump Republicanism Can Still Matter" in *Politico*
August 15, 2019	Tom Nichols (*USA Today*) publishes "Why this Never Trump ex-Republican will vote for almost any 2020 Democratic nominee"
November 1, 2019	Bret Stephens (*New York Times*) publishes "The NeverTrump Vindication"

Source: Compiled and created by the authors.

voice at the *New York Times*, wrote a column assessing whether Trump was a "fascist." This article came on the heels of Trump mocking Serge Kovaleski, a *New York Times* reporter with arthrogryposis. Douthat concluded Trump did not fit the label, but stated that "it seems fair to say that he's closer to the 'proto-fascist' zone on the political spectrum than either the average American conservative or his recent predecessors in right-wing populism."[16]

JOIN OR DIE: #NEVERTRUMPISM
WITHIN THE GENERAL ELECTION

When Trump officially secured the Republican nomination in July of 2016, he upended decades of a carefully crafted unified voice and partisan loyalty within conservative media. Until now, #NeverTrumpers had merely cast doubts, raised concerns, and provided skepticism about Trump's candidacy. Now that these warnings had fallen on deaf ears, #NeverTrump conservatives found themselves at an existential crossroads: toe the party line and support Trump in the general election or oppose him and risk readership and potentially social alienation. Crucially, this choice would be more difficult for outlets that catered entirely to conservatives (unlike the *New York Times* and *Washington Post*) and even more so for outlets with a populist, culture-war tone. What would the official nomination of Trump mean for conservative journalists who had previously expressed discontent with his candidacy?

Some conservative outlets like *The Washington Examiner* and the *New York Post* (both had endorsed Trump in the primary), declined to make an official statement going into the general election, thus making their support or opposition for him unclear. Still, others felt compelled to continue speaking out against the Republican nominee by endorsing out-party members or explicitly encouraging their readers not to vote for Trump (i.e., anti-endorsement). Traditionally right-leaning regional outlets, such as the *Houston Chronicle* and the *Columbus Dispatch,* officially endorsed Hillary Clinton in early October 2016. Tellingly, some print publications, such as the *Arizona Republic*, who threw their weight behind Clinton in a general election matchup, had never endorsed a Democrat in its history. Although it seems unlikely that media endorsements alone would alter the outcome of a presidential election, research does suggest that they are most impactful on the public when the endorsement is out of character for the outlet, as these certainly were.[17] In addition to these unexpected anti-endorsements from conservative newspapers, Clinton garnered a historic number of media endorsements overall. The gap between her "expected" endorsements and her actual endorsements was unprecedented, according to the website FiveThiryEight.com.[18]

News consumers also witnessed individual writers within larger conservative organizations express #NeverTrump sentiment, if only speaking for themselves. For example, in his October 8 article "Unfit" for *Commentary* magazine, John Podhoretz wrote "Trump is unfit to be the President of the United States . . . for reasons that have nothing to do with policy. Simply put, he is an unspeakable human being."[19] Five days before the 2016 general election, Rod Dreher from the *American Conservative* wrote an article titled

"The Most Conservative Case Against Donald Trump." In it, Dreher minced no words in stating "I think the chance of war and civil unrest under a Trump presidency is much greater than under a Clinton one. These are the evils, or potential evils, greater than any of the certain evils that a Clinton administration would bring. We can't take that chance."[20]

Opposition from individual journalists and media personalities were also published online via personal social media pages, unconnected with their news organization. While the Republican National Convention was still ongoing, conservative columnist Ross Douthat at the *New York Times* wasted no time in voicing outrage of Trump's nomination by tweeting, "Every major figure who participated in this grotesquerie has disgraced themselves on a level unique in the history of our Republic."[21] In October 2016, Bill Kristol of *The Weekly Standard* tweeted, "'Trump: I am your voice.' Not my voice. Not most Americans' voice. Isn't it time for a Republican revolt against his remaining GOP's voice?"[22]

The emergence of such strong discontent among conservative news outlets and individual journalists was and continues to be reflective of the increasing varieties of news distribution mechanisms.[23] That is to say, if conservative readers of the *New York Times* find fault with Douthat's assessment of Trump, for instance, they can turn elsewhere for attitudinally congruent campaign coverage to reinforce that disposition. This type of media fractionalization provides the foundation for narrowcasting, a technique that involves the targeting of campaign information to specific demographics of voters via niche media markets.[24] During the 2016 presidential primary season, narrowcasting provided the mechanism that allowed some conservative news outlets to deviate from presenting a "united front" in support of Trump. This ability to express dissimilar opinions early in the election cycle was precisely the root of the #NeverTrump movement.

Still, November 8, 2016, was a day of reckoning for #NeverTrump journalists. Some in the movement immediately changed course (table 1). A prominent example of this came from *National Review*, who had published an issue called "Against Trump" during the Republican primary in which the editors and a symposium of columnists outlined a case against the candidate.[25] On November 11, 2016—a mere three days after the general election—Maggie Gallaher of *National Review* published "It's time to disband Never Trump" suggesting that others "congratulate President-elect Trump, and work to help him make American great again."[26] Going forward, the magazine would take on more of an "anti-anti-Trump" flavor, in which journalists turned their criticism of Trump into criticism of Trump's critics.

Some #NeverTrumpers attempted to resist the new president for a period of time but subsequently flipped to an overtly pro-Trump stance. Erick Erickson—who once disinvited Trump to a Red State gathering—penned

"I'll be voting for President Trump and Vice President Pence in 2020" on his blog The Resurgent in February of 2019.[27] Others in the media, such as Jennifer Rubin, a conservative columnist at the *Washington Post*, and Brett Stephens, a conservative columnist at the *New York Times*, continued to look on in horror, expressing outrage in their respective publications and on social media. While Stephens and Rubin arguably subscribe to a more traditional conservatism than Erickson, the fact that their journalistic homes do not exist to serve an exclusively conservative audience, let alone a populist conservative audience, allowed for continued criticism of Trump.

Below we highlight two dramatically different case studies in the #NeverTrump conservative media movement. These accounts serve to illuminate the simultaneous economic and ideological pressures that acted upon conservative media outlets throughout the election, and their differential responses to each.

BREAKING FROM TRADITION: THE CASE OF *THE WEEKLY STANDARD*

The Weekly Standard, a print magazine (and website) launched by Rupert Murdoch's News Corp in 1995, was home to prominent voices in the conservative movement until 2018. The magazine and its columnists have often been referred to as "neoconservative." Although this philosophy has many moving parts, the label generally applies to those on the Right who believe peace can best be achieved when anti-democratic evil is confronted through the United States' unique military strength. Modern neoconservative ideology came about in the 1960s and 1970s when a faction of hawkish liberals—disenchanted with the Democrat's "soft" stances on communism and crime—moved to the Republican Party. However, many consider the philosophy to have peaked during the George W. Bush years when neoconservatives played roles in the White House during the planning of the Iraq War. In addition, neoconservatives in the news media—particularly those at *The Weekly Standard*—vociferously defended the war. The publication was often referred to as the "In-flight magazine of Air Force One," indicating its importance in the policymaking of the Bush administration.[28] Despite praise for its writing and its prominence in conservative circles in the 2000s, *The Weekly Standard* had poor financials, and was eventually sold in 2009 to Philip Anschutz, a conservative billionaire and head of the Anschutz Corporation, whose subsidiaries included the *Washington Examiner*, another right-wing outlet.

When the 2016 election reared its head, *The Weekly Standard* took an aggressively #NeverTrump stance. Despite his promises to deregulate many aspects of government, cut taxes, and appoint conservative judges, Trump's authoritarian impulses, as well as his affinity for dictators and immoral behavior, posed a threat to neoconservative principles. Bill Kristol, the publication's founder, frequent columnist and editor-at-large, explicitly described himself as "NeverTrump" in his writing and on social media.[29] Kristol ended up supporting Evan McMullin in the general election. Stephen Hayes, a prominent columnist who would become editor-in-chief after Trump's election, penned the article, "Donald Trump is crazy and so is the GOP for embracing him."[30] This reaction was in line with the outlet's origins and philosophy. John Podhoretz, one of the publications' first writers, wrote that "not being a team player was part of the DNA of the *Standard* from the outset, for better or for worse. Our loyalty was to the ideas in which we believed, not to the Republican Party."[31]

Meanwhile, the *Washington Examiner*—which had previously endorsed John McCain and Mitt Romney—did not make an endorsement. This decision could be perceived as an attempt to balance partisanship, profit and morality—at least until the general election was over. The two publications appeared to be moving in different political directions. *The Washington Examiner* seemed to be positioning itself such that it could safely and seamlessly follow the country's political trajectory without risking profits and readership. *The Weekly Standard* stood by its ideological leanings, readership be damned.

In early December of 2018, rumors began circulating that *The Weekly Standard* would be shutting down. A source at the magazine claimed the owners "have worked to sabotage TWS every step of the way" in what Vox called an attempt to "harvest the magazine's subscriber base to help support the *Washington Examiner*, which is now expanding into a nationally distributed magazine."[32] In addition to its dwindling subscriber base, which had become common in the magazine industry, *The Weekly Standard*'s opposition to Trump may have been a liability as the tides turned and Republicans in Congress showed little resistance to him.[33] The magazine was now out of sync with the executive branch that it once influenced, sizable swaths of Republican voters *and* elected Republicans who were now forced to support the "party of Trump." Its final issue was printed in December 2018.

It is difficult to know the exact mechanism for the magazine's demise. John Podhoretz called it a "murder" and hypothesized that it had more to do with "deep pettiness" and "bureaucratic revenge" from higher-ups rather than the publication's antagonism toward the president.[34] But it may well have been due to natural changes in the media landscape and the economic risks of continuing to promote #NeverTrumpism to an audience that was "used to reading positive coverage of Republican presidents and withering criticism of Democrats."[35]

After shutting its doors, Bill Kristol and Charlie Sykes, a #NeverTrumper known for his career in radio, founded The Bulwark, a website whose contempt for Trump could be seen implicitly in its originally stated goal to "push back against the moral and intellectual corruption that now poses and existential threat to conservatism as a viable political force."[36] Perhaps the website's most scathing, explicit critique of the president came after his threat to target Iranian cultural sites if the country retaliated for the killing of Qasem Solemiani. A response piece entitled "Illegal. Barbaric. And Foolish" ends by stating that "once again, Trump has reminded us why he is unfit to be the commander in chief—not only because of his poor intellect and poor management style, but also because he is a contemptible man with no regard for law or morality, prudence or strategy."[37] For their staff and audience, #NeverTrumpism lives on. However, the death of *The Weekly Standard* perhaps served as a warning sign that the #NeverTrump movement was on life support.[38]

TO #NEVERTRUMPISM AND BACK:
THE CASE OF GLENN BECK

Although #NeverTrumpism is indeed concentrated in print journalism, it could also be seen in AM talk radio, where conservative commentary thrives. Perhaps the most puzzling individual in this space is Glenn Beck. Although he had been involved in various radio shows since the 1980s, Beck came to national television prominence for hosting the Glenn Beck Program, which was moved from CNN Headline News to FoxNews in 2009 during the early years of the Obama presidency.

Although Beck once indicated that his programming is not to be taken too seriously, it nonetheless projected an angry, right-wing, populist tone.[39] Beck depicted a doomsday vision of society, often using chalkboard drawings to craft relationships between government officials and supposedly dodgy organizations to weave a narrative of elite conspiracy. His penchant for comparing just about anything to Hitler and the Third Reich was discussed outside the confines of conservative media and in late night comedy.[40] Although some tried to out Beck as a political "fraud" and "dangerous faker" chasing a paycheck, his show was the third most watched program on cable news at its peak.[41]

In 2016, a number of years after Beck's program declined in ratings and moved from FoxNews to his online platform The Blaze, the provocateur took a sharp turn. He joined those at *National Review* for their column "Conservatives Against Trump" warning that Trump had supported big government in the past and that his nomination would be a "crisis for conservatism."[42] In typical Glenn Beck fashion, he began comparing Trump to Hitler.[43] Beck's right-wing, populist style made his move to #NeverTrumpism particularly intriguing, considering journalist and professor Peter Beinart suggested that "Beck, in fact, pioneered some of Trump's most disturbing themes."[44]

For some time, Beck continued to criticize Trump and make amends for his inflammatory past programming. In an interview with the *New York Times Magazine* shortly after the 2016 general election, Beck claimed that Trump "could be one of the most dangerous presidents to ever come into the Oval Office" and pleaded with the *Times'* liberal leadership to learn from his mistakes and "be better" than him. His concern and seemingly earnest apologies continued. In March of 2017, he told journalist Peter Kafka, "I'm a constitutional conservative . . . I will take responsibility for the things that I did. . . . I'm looking for people in media, on the right *and* the left, who have the balls to stand up to their own audience [and] say, 'This is what we did wrong,' 'This is what I did wrong,' 'This is what I didn't get.'"[45]

In May of 2018, after months of Beck's soul-searching apology tour in mainstream media circles, he again took a curious turn during his radio show when he pulled out a "Make America Great Again" hat, placed it on his head and told his listeners that he would "gladly" vote for Trump in 2020. David Frum, a conservative Republican and former speechwriter for George W. Bush responded to this announcement by tweeting "Glenn Beck succumbs to the imperatives of the conservative entertainment complex," indicating that Beck was indeed incentivized by money and ratings rather than a principled worldview.[46] An (anonymous) friend of Beck's told *The Daily Beast* that his sudden transformation was a "desperate and predictable act of a man hanging on to his last shred of relevance by a thread. Trying desperately to woo back the massive number of fans lost when he opposes Trump. Sad."[47]

Beck's support for Trump continues at the time of writing. Speaking about the 2020 election, Beck told Sean Hannity in March of 2019 that "if the Republicans don't win this next election, I think we are officially at the end of the country as we know it . . . it has to mean the reelection of Trump."[48] While it is surely possible that Beck's alarm over Trump's election was sincere, his switch to Trump supporter three years into the presidency is more likely a calculated business decision. Unlike #NeverTrump conservatives who write for mainstream newspapers such as *The New York Times* and *The Washington Post*, Beck relies on a niche, populist audience that is drawn to controversy, conspiracy, and anger—the same environment that defines the Trump presidency.

#NEVERTRUMP, BY ANY OTHER NAME

To equate the inauguration of Donald Trump with the end of the #NeverTrump conservative media movement would be entirely shortsighted. Nevertheless, the movement has clearly branched off in a number of directions. Some previously outspoken #NeverTrump journalists acquiesced with the presidential selection, rebranding themselves as "LimitedTrumpers" in order to give Trump the benefit of the doubt as his tenure commenced.[49] For Nicholas Connors at The Bulwark (see *The Weekly Standard* case study above), however, the benefit of the doubt did not last long. In fact, many in print journalism ultimately held their ground and remained solidly anti-Trump. George Will, a columnist for the *Washington Post* who left the Republican Party in 2016, referred to the party as a "cult" with an "absence of ideas."[50] In June of 2019, months ahead of Trump's official 2020 Presidential campaign launch, the *Orlando Sentinel,* which had typically endorsed Republican candidates until recent years, boldly proclaimed, "There's no point pretending we would ever recommend that readers vote for Trump."[51]

Perhaps most interesting to this story are the once pro-Trump journalists and broadcasters who had a change of heart after three years of controversy and ongoing impeachment proceedings. For example, talk-radio host and 2016 Trump supporter Craig Silverman of Denver's conservative KNUS station admitted stepping off the "Trump train" since the general election.[52] In November of 2019, Silverman's mic was cut off and he was fired on the spot for discussing impeachment on air. Although the station management disputes his claims, Silverman stated that "Salem (Media Group) from corporate in California on down is seriously pro Trump. So does it have to do with Donald Trump? I think so. I wanted to talk about the impeachment inquiry and a lot of these facts are very damning against Donald Trump."[53]

Similarly, several broadcasters affiliated with *Fox News*, an organization well-known for its predominantly conservative audience, recently broke from such institutional norms.[54] After years of skepticism toward President Trump, much of which was reciprocated through Trump's own Twitter feed, longtime FoxNews host, Shepard Smith, announced in October of 2019 his exit from the news organization.[55] Likewise, FoxNews anchors Neil Cavuto and Brit Hume recently expressed frustration toward Trump's presumed connection between their ratings and loyalty or favoritism toward his presidency. In an August 2019 tweet directed at the president, Hume noted that "FoxNews isn't supposed to work for you." Two days later, Cavuto took to the airwaves to clarify "Mr. President, we don't work for you. I don't work for you. . . . My job is to cover you, not fawn over you or rip you. Just report on you."[56]

Still, some journalists seem impervious to the influence of Donald Trump and the trajectory on which he is steering the Republican Party. Consider Republican radio and broadcast news commentator Scottie Nell Hughes. Despite litigation involving FoxNews and her own claims of being blacklisted from conservative media, Hughes, who is now affiliated with RT America, has already pledged support for Trump in 2020.[57] Conservative personality

Meghan McCain was persistent in expressing opposition to Trump's bid for the presidency, particularly during the primary cycle when he declared that her father was not a war hero.[58] Notwithstanding, McCain has recently stated that she will continue to vote Republican going forward, though some of her more recent remarks have hinted at a tipping point for her support for the "party of Trump."[59] One might argue that Trump's bully reputation, both in the boardroom and the White House, extends to his control of conservative newsmakers as well.[60]

The #NeverTrump uprising witnessed during the 2016 Presidential election is unlike any other in US history. While the movement presently shows signs of continuing on, albeit under different circumstances, the manner in which American conservative media expressed #NeverTrump sentiment in 2016 will not be replicated in 2020. Although the original coalition was led mostly by intellectual neoconservatives, a few others such as Glenn Beck and Erick Erickson were also dedicated to the cause. At the time of writing, however, most of the conservative journalists who continue to convey #NeverTrumpism hail from elite print publications and mainstream newspapers, outlets whose audiences do not generally reflect the populist masses. For these individuals who have maintained a position of anti-Trumpism, the result has at times led to attacks from the rest of conservative media, many of whom seem to be working overtime to protect Trump and his supporters by criticizing those who speak out against them.[61]

Yet the hot and blinding spotlight of the campaign trail has the propensity to spark fervor into those "born-again #NeverTrumpers."[62] In this vein, *The Bulwark* author Nicholas Connors has proposed the reframing of #NeverTrumpers as "Country First Republicans."[63] Journalists who choose to push such rhetoric during the 2020 election envision the removal of Trump through an emphasis on collective identity and post-Trump rehabilitation of the GOP. The ability of conservative media to collectively accept or reject this narrative will unquestionably shape alignments within the Republican Party and, ultimately, play a major role in directing its electoral outcomes.

NOTES

1. Michael Lewis-Beck, William G. Jacoby, Helmut Norpoth, and Herbert F. Weisberg, *The American Voter Revisited* (Ann Arbor, MI: University of Michigan Press, 2008).

2. The Righting, "An A-Z Guide to Right Wing Media," *The Righting*, https://www.therighting.com/media-guide/, accessed on February 25, 2020.

3. Robert Merry, "The Man Who Built *The Wall Street Journal* Editorial Page," *The American Conservative*, May 16, 2019, https://www.theamericanconservative.com/ articles/the-man-who-built-the-wall-street-journal-editorial-page/.

4. Editorial, "Trump and His Apologists," *The Wall Street Journal*, July 19, 2015, https://www.wsj.com/articles/trump-and-his-apologists-1437345060.

5. Daniel McCarthy, "Donald Trump Leads a Failed Field," *The American Conservative*, July 17, 2015, https://www.theamericanconservative.com/mccarthy/d onald-trump-leads-a-failed-field/.

6. Isaac Cohen, "Donald Trump's Surprisingly Progressive Past," *National Review*, July 10, 2015, https://www.nationalreview.com/2015/07/donald-trump-pro gressive-issues/.

7. Noah Rothman, "Donald Trump Is Making Fools of His Fans," *Commentary*, August 27, 2015, https://www.commentarymagazine.com/politics-ideas/campaigns-elections/donald-trump-conservative-or-liberal/.

8. Marjorie Randon Hershey, *Party Politics in America*, 15th edition (Boston, MA: Pearson, 2013).

9. Tracy Jan and Annie Linskey, "Republican Groups Aim to Bring Down Donald Trump," *Boston Globe*, November 24, 2015, https://www.bostonglobe.com/ news/politics/2015/11/24/gop-establishment-fears-donald-trump-could-permanently -tarnish-republican-party-image/EbCIEyJlbD1xF74eXe1LfP/story.html.

10. Hannah Hartig, John Lapinski, and Stephanie Psyllos, "Poll: Trump Reaches 50 Percent Support Nationally for the First Time," *NBC News*, April 26, 2016, https ://www.nbcnews.com/politics/2016-election/poll-trump-reaches-50-percent-support-nationally-first-time-n562061.

11. Kenneth T. Walsh, "Trump Attacks Fellow Republicans," *U.S. News and World Report*, May 26, 2016, https://www.usnews.com/news/articles/2016-05-26/tr ump-attacks-fellow-republicans; Kathleen Gray and Brent Snavely, "Trump to Mich Crowd: 'I'm an Outsider Fighting for You,'" *USA Today*, October 1, 2016, https://ww w.usatoday.com/story/news/nation-now/2016/10/01/donald-trump-novi-michigan-rally-campaign/91382940/; Ian Schwartz, "Trump: Mexico Not Sending Us Their Best; Criminals, Drug Dealers and Rapists Are Crossing Border," *RealClearPolitics*, June 16, 2015, https://www.realclearpolitics.com/video/2015/06/16/trump_mexico_n ot_sending_us_their_best_criminals_drug_dealers_and_rapists_are_crossing_border. html; J. M. Berger, "How White Nationalists Learned to Love Donald Trump," *Politico*, October 25, 2016, https://www.politico.com/magazine/story/2016/10/do nald-trump-2016-white-nationalists-alt-right-214388.

12. Gray and Snavely, "Trump to Mich Crowd."

13. David Brooks, "No, Not Trump, Not Ever," *The New York Times*, March 18, 2016, https://www.nytimes.com/2016/03/18/opinion/no-not-trump-not-ever.html.

14. Jeremy Diamond, "Trump: I Could Shoot Somebody and Not Lose Voters," *CNN*, January 24, 2016, https://www.cnn.com/2016/01/23/politics/donald-trump-sh oot-somebody-support/index.html.

15. Nick Gass, "Trump Defends Loyalty Oaths: 'We're Having Such a Great Time,'" *Politico*, March 8, 2016, https://www.politico.com/blogs/2016-gop-primary -live-updates-and-results/2016/03/donald-trump-loyalty-oaths-220416.

16. Ross Douthat, "Is Donald Trump a Fascist?" *The New York Times*, December 3, 2015, https://www.nytimes.com/2015/12/03/opinion/campaign-stops/is-donald-tr ump-a-fascist.html.

17. Chun-Fang Chiang and Brian Knight, "Media Bias and Influence: Evidence from Newspaper Endorsements," *The Review of Economic Studies*, 78, no. 3 (October 2008): 795–820; Fernanda Leite Lopez de Leon, "The Tuesday Advantage of Politicians Endorsed by American Newspapers," *The BE Journal of Economic Analysis & Policy*, 13, no. 2 (October 2013): 865–86.

18. Milo Beckman, "Clinton Leads Trump—And Obama and Reagan—In the Newspaper Endorsement Race," *FiveThirtyEight*, October 28, 2016, https://fivethi rtyeight.com/features/clinton-leads-trump-and-obama-and-reagan-in-the-newspaper-endorsement-race/.

19. John Podhoretz, "Unfit," *Commentary*, October 8, 2016, https://www.com mentarymagazine.com/politics-ideas/campaigns-elections/donald-trump-unfit/.

20. Rod Dreher, "The Most Conservative Case Against Donald Trump," *The American Conservative*, November 3, 2016, https://www.theamericanconservative .com/dreher/the-most-conservative-case-against-trump/.

21. Ross Douthat, @DouthatNYT, Twitter Post, July 19, 2016, 7:58 PM, https:// twitter.com/DouthatNYT/status/755597720300101632?ref_src=twsrc%5Etfw%7Ct wcamp%5Etweetembed%7Ctwterm%5E755597720300101632&ref_url=https%3A %2F%2Fwww.vox.com%2F2016%2F7%2F20%2F12232638%2Fconservative-write rs-rnc-trump.

22. Bill Kristol, @BillKristol, Twitter Post, October 7, 2016, 4:49 PM, https://tw itter.com/billkristol/status/784541114585976832.

23. Doris A. Graber and Johanna L. Dunaway, *Mass Media and American Politics*, 10th edition (Washington, DC: CQ Press, 2018).

24. Hershey, *Party Politics in America.*

25. "Conservatives against Trump," *National Review*, February 15, 2016, https:// www.nationalreview.com/magazine/2016/02/15/conservatives-against-trump/.

26. Maggie Gallagher, "It's Time to Disband NeverTrump," *National Review*, November 11, 2016, https://www.nationalreview.com/2016/11/never-trump-repu blicans-donald-trump-needs-help-economy-health-care-reform/.

27. Eric Erickson, "I'll Be Voting for President Trump and Vice President Pence in 2020," *The Resurgent*, February 11, 2019, https://theresurgent.com/2019/02/11/ ill-be-voting-for-president-trump-and-vice-president-pence-in-2020/.

28. Jason Schwartz, "Weekly Standard Faces Uncertain Future After Holding Its Ground Against Trump," *Politico*, December 4, 2018, https://www.politico.com/story /2018/12/04/weekly-standard-future-media-trump-1045356.

29. William Kristol, "#NeverTrump: A Final Word," *The Weekly Standard*, November 7, 2016, https://www.washingtonexaminer.com/weekly-standard/neve rtrump-a-final-word.

30. Stephen Hayes, "Donald Trump Is Crazy and so Is the GOP for Embracing Him," *The Weekly Standard*, July 22, 2016, https://www.washingtonexaminer.com/ weekly-standard/donald-trump-is-crazy-and-so-is-the-gop-for-embracing-him.

31. John Podhoretz, "The Murder of *The Weekly Standard*," *Commentary*, December 14, 2018, https://www.commentarymagazine.com/politics-ideas/murder -weekly-standard/.

32. Jane Coaston, *"The Weekly Standard*, a Conservative Magazine Critical of Trump, Is Officially Shutting Down," *Vox*, December 14, 2018, https://www.vox .com/2018/12/14/18140925/weekly-standard-trump-media-shut-down.

33. Schwartz, "Weekly Standard Faces Uncertain Future."

34. Podhoretz, "The Murder of *The Weekly Standard*."

35. James Antle, "How *The Weekly Standard* Lost Its Influence," *The Week*, December 17, 2018, https://theweek.com/articles/812765/how-weekly-standard-lost -influence.

36. Sean Illing, "How Conservative Media Became a Safe Space," *Vox*, January 9, 2019, https://www.vox.com/2019/1/18/18175582/trump-fox-news-conservative-med ia-charlie-sykes.

37. Shay Khatiri, "Illegal. Barbaric. And Foolish," *The Bulwark*, January 7, 2020, https://thebulwark.com/illegal-barbaric-and-foolish/.

38. David Azerrad, "Op Ed: The NeverTrump Movement Is on Life Support," *The Los Angeles Times*, April 26, 2019, https://www.latimes.com/opinion/op-ed/la-oe-a zerrad-end-of-nevertrump-20190424-story.html.

39. Brian Stetler and Bill Carter, "Fox News' Mad, Apocalyptic, Tearful Rising Star," *The NewYork Times*, March 29, 2009, https://www.nytimes.com/2009/03/30/ business/media/30beck.html.

40. Dana Milbank, "Glenn Beck Is Obsessed with Hitler and Woodrow Wilson (I'm Just Saying)," *The Washington Post*, October 3, 2010, https://www.washingt onpost.com/wp-dyn/content/article/2010/09/30/AR2010093005267.html?hpid=opin ionsbox1&sid=ST2010093005292.

41. Bob Cesca, "Exposing Glenn Beck as a Dangerous Fraud," *Huffington Post*, May 25, 2011, https://www.huffpost.com/entry/exposing-glenn-beck-as-a_b _528966; Matea Gold, "Fox News' Glenn Beck Strikes Ratings Gold by Challenging Barack Obama," *The Los Angeles Times*, March 6, 2009, https://www.latimes.com/a rchives/la-xpm-2009-mar-06-et-foxnews6-story.html.

42. "Conservatives Against Trump."

43. David Folkenflick, "Smaller Audience, Bigger Payoff for Glenn Beck," *NPR*, September 21, 2012, https://www.npr.org/2012/09/21/161495610/smaller-audience -bigger-payoff-for-glenn-beck; Melissa Chan, "Glenn Beck Compares Donald Trump to Hitler," *Time*, March 6, 2016, https://time.com/4248841/glenn-beck-donald-trump -hitler/.

44. Peter Beinart, "Glenn Beck's Regrets," *The Atlantic*, January/February 2017, https://www.theatlantic.com/magazine/archive/2017/01/glenn-becks-regrets /508763/.

45. Eric Johnson, "Glenn Beck Says He Doesn't Care If He Alienates Trump Voters," *Vox*, March 16, 2017, https://www.vox.com/2017/3/16/14928412/glenn- beck-donald-trump-south-by-southwest-sxsw-recode-podcast.

46. David Frum, @davidfrum, Twitter Post, May 18, 2018, 12:33PM, https://tw itter.com/davidfrum/status/997560930648158208?lang=en.

47. Lloyd Grove, "Glenn Beck Changes Sides Again. Does Anyone Believe Him?" *The Daily Beast*, May 18, 2019, https://www.thedailybeast.com/glenn-beck -changes-sides-again-does-anyone-believe-him.

48. Ian Schwartz, "Glenn Beck: If Trump Doesn't Win 'We Are Officially at the End of the Country as We Know It,'" *RealClearPolitics*, March 18, 2019, https://ww w.realclearpolitics.com/video/2019/03/18/glenn_beck_if_trump_doesnt_win_we_are _officially_at_the_end_of_the_country_as_we_know_it.html.

49. Nicholas Connors, "It's Not 'Never Trump.' It's Country First," *The Bulwark*, November 21, 2019, https://thebulwark.com/its-not-never-trump-its-country-first/.

50. Josh Feldman, "George Will: The Republican Party's Become a Cult," *Mediate*, June 5, 2019, https://www.mediaite.com/tv/george-will-the-republican-partys-become-a-cult/.

51. Orlando Sentinel Editorial Board, "Our Orlando Sentinel Endorsement for President in 2020: Not Donald Trump," *Orlando Sentinel*, June 18, 2019, https://ww w.orlandosentinel.com/opinion/editorials/os-op-sentinel-not-endorsing-donald-trump -2020-20190618-63ya7cyb5ngf3irllodwxnznui-story.html.

52. Caitlin Yilek, "'You're Done': Radio Host Fired Mid-show after Slamming Trump," *The Washington Examiner*, November 18, 2019, https://www.washingtonexa miner.com/news/youre-done-radio-host-fired-mid-show-after-slamming-trump.

53. Saja Hindi, "KNUS Disputes Craig Silverman's Claim His Show Was Cancelled Over Trump Comments, Says He's Welcome Back on the Airwaves," *The Denver Post*, November 7, 2019, https://www.denverpost.com/2019/11/17/craig -silverman-denver-radio-fired-trump/; Michael Abeyta, "Sudden Firing of KNUS's Craig Silverman Causes Controversy," *CBS Denver*, November 17, 2019, https://de nver.cbslocal.com/2019/11/17/firing-knus-craig-silverman/.

54. Jesse Holcomb, "5 Facts about Fox News," *Pew Research Center*, January 14, 2014, https://www.pewresearch.org/fact-tank/2014/01/14/five-facts-about-fox-news/.

55. Michael M. Grynbaum, "Shepard Smith, Fox News Anchor, Abruptly Departs from Network," *The New York Times*, October 11, 2019, https://www.nytimes.com/2 019/10/11/business/media/shepard-smith-fox-news.html.

56. Aaron Rupar, "Why Trump Is Furiously Attacking Fox News," *Vox*, September 3, 2019, https://www.vox.com/2019/9/3/20836724/why-trump-is-atta cking-fox-news-explained.

57. Jeremy Barr, "Former CNN Contributor Scottie Nell Harris Joins RT America as Anchor," *Hollywood Reporter*, September 6, 2018, https://www.hollywoodrepo rter.com/news/cnn-contributor-scottie-nell-hughes-joins-russian-network-rt-america -1140317.

58. Jonathan Martin and Alan Rappeport, "Donald Trump Says John McCain Is No War Hero, Setting Off Another Storm," *The New York Times*, July 18, 2015, https://www.nytimes.com/2015/07/19/us/politics/trump-belittles-mccains-war-record .html.

59. Cydney Henderson, "Why Meghan McCain Is Kind of 'Grateful' That Donald Trump Is President," *USA Today*, April 10, 2019, https://www.usatoday .com/story/life/tv/2019/04/10/why-meghan-mccain-grateful-donald-trump-president/ 3427599002/; Caitlin O'Kane, "Meghan McCain on Whether She'll Vote Democrat in 2020: Joe Biden 'Could Be Very Healing for the Country,'" *CBS News*, September 26, 2019, https://www.cbsnews.com/news/meghan-mccain-the-view-host-talks-vo ting-for-joe-biden-in-2020-election-on-watch-what-happens-live/.

60. Noah Lawrence, "Trump Is a Bully. Here Are Three Ways to Take Him On," *Newsweek*, February 5, 2019, https://www.newsweek.com/trump-bullying-pelosi-202 0-elections-1318665.

61. Max Boot, "National Review's Ugly Attack on Me Reflects the Trumpification of Conservatism," *The Washington Post*, August 13, 2019, https://www.washingt onpost.com/opinions/2019/08/13/national-reviews-ugly-attack-me-reflects-trumpifi cation-conservatism/.

62. Bob Brigham, "John Bolton Is Now a 'Born-Again Never Trumper,'" Conservative Expects 'Devastating Insider's Indictment,'" *Raw Story*, November 2, 2019, https://www.rawstory.com/2019/11/ john-bolton-is-now-a-born-again-never-tr ump-conservative-expects-devastating-insiders-indictment/.

63. Connors, "It's Not 'Never Trump.' It's Country First."

Chapter 5

#NeverTrumpers and the Think Tank Resistance

Heather E. Yates

Periodically, political developments dramatically change the landscape in which organized interests operate—the 2016 presidential campaign was clearly one of those moments. The campaign and subsequent election of Donald Trump represented a tectonic shift, altering the political environment in which groups were accustomed to working. At the outset, it was clear that Trump placed minimal value on traditional norms and ground rules of the American presidency. During his term, he has refused to recuse himself from business interests, attempted to interfere with federal investigations, and leveled personal attacks on the independent media and press.[1]

Trump's behavior spurred concern among many within the GOP establishment about the future of the party. While some think tanks found it politically expedient to acquiesce to Trump, others took a step back, fearful that his presidency would dismantle Ronald Reagan's conservative movement. Republicans, many of whom have been deeply committed to the prevailing version of traditional American conservatism, went so far as to characterize Trump as an existential threat to the movement.[2] Concerned thought leaders viewed Trump as an inauthentic conservative who would not promote their interests in Washington, and, moreover, poses a danger to the U.S. democratic system itself. Prominent so-called #NeverTrumpers include a cohort of long-standing establishment-oriented officials who professed their criticisms from positions in various think tanks or even organized for the principle purpose of opposing Trump and what they believe he represents. The conservative resistance is not necessarily operating from a space of personal animus, but is motivated by a collective worry for the future of the conservative tradition that has defined the movement and the GOP for generations.

This chapter examines the role think tanks have played in the #NeverTrump resistance. As political actors, think tanks see themselves as drivers of public dialogue who produce specialized knowledge in service to the public inter-est.[3] Their principle goal is to educate elected officials, the general public, and the private sector on policy related to their specialized areas expertise.[4] The scope and purpose of their activities often incorporates an agenda of public engagement, research brokering, contract work, and policy research. Publications typically advocate for specific policy positions and research is publicly available mostly through institute websites and press releases. Think tanks, in particular, often take direct, independent action separate from the conventional legislative and political outlets in order to achieve defined political or social goals.[5] Depending on their policy focus, think tanks may criticize presidents on matters of policy, but criticism of Trump generally rests on a more fundamental foundation that runs deeper than policy-based disagreements. Indeed, several think tanks publicly opposed Donald Trump on the grounds that they believe he poses an existential threat to fundamental conservative principles, long-standing political norms, and American democ-racy itself.

As mentioned previously, think tanks will take either direct or indi-rect action in order to advance their political goals. With regards to the #NeverTrump think tank resistance, both methods are practiced. There are no better examples of direct action in response to President Trump than that as exercised by the Cato Institute, its close affiliate the Niskanen Center, and the constellation of newly formed #NeverTrump groups like "Checks and Balances," Defending Democracy Together, and Republicans for the Rule of Law. In terms of indirect action, the Heritage Foundation warrants attention because even though it remains publicly supportive of the administration's policies in general, it has often leveraged indirect resistance, such as in 2017 when it forcibly removed its pro-Trump president Jim DeMint. Given the worry that Trump is denigrating democratic institutional norms, resistance from institutes like Cato and Niskanen functions like that of an independent ombudsman, monitoring the president's blatant maladministration. These are particularly useful examples because they openly oppose President Trump on their websites, in op-eds, and in scholarship on policy matters such as tariffs, his mishandling of immigration at the southern border, and the mili-tary escalation with Iran. To be clear, the #NeverTrump resistance in think tanks is different from conventional political disagreement in that the very public and very strident opposition to Trump expressed by these institutes is chiefly about sounding the alarm, raising red flags, regarding what they see as immense threats posed by the president and those who support him and his policies.

The Niskanen Center has played a particularly important role in cultivating political action of the resistance, working in partnership with William Kristol and with the support of rank-and-file Reagan Republicans such as George

Conway III, who see that the conservative movement is badly strained. It is important to note that these organizations not only openly oppose Trump's personal and political behavior behind closed doors but they also broadcast their opposition "loud and clear" through mainstream press outlets and other media platforms, in an effort to shape and shift public attitudes and opinions. Their strident critiques of Trump's behavior and wanton disregard for institutional norms are unforgiving as they believe he poses a fundamental danger to the office of the presidency, the constitutional order, and American democracy itself.

THINK TANK ACTIVISM TURNS TO THINK TANK RESISTANCE

Brink Lindsey, vice president of the Niskanen Center, has argued that "the Trump presidency is not a freak accident, but rather the culmination of developments that have been corrupting the conservative movement and the Republican Party for many years."[6] Lindsey's comment on the state of the GOP solicits an examination of the developments that have led to the current political context in which Trumpism, and #NeverTrumpism for that matter, exists. He emphasizes, in particular, the detrimental influence of the Tea Party movement on the Republican Party as it has disrupted the party system after President Obama's election and contributed to the environment that made Trump's candidacy feasible. The Tea Party's ideological sentiments pushed the party rightward and elevated an intra-party schism, which revolved around the principle meaning of what it means to be a conservative and who would be its rightful standard-bearer. The result is that we are left with two wings of the Republican Party. The rightward push crafted an alliance of uncompromising, anti-government free-market enterprisers with conservative cultural warriors (with wide appeal to grassroots supporters turned activists) on the one side and establishment-oriented, moderate Republicans on the other.[7] At first, the Tea Party emerged as an economic populist, free-market enterprise mobilizing on a platform of astroturf activism, which was financed by the Koch Brothers' groups such as Americans for Prosperity. As it gained strength, however, the movement metamorphosized into a populist, anti-Obama faction that advocated for cultural warfare and served as a bastion for grievance mongering.[8]

This new angle gave oxygen to an insurgent political movement from the fringe, pushing the party rightward, mainstreaming the radical brand of Republican politics. However, there were fissures inside of the Tea Party movement between its elite—deep-pocketed benefactors such as the Koch Brothers and affiliated groups—and grassroots supporters and activists in the field. For the benefactors, it was about specific tax relief policies privileging the nation's top earning class. For the bulk of supporters of the Tea Party insurgency, the anti-establishment protest evolved into an anti-Obama movement. (Much of the racial antagonism which flourished under its banner is beyond the scope of this chapter, but necessitates mention here).

Electorally, the Tea Party caused self-inflicted damage to the party by undercutting long-time GOP incumbents in the primaries and by fostering distrust between its base supporters toward incumbent Republican office holders and the entire Washington establishment. However, the anti-establishment, insurgent styled politics found a champion in Donald Trump and suddenly the Tea Party faction of the party became the political establishment.

Conservative think tanks are also credited with having a hand in driving political polarization in American politics and creating a political climate that made Donald Trump's nomination in 2016 possible.[9] A significant antecedent to the politics of #NeverTrump was the transformation of public discourse on policy matters due in part to the role of conservative think tanks. They are created to, on ideological and empirical terms, challenge and disrupt what they consider the liberal political establishment. Think tanks stand on a long evolved anti-establishment, anti-elite pedigree stretching back to the Roosevelt era, and anti-New Deal sentiment.[10] Conservative think tanks, as originally conceived, were about disruption to the status quo. Now they have become the status quo.[11] They transformed the Washington intellectual landscape in their function as a counterweight to the perceived outsized influence of the FDR liberal elite, and effectively reshaped the public discourse around policy the way Reagan transformed conservatism.[12] Classic American conservatism under Reagan merged together Edmund Burke traditionalists and classical liberals (free-market capitalists) with ideological commitments to tradition and virtue and the value of wealth creation in a free-market economy coupled with an emphasis on individual liberty.[13] This foundation sustained the conservative establishment for several decades, and represents what is at stake under Trump's presidency. It is from this perspective that some establishment-oriented Republicans and traditional party conservatives are pushing back.

#NEVERTRUMP RESISTANCE IS ABOUT
SAVING THE PARTY OF REAGAN

Those #NeverTrump Republicans connected to conservative think tanks are committed to Reagan's vision of the Republican movement, one that unified several strands of conservatism under a single banner of the Republican Party.[14] The #NeverTrump faction among the Republican and libertarian policy institutes rejected what they viewed as Trump's political naiveté into the traditional Reagan Republican agenda.[15] As a private citizen, Donald Trump's civic record is mixed, with soft ideological commitments and frequent party switching, making conservative think tanks skeptical of his rhetoric and true intent with regards to the conservative agenda. The Trump resistance from inside think tanks presents itself as the guardian of the Reagan-era American conservative platform. As such, their opposition is characterized as a preservation mission, with the goal of reclaiming the party of Reagan. Traditional conservative Republicans refuse to be displaced by the Tea Party brand of Republicanism. Historically, when intra-party dealignments occur, they lead to secular realignments as a result of partisan defections, when individuals find refuge in a different party organization or withdraw from political life altogether. In contrast, most of the #NeverTrump resistance comes from two communities inside the conservative think tank universe: Reagan Republicans and free-market libertarians. Many prominent conservatives who served in Reagan's administration (and consider themselves first-generation Reagan conservatives), see Trump as an existential threat to the traditional platform of limited government, strong national defense, free markets, and individual liberty.

Conservative and libertarian policy institutes oppose President Trump mostly on ideological grounds and are principally motivated to defend what they see as a threat to the traditional conservative agenda. Their main concerns are focused on how Trump seems to be capturing the Republican Party and reshaping it in his own image. The sense of urgency emanates from what was interpreted as an abandonment of the post-Regan conservative platform and the insurgent styled disruption manifested in the Tea Party candidacies of Marco Rubio (R-FL), and Ted Cruz (R-TX).[16] The conservative #NeverTrump resistance expresses a collective concern, if not fear, that Donald Trump is dismantling traditional conservative values that have anchored the Republican Party for decades.

UNEASY ALLIANCE AT THE HERITAGE FOUNDATION

In the new political era defined by Trump and clashes among conservatives, some think tanks exhibited internal turmoil more publicly than did others. Because think tanks are not membership-based organizations, internal disputes emerged among leaders and stakeholders and appeared to revolve around public narratives capturing everything from management disputes to mission statements.

The Heritage Foundation achieved prominence during the proliferation of conservative think tanks in the 1970s. Incorporated in 1973, it has established itself as one of the most influential conservative policy institutes. Heritage's core purpose is articulated in terms of Reagan-era conservatism, reflected in its mission statement which conveys commitment to "conservative public policies based on the principles of free enterprise, limited government, individual freedom and traditional American values, and a strong national defense."[17] While the Heritage Foundation has worked with administrations from both parties, it has more influence with Republican officeholders, who have helped the Heritage Foundation establish its reputation as a respected conservative-leaning policy institute. Its public agenda and research features topics devoted to what it calls "responsible conservatism." The Heritage Foundation has established working relationships within the media and academic spheres, the business sector, and financial industries.[18] Suffice it to say that, as a policy institute, The Heritage Foundation is an enduring fixture in Washington.

While the Heritage Foundation has enjoyed considerable influence on Trump's policy agenda during his first term, it has not publicly presented as a pro-Trump institution. However, during the past few years, we have seen pro-Trump leadership at its helm. Its now former president, Jim DeMint was recognized to be an ardent supporter of President Trump, a position cultivated through personal friendships with Vice President Mike Pence and many White House staff.

However, over time the Heritage Foundation's advisory board grew increasingly uncomfortable with DeMint's political posturing, as they perceived him as leveraging the think tank's platform and reputation for access to President Trump and those close to him. In the spring of 2017, only a few months after Trump's inauguration, DeMint was summarily ousted from his post as president of Heritage. It was an unexpected development from the think tank that had been working closely with the administration. The unexpected dismissal of DeMint gave the indication that the Heritage Foundation's internal leadership was uncomfortable with the close association between its policy institute and Donald Trump.

Public accounts suggest that the institute's board members believed DeMint's personal politics and ambitions jeopardized the institute's purpose and threatened to take the think tank in an unsanctioned direction. Details indicate that DeMint's dismissal was a decision caused by the Republican attempt to repeal-and-replace Obamacare in March 2017 and that DeMint had committed the organization to policy positions the board did not support.[19] The public narrative suggests that the Heritage Foundation was protecting its own policy turf against internal power plays that would have forced the its endorsement of policies it did not support.[20] Articulated concerns focused on the fact that DeMint appeared to utilize the Foundation as his personal political long-arm, and the complaints against him include concerns he neglected the research and scholarly aims of the institute.[21] DeMint's leadership was accused of converting the Heritage Foundation into an ardent ideologically driven political tool in service of Trump's personal agenda to repeal Obamacare.[22] Even though the Heritage Foundation carries considerable influence with the Trump administration, its decision to remove DeMint suggests that it is not willing to be politically aligned, at least in terms of personnel, with the White House.

LIBERTARIAN ALLIES OF THE CONSERVATIVE RESISTANCE

Libertarians and Republicans appreciate a reasonably affable partnership in terms of a shared commitment to conservative principles. However, in era of Trump, some #NeverTrump libertarians began questioning whether the president shared their commitment to rule of law, institutional norms, and democratic practices.[23] When it was clear that Trump had secured the Republican nomination, and a scheme to orchestrate a brokered convention to disrupt Trump's bid for the White House failed, it was not surprising that #NeverTrump Republicans partnered with libertarian allies to develop and implement a long-term strategy centered on shoring up the conservative movement.[24] The response was a concerted #NeverTrump effort with the leadership of libertarian-leaning think tanks such as the Cato Institute and its close affiliate, the Niskanen Center.[25]

The Cato Institute articulates its commitment to engaging the public in the promotion of individual liberty, limited government and free markets.[26] It is also an active organ in the anti-Trump resistance, publishing papers and disseminating research to engage the public. In the era of Trump, research fellows at both think tanks are publicly critical of Trump on myriad policy matters, and most bitterly vocal on the view that Trump is endangering constitutional norms. From the official platforms of Cato and the Niskanen Center, their analysts publish scathing #NeverTrump critiques.[27] Since he took office, the Cato Institute operates as an active hub for the anti-Trump intellectual movement, serving as a repository for research cataloging the harms inflicted by him to democratic norms and institutions.[28]

The public anti-Trump sentiment at the Cato Institute is stinging. Graham Vyse, a Cato analyst, equated Trump with authoritarianism, asserting the president's "contempt for the Constitution and democratic norms is exceeded only by his ignorance of them."[29] Vyse went on to outline the case for Trump's penchant for authoritarianism, "He's an authoritarian by instinct who swoons over dictators and lashes out at the independent judiciary, rejects Congress as a co-equal branch of government, and fancies himself above the law."[30] On the topic of Congress, other analysts have called out Trump's use of social media to denigrate democratic institutions, especially when he targeted sitting members of Congress. A senior fellow, Thomas Firey, criticized Trump's use of Twitter to vilify four Democratic minority congresswomen in his tweet that said they should "go back" to the countries "they originally came from. Firey wrote, "This post focuses on a different problem with the tweet, one that has gotten overlooked: it was a direct attack on representative government and the US Constitution."[31] Senior research fellows like Michael Tanner implicated Congress in its acquiescence to Trump's declaration of a domestic emergency to redirect federal budget funds to his pet campaign promise of building a southern border wall. "Now, we have President Trump claiming the authority to reallocate funds that Congress (a) specifically appropriated for other purposes and (b) specifically refused to appropriate for the uses the president wants. Congress may actually have voluntarily surrendered its authority."[32]

While the Cato Institute is active with disseminating research on the adverse effects of Trump's policies, The Niskanen Center, whose articulated mission echoes the principles of the Cato Institute, also branded itself a refuge, or an ad hoc headquarters, for the #NeverTrump resistance.[33] It functions as a staging ground for mobilizing the resistance into political action, with a pointed message of purpose on its website, "to advance an open society by active engagement in the war of ideas . . . mobilize other groups to support those proposals."[34] The sense of urgency emanates from what is interpreted as an abandonment of the Reagan conservative platform and a counter to the disruptive Tea Party faction. After taking an inventory of the 2016 election, the Niskanen Center's intellectual emphasis was reoriented toward political action. "We [Republicans] cannot simply wait for Trump to pass from the scene, or for Democrats to win big, and hope that things will somehow go back to normal."[35] Niskanen's statement signaled the institute will be engaging in more direct political action to supplement the scholarly resistance.

With this focus in mind, Niskanen analysts are openly critical of Trump on what they see is his corrupting influence on the Republican Party by imperiling the partnership between libertarian free-market principles and traditional GOP conservatism. As one Niskanen analyst observed, "The imminent integration between Trump's business enterprises (notwithstanding the ludicrous suggestion that letting his children run them will prevent that integration) and his official position is a serious danger."[36] There is palpable concern that Trump, as the GOP's standard-bearer, who sets the tone and priorities for the party, is effectively re-branding the GOP in his own image. As Niskanen's president, Jerry Taylor, commented, "despite scandal and chaos and incompetence engulfing the White House, the president nevertheless tightened his grip on the party by merging his campaign with the national party while actively working to thwart a challenger."[37]

In addition to their apprehensions, other Niskanen scholars echo their Cato Institute peers regarding concern for democratic norms. While Cato's public research has emphasized Trump's proclivity toward authoritarianism, Niskanen scholars criticize Trump's abuse of the independent press and its journalists. A resident analyst, Paul Gowder writes, "equally alarming are Trump's efforts to undermine the free press [. . .] and this appears to be a conscious strategy of Trump's, who has been attacking the media in speeches and on Twitter, who put the press in a pen at his rallies to be abused by the attending mobs."[38] Gowder's essay details a comprehensive indictment of the risks Trump poses to American democracy, and concludes that, "However, given Trump's pattern of behavior, and its striking resemblance to authoritarian precedent, it would be imprudent and irresponsible not to consider the possibility that something like this [collapse] could happen."[39]

The Niskanen Center's 2019 conspectus report addressed this crisis for traditional conservatism when it wrote, "the politics of the 21st century increasingly pits defenders of the open society against a new breed of populists animated by a vision of a closed and exclusive national community."[40] As the perception of threat grew, the Niskanen Center became something of the unofficial headquarters of the intellectual rebuke of Trump, offering a space for those "whose loyalties to [the] movement and party are now badly strained or even severed."[41] After the initial distress associated with Trump's election subsided, a sense of urgency was felt most intently among conservatives. There was a pressing need to examine the implications of a Trump presidency as the Niskanen Center president acknowledged, "It is a dark time for those who consider themselves 'Never Trumpers' or moderates. That community now has been blown apart."[42]

Unwilling to be sidelined, a group of Republican consultants, conservative media personalities and a few public officials, together with their libertarian allies organized regular meetings at the Niskanen Center, calling their gatherings the "the Meeting of the Concerned."[43] Details made public indicate that the meetings were focused on the future of the Republican Party, and less focused on Donald Trump. Their resistance is as much about defending traditional conservative ideology as it is about promoting conservative policy. As the Niskanen vice president put it, "At stake is not simply the redemption of a great political party, or the effective representation of important constituencies and values . . . the continued stability and integrity of republican self-government in America are on the line."[44] Furthermore, the #NeverTrump think tank resistance set its focus for what comes after Trump and his presidency. At a small conference hosted at the Niskanen Center in the fall of 2018 titled "Starting Over: The Center-Right After Trump" they began to calculate a strategy forward. As one Republican consultant at the conference observed, "as the leader of the party he's [Trump] shaping what the party stands for, but he's not going to be president forever, if you look at the next generation of Republican leaders, people who are likely to be our nominee in 2024 and 2028, they generally represent a classical version of conservatism."[45] The #NeverTrump resistance is strategizing its field operation for the 2020 campaign because, as one analyst put it, "The electoral process is another important coordinating institution for mass resistance to would be autocrats."[46]

"CHECKS AND BALANCES"

As detailed earlier, a shared concern motivating the conservative #NeverTrump resistance is the threat to constitutional and democratic norms. Conservative #NeverTrumpers who are not affiliated with existing think tanks are also mobilizing for direct political action. Conservative figures such as George Conway III and Bill Kristol congregate among various social networks and have launched ad hoc groups for the purposes of further mobilizing the #NeverTrump resistance. Their message is straightforward: not all conservatives, libertarians, and self-identified Republicans are Trump supporters by default, and there is a resistance among the ranks.[47] These sorts of freelance resisters have fashioned themselves a public platform from which to not only publicly criticize Trump, but to actively challenge him electorally.

In November 2018, just ahead of its annual legal conference in Washington several prominent members of Federalist Society officially made public the creation of a new group called "Checks and Balances" to raise awareness of Trump's malfeasance.[48] Its charter signatories feature several prominent conservative legal minds and rank-and-file Republicans including George Conway, the spouse of close Trump aid and White House counsel Kellyanne Conway. Other founders include former White House officials such as Homeland Security Secretary Tom Ridge, Reagan's Deputy Counsel Phillip Brady, Bush's Legal Advisor and Senior Counsel John Bellinger and Bush's Assistant Attorney General Peter Keisler.[49] While the group does not have any formal tax code designation or engage in specific actions or projects, its principle method is to circulate position statements in the press and media, using methods similar to conservative think tanks trying to drive a public discourse that raises public awareness about the president's violations of legal and constitutional norms.[50]

The mission statement articulates a call to action and characterizes its existence as a voice and a safe outlet for anyone who wishes to have a platform to hold the president accountable. The group's articulated purpose reiterates the conservative platform they are committed to defending; "we believe in rule of law, the power of truth, the independence of the criminal justice system, the imperative of individual rights, and the necessity of civil discourse."[51] They go on to articulate their principles of political philosophy, "We believe in the Constitution, We believe in free speech, a free press, separation of power, and limited government."[52]

"Checks and Balances" self identifies as group of attorneys and legal experts who believe they need to hold Trump accountable, "We seek to provide a voice and a network for like-minded attorneys to discuss these ideas, and we hope that they will join with us to stand up for these principles."[53] Members are unified in their concerns that, "the president is abusing the office of the presidency for personal political objectives."[54] They make their opposition very clear in that Trump's behavior and wanton disregard for institutional norms pose a danger to the presidency, and more generally, American democratic institutions.

The members of this network also distinguish themselves from their professional affiliations. Although they are outspoken critics of the president, they do so in their own capacity. "Each of use speaks and acts solely in our individual capacities, and our views should not be attributed to any organization we may be affiliated with."[55] In their own capacity, they issue innumerable public statements protesting President Trump and his behavior. John Bellinger commented that members were moved to action because, "There is a deep-seated concern and uneasiness in conservative legal circles with the president's attacks on our institutions, including the press and the Department of Justice, and a belief that conservative lawyers are not speaking up enough."[56] These anti-Trump sentiments are more substantive than political opposition—the public comments suggest they believe a civic obligation to speak out against the president. To that point, another member, Paul Rosenzweig said, "all of us believe in conservative legal principles and in the need to stand up for them no matter who is the president."[57]

Their statements convey a collective concern that silence enables the perceived abuses to continue unabated and, like political action at the Niskanen Center, there is a sense of urgency to speak out on behalf of the conservative principles like of rule of law and individual liberty. One of the group's more recognizable associates, George Conway, is a remarkable opponent of the president given his spouse's White House post. As a private citizen, Conway criticizes Trump and his own party for its complacency. In one of his television interviews granted to MSNBC, Conway articulated his bewilderment and frustration at the Republican Party, "I'm horrified. I'm appalled. If you had told me three years ago that it would come to this, I wouldn't have believed it. If Barack Obama had done these things, they'd be out for blood. And they'd be right." Adding the sense of urgency, he stated, "It's the moment. I don't frankly want to be on TV. I just don't get why people don't see this, or are refusing to see this. It's appalling to me."[58] Additionally, Conway has authored or coauthored op-eds in prominent publications outlining specific actions by Trump which he believes are in direct conflict with the U.S. Constitution and the powers of the presidency on everything from the Mueller investigation to Trump's proposal of eliminating 14th amendment birthright citizenship.[59] Meanwhile, Conway has taken his #NeverTrump salvos to Twitter, where he routinely confronts the president in real time on the perceived rank incompetence of the president and abuses that he views are threatening democratic norms.[60]

The formation of "Checks and Balances" is extraordinary because the Federalist Society is one of the most influential conservative legal organizations in the United States. Established in 1982 as a 501c3 educational organization, it advocates for originalist constitutional interpretations and promotes the adherence to judicial restraint and has become one of the most influential organizations in vetting and recommending judicial appointments to presidential administrations.[61] This influence notwithstanding, it serves as a good example of the how some Reagan conservatives are mobilizing in the #NeverTrump resistance.

DEFENDING DEMOCRACY TOGETHER

Inspired by the Niskanen Center, Bill Kristol, in collaboration with long-time Washington think tank veteran, Sarah Longwell, organized another #NeverTrump think tank called the Defending Democracy Together Institute (DDTI) and two advocacy groups called Republicans for the Rule of Law and Defending Democracy Together (DDT). The organization, DDT, formed around the time that Kristol's publication *The Weekly Standard* stopped production. In the Trump era, some conservative periodicals became vehicles to criticize Donald Trump. Any criticism of the president was met with hostile reception and likely contributed to many publications going under. As Kristol recounts, "The Standard's demise [resulted from] the hostility it faced as an anti-Trump organ operating inside the Trump-dominated right."[62] Despite the open hostility toward critical publications of Trump, Kristol and conservative allies pressed forward to establish the groups to promote conservative activism through public engagement and discourse, and raise public awareness through political action.

The DDT institute is a 501c3 educational organization "dedicated to defending America's democratic norms, values, and institutions and fighting for consistent conservative principles like rule of law, free trade, and expanding legal immigration."[63] It operates as the intellectual center affiliated with the advocacy group to "resist Trump and Trumpism inside the Republican Party."[64] Furthermore, DDT is structured like a policy issue cooperative. There are six articulated areas that have dedicated focus: the rule of law; birthright citizenship (which Trump wants to eliminate); immigration and naturalization; fighting tariffs; an anti-Putin platform; and defending American allies.[65] Each niche area showcased on the organization's website takes interested participants to an informal network of supporters where they can sign up for digital newsletters, with the exception of Republicans for the Rule of Law. With each issue area outlined, DDTs scope and purpose of its strategy is reinforced, it serves as a reminder of values and policy platforms of the pre-Trump Republican Party. In terms of raising awareness, its educational tactics are based in research, education, and grassroots activism.[66] In addition to the foundation of the organization's mission, Kristol articulates that DDT exists in order to actively combat the dangers posed by Trump's abuse of power that jeopardizes election integrity, federal agencies, and the Republican Party itself.[67]

The one niche area where DDT established an affiliated 501c4 advocacy group is with the Republicans for the Rule of Law. Although listed as one of DDTs subsidiary projects, it is the only one with a designated code that permits direct advocacy and political organizing, rather than simply public education. It suggests that the Republicans for the Rule of Law will be engaging in political activism in the 2020 presidential campaign cycle. Specifically, the group Republicans for the Rule of Law was incorporated for DDTs project-specific action on legal advocacy and lobbying (with non-disclosed donors) with the possibility of engaging members of Congress more directly on issues pertaining to civil rights, institutional transparency, and preserving an independent judiciary.[68] Of the think tanks discussed in this chapter, the DDT trifecta is the most formalized operation. It is organized into separate legal designations to raise and spend money in political pursuits to defeat Donald Trump.

CLOSING THOUGHTS ABOUT
RESISTANCE IN THE TRUMP ERA

Trumpism has complicated the think tank universe. Conservative policy institutes operate on a decades long practices of disrupting the political establishment, especially when that establishment was dominated by the New Deal coalition. With the rise of Trump, many organizations are forced to choose between a newly populist Republican president and the traditional conservative norms and policies they advocated for over a generation. They must attempt to disentangle the GOP from the populist insurgency that has supplanted traditional conservative and libertarian think tank leanings.

As some conservative groups see it, the Republican Party is embroiled in a crisis of principles. The longer Trump remains the party's standard-bearer, the more he actively redefines conservatism, nudging it further away from Reagan's vision. The polarizing effect Trump has had in the group universe is undeniable. The conservative #NeverTrump resistance functions much like a watchdog and as an external mechanism of accountability to address the void of institutional controls created by intra-party and hyper-partisan conflict in Washington.

In summary, during the campaign, think tanks were relatively subdued because then candidate Trump was difficult to predict (and the prospects of his election seemed unlikely). For groups to prognosticate about his governing style was unproductive and hyperbolic. Now that he has been in office for a term and seeking reelection, Trumpism has distorted the political landscape in which groups and think tanks operate to influence public awareness. During the presidential campaign, the organized resistance against Trump's candidacy surfaced mostly from the foreign policy wing of the Republican Party. Since then, libertarian-oriented think tanks have provided much of the oxygen for the ideological resistance to the Trump administration, though they are joined by more traditionally conservative groups as well.

Mostly, in the era of Trump, think tanks are actively and directly engaging the public to disseminate and circulate information, research policy positions, and making incisive suggestions. They are not engaged in the politics of pressure, but the politics of public education, and as detailed with organizations like Republicans for the Rule of Law, the #NeverTrump movement is expanding beyond think tank activism. They are engaging in political electioneering—trying to appeal to public awareness and advocate for the restoration of conservative principles at the ballot box.

NOTES

1. Christine Todd Whitman, "Calling My Fellow Republicans: Trump Is Clearly Unfit to Remain in Office," *Los Angeles Times*, July 22, 2018, https://www.lat imes.com/opinion/op-ed/la-oe-whitman-trump-helsinki-gop-response-20180722-s tory.html.

2. Tess Bonn, " 'Never Trump' Conservative Says GOP Could Pose 'Existential Threat' to US," *The Hill.* December 5, 2018, https://thehill.com/hilltv/rising/4 19826-never-trump-conservative-calls-gop-existential-threat-to-us; Brink Lindsey, "Republicanism for Republicans," *National Affairs*, Winter 2019, https://www.nat ionalaffairs.com/publications/detail/republicanism-for-republicans.

3. David M. Ricci, *The Transformation of American Politics: The New Washington and the Rise of Think Tanks* (New Have: Yale University Press, 1993).

4. Donald E. Abelson, *Do Think Tanks Matter? Assessing the Impact of Public Policy Institutes* (Ontario, Canada: Queen's School of Policy Studies, 2002).

5. Burdett A. Loomis and Allan J. Cigler, "Introduction: The Changing Nature of Interest Group Politics," in *Interest Group Politics*, eds. Burdett A. Loomis and Allan J. Cigler, 8th edition (Washington DC: CQ Press, 2012), 1–34; Alexander Fouirnaies and Andrew B. Hall, "How Do Interest Groups Seek Access to Committees?" *American Journal of Political Science*, 62, no. 1 (January 2018): 132–47.

6. Lindsey, "Republicanism."

7. Theda Skocpol and Vanessa Williamson, *The Tea Party and the Remaking of Republican Conservatism* (New York: Oxford University Press, 2012), 157–88.

8. Skocpol and Williamson, "Tea Party," 157; Katherine J. Cramer, *The Politics of Resentment: Rural Consciousness in Wisconsin and the Rise of Scott Walker* (Chicago: University of Chicago Press, 2016).

9. Jason Stahl, "How Conservative Think Tanks Helped Create the Age of Trump," CEHD Vision 2020 Blog, The University of Minnesota, August 12, 2016, https://cehdvision2020.umn.edu/blog/conservative-think-tanks/; Jason Stahl, *Right Moves: The Conservative Think Tank in American Political Culture Since 1945* (Chapel Hill: University of North Carolina Press, 2016), 9–21.

10. Stahl, *Right Moves*.

11. Stahl, *Right Moves*.

12. Stahl, *Right Moves*.

13. Gleaves Whitney, "Ronald Reagan and the Conservative Movement," *Hauenstein Center for Presidential Studies*, June 9, 2004, https://scholarworks.gvsu.edu/cgi/viewcontent.cgi?article=1093&context=ask_gleaves.

14. Whitney, "Ronald Reagan."

15. Daniel McCarthy, "A New Conservative Agenda: A Governing Philosophy for the Twenty-First Century," *First Things*, March 2019, https://www.firstthings.com/article/2019/03/a-new-conservative-agenda.

16. McCarthy, "Conservative Agenda."

17. "About Heritage," accessed on March 1, 2020, https://www.heritage.org/about-heritage/mission.

18. Jeffrey B. Gayner, "The Contract with America: Implementing New Ideas in the U.S.," *The Heritage Foundation*, October 12, 1995, https://www.heritage.org/political-process/report/the-contract-america-implementing-new-ideas-the-us.

19. Eliana Johnson and Nancy Cook, "The Real Reason Jim DeMint Got the Boot," *Politico*, May 2, 2017, https://www.politico.com/story/2017/05/02/why-jim-demint-was-ousted-from-heritage-237876.

20. John McCormack, "The Heritage Foundation's Sudden Shakeup," *The Washington Examiner*, May 8, 2017, https://www.washingtonexaminer.com/weekly-standard/the-heritage-foundations-sudden-shakeup.

21. Johnson and Cook, "Real Reason."

22. Johnson and Cook, "Real Reason."

23. Daniel Cox, Juhem Navarro-Rivera, and Robert P. Jones, "In Search of Libertarians in America," *The Public Religion Research Institute*, October 29, 2013, https://www.prri.org/research/2013-american-values-survey/; William A. Galston,

"Libertarian Values & a Divide in the Republican Party," *Brookings*, October 30, 2013, https://www.brookings.edu/blog/fixgov/2013/10/30/libertarian-values-a-divide -in-the-republican-party/.

24. Brian Doherty, "Does the Libertarian Party Finally Have a Chance?" *Politico Magazine*, May 26, 2016, https://www.politico.com/magazine/story/2016/05/never -trump-2016-elections-libertarians-213917; Miranda Green, "Some #NeverTrump Republicans Consider 3rd Party," *ABC News San Diego*, May 4, 2016, https://www .10news.com/decodedc/some-die-hard-nevertrump-republicans-consider-third-party-run; Alan Rappeport, "Libertarians See a Chance Amid Discontent Over Donald Trump and Hillary Clinton," *The New York Times*, May 29, 2016, https://www.nyt imes.com/2016/05/30/us/politics/libertarians-see-chance-amid-discontent-over-don ald-trump-and-hillary-clinton.html.

25. Leigh Ann Caldwell, "Will Republicans Find Solace in The Libertarian Party?" *NBC News*, March 24, 2016, https://www.nbcnews.com/politics/2016-electio n/will-republicans-find-solace-libertarian-party-n544496.

26. "About Cato," accessed March 1, 2020, https://www.cato.org/about.

27. "The Range of Cato's Work," https://www.cato.org/mission; Ilya Somin, "No, Libertarians Have Not Thrown in with Trump," *Cato Institute*, January 30, 2018, https://www.cato.org/publications/commentary/no-libertarians-have-not-throw n-trump.

28. Aaron Powell and Matthew Feeney, "Trump's Assault on America's Institutions," Free Thoughts Podcast, January 19, 2018, https://www.libertarianism .org/media/free-thoughts/trumps-assault-americas-institutions.

29. Graham Vyse, "Libertarians Should Stand Against Authoritarianism," *Cato Unbound*, October 15, 2019, https://www.cato-unbound.org/2019/10/15/graham-vys e/libertarians-should-stand-against-authoritarianism.

30. Vyse, "Libertarians Should Stand."

31. Thomas Firey, "The Other Problem with Trump's Tweet," Cato at Liberty, July 26, 2019, https://www.cato.org/blog/other-problem-trumps-tweet.

32. Michael D. Tanner, "Congress Is Complicit in Trump's Power Grab," February 20, 2019, https://www.cato.org/publications/commentary/congress-compli cit-trumps-power-grab.

33. David M. Drucker, "Little-Known DC Think Tank Becomes Brain Trust of 'Never Trumpism,'" *The Washington Examiner*, February 1, 2019, https://www.was hingtonexaminer.com/news/campaigns/little-known-dc-think-tank-becomes-brain -trust-of-never-trumpism.

34. "About," accessed March 1, 2020, https://www.niskanencenter.org/about.

35. Lindsey, "Republicanism."

36. Paul Gowder, "The Trump Threat to the Rule of Law and the Constitution," *The Niskanen Center-Commentary on Open Society*, February 3, 2017, https://www .niskanencenter.org/trump-threat-rule-law-constitution/.

37. Tim Alberta, "The End of the Libertarian Dream?" *Politico*, March/April 2017, https://www.politico.com/magazine/story/2017/03/libertarian-politics-succes s-failure-donald-trump-era-214847; Conor Friedersdorf, "Where Libertarians Stand as Donald Trump Rises," *The Atlantic*, March 31, 2016, https://www.theatlantic.c

om/politics/archive/2016/03/where-libertarians-stand-as-donald-trump-rises/47613
9/; Henry Olsen, "What Happened to the 'Libertarian Moment'?" *The National
Review*, November 20, 2017, https://www.nationalreview.com/2017/11/libertarian
-conservatives-influence-republican-party-shrinking/; Kevin D. Williamson, "The
Passing of the Libertarian Moment," *The Atlantic*, April 2, 2018, https://www.the
atlantic.com/politics/archive/2018/04/defused/556934/; "Trump Is the Opposite of a
Libertarian," *Libertarian*, March 28, 2018, https://www.lp.org/trump-opposite-libe
rtarian/.

38. Gowder, "Trump Threat."

39. Gowder, "Trump Threat."

40. "Conspectus Annual Report," *The Niskanen Center*, 2019, https://www.nis
kanencenter.org/wp-content/uploads/2019/09/Niskanen-conspectus-2017-final-1.pdf.

41. Lindsey, "Republicanism."

42. Jonathan Miller, "A Place for the GOP to Mull Life After Trump," *Roll Call*,
May 1, 2019, https://www.rollcall.com/news/congress/place-gop-mull-life-trump.

43. Mark Leibovich, "Meet the Other Resistance: The Republican One," *The New
York Times Magazine*, April 24, 2019, https://www.nytimes.com/2019/04/24/magaz
ine/republican-primary-trump-resistance.html.

44. Lindsey, "Republicanism."

45. Miller, "Place for the GOP."

46. Gowder, "Trump Threat."

47. George Conway, Steve Schmidt, John Weaver, and Rick Wilson, "We Are
Republicans, and We Want Trump Defeated," *The New York Times*, December 17,
2019, https://www.nytimes.com/2019/12/17/opinion/lincoln-project.html.

48. Adam Liptak, "Conservative Lawyers Say Trump Has Undermined the Rule
of Law," *The New York Times*, November 14, 2018, https://www.nytimes.com/2018
/11/14/us/politics/conservative-lawyers-trump.html.

49. "About," accessed March 1, 2020, https://checks-and-balances.org/about/.

50. Preet Bharara and Christine Todd Whitman, et al., "Proposals for Reform:
National Task Force on Rule of Law & Democracy," Brennan Center for Justice,
October 2, 2018, https://www.brennancenter.org/our-work/policy-solutions/prop
osals-reform-national-task-force-rule-law-democracy; Deanna Paul, "Kellyanne
Conway's Husband and Reagan's Counsel Are Among Lawyers Warning that Trump
Imperils Democracy," *The Washington Post*, November 14, 2018, https://www.was
hingtonpost.com/politics/2018/11/14/kellyanne-conways-husband-reagans-counsel
-are-among-lawyers-warning-that-trump-imperils-democracy/.

51. "About," https://checks-and-balances.org/about/.

52. "About," https://checks-and-balances.org/about/.

53. "About," https://checks-and-balances.org/about/.

54. Press release, "New Statement from Checks and Balances on President
Trump's Abuse of Office," October 10, 2019, https://checks-and-balances.org/new
-statement-from-checks-and-balances-on-president-trumps-abuse-of-office/.

55. "About," https://checks-and-balances.org/about/.

56. Paul, "Kellyanne Conway's Husband."

57. Paul, "Kellyanne Conway's Husband."

58. Rob Tornoe, "George Conway Moves from Twitter to MSNBC: I'm 'Horrified' and 'Appalled,'" *The Philadelphia Inquirer*, November 13, 2019, https://www.inquirer.com/politics/nation/george-conway-msnbc-impeachment-hearings-kellyanne-trump-twitter-20191113.html.

59. George Conway III and Neal Katyal, "Trump's Proposal to End Birthright Citizenship Is Unconstitutional," *The Washington Post*, October 30, 2018, https://www.washingtonpost.com/opinions/trumps-proposal-to-end-birthright-citizenship-is-unconstitutional/2018/10/30/4615ab5c-dc85-11e8-b3f0-62607289efee_story.html; Neal Katyal and George Conway III, "Trump's Appointment of the Acting Attorney General Is Unconstitutional," *The New York Times*, November 8, 2018, https://www.nytimes.com/2018/11/08/opinion/trump-attorney-general-sessions-unconstitutional.html.

60. @gtconway3d, https://twitter.com/gtconway3d.

61. Liptak, "Conservative Lawyers Say Trump Has Undermined the Rule of Law"; Marcia Coyle, "New Conservative Lawyers' Group 'Checks and Balances' Bristles at Trump," *The National Law Journal*, November 14, 2018, https://www.law.com/nationallawjournal/2018/11/14/new-conservative-lawyers-group-checks-and-balances-bristles-at-trump/.

62. Christal Hayes and Aamer Madhani, "'May It Rest in Peace' Trump Celebrates End of Weekly Standard, a Critical GOP Magazine," *USA Today*, December 14, 2018, https://www.usatoday.com/story/news/politics/2018/12/14/weekly-standard-conservative-magazine-closes-never-donald-trump-bill-kristol/2312627002/.

63. "About Us," accessed March 1, 2020, https://www.defendingdemocracytogether.org/about-us/.

64. Leibovich, "Meet the Other Resistance."

65. "Projects," accessed March 1, 2020, https://www.defendingdemocracytogether.org/#projects.

66. "About Us," https://www.defendingdemocracytogether.org/about-us/.

67. "About Us," https://www.defendingdemocracytogether.org/about-us/.

68. "Projects," https://www.defendingdemocracytogether.org/#projects.

Chapter 6

Elephants Grumble

The Republican Establishment's Resistance to Donald Trump

Jason S. Byers

On November 8, 2016, Donald Trump defeated Hillary Clinton to become the next president of the United States. He was able to climb out of relative political obscurity with the help of an emerging populist movement within the American electorate, win the Republican nomination, and ride the insurgency wave into the White House. President Trump's victory sent political shock-waves across the country, based on the fact that almost every news media outlet in the country had predicted a sizeable victory for Hillary Clinton, with some claiming that her probability of victory was anywhere between 70 and 99 percent.[1] Nevertheless, on January 20, 2017, Donald J. Trump was sworn in as the forty-fifth president of the United States.

Donald Trump's ascension to the presidency was the result of a highly contentious electoral battle. Opposition from Democrats was expected, of course; what was unexpected was the often-unrelenting opposition Trump received from some within his own political party. Trump received fierce scrutiny from well-established members of the GOP throughout his campaign, and the opposition has continued (for some) throughout the first term of his administration. The most adamant public opposition to President Trump has come from so-called #NeverTrumpers—prominent figures long synonymous with the GOP (such as the Bush family, Senators John McCain and Mitt Romney, Michael Steel, Rick Wilson, and others)—rather than from more obscure fringe partisan factions.

Throughout the presidential nomination and general election campaigns and during the first three years of his administration, President Trump has faced harsh criticism from those within the GOP establishment. The tone and tenor of this relationship has varied, however, with much of the harshest criticism dissipating over time. As it relates to the #NeverTrump movement or the #NeverTrumpers, "the establishment" refers to mainstream, committed, often long-standing members of the GOP who helped maintain, build, expand, and run the party prior to the emergence of Donald Trump. These members generally support and promote traditional conservative values— small government, the traditional family, free markets, and Christian principles—many of which may appear to contradict the policies, rhetoric, and behavior of Trump, his campaign, and administration.

The "old guard" was chiefly concerned with the insurgent campaign of Donald Trump and the tone and tenor of the particular brand of populist message he presented. As such, their main focus was protection of the party as it pertained to the short-term goals of electoral success in 2016, but also the long-term preservation of the principles and norms that have sustained the GOP throughout the post–World War II era.[2] Many members of the establishment were concerned with the potential damage that a Trump presidency would have on the GOP brand. They also viewed Trump's behavior as degrading fundamental norms within society. Public opinion data reveal a wide schism between elite and mass publics. When examining voters who would be considered a part of the GOP establishment, such as those that identify strongly with the Reagan presidency compared to those who would more readily identify with Trump, four of every five Trump Republicans claimed that the changes he would instill in the party were for the betterment of the party, whereas only 35 percent of Reagan Republicans agreed with the same sentiment.[3]

Early on, Donald Trump was not warmly welcomed by conservative elites, but in short time he had staged a successful insurgency movement which gained control of the GOP. Insurgents, as it pertains to the recent reshaping of the Republican Party, rebelled against the establishment and have viewed Trump as the titular leader in this effort. Within this framework, it becomes clear why members of the establishment decided to fight against the Trump campaign in order to secure the viability of their position in the party. These elites understood that Trump and his supporters sought to supplant the elite power structures and, along the way, challenge many of the core values of the Republican Party.

In this chapter, I briefly describe how Donald Trump secured the Republican nomination and has continued to dominate the GOP throughout his first term. Second, I discuss the principal members of the #NeverTrump movement, especially those we would consider part of the Republican Party establishment. Third, I examine the impact of President Trump on the Republican Party as a whole and evaluate if there will be any lasting effects in terms of political dealignment or nationalization. Lastly, I examine where the #NeverTrump movement currently stands with respect to these key members of the Republican Party establishment.

THE GOP ESTABLISHMENT AND THE 2016 ELECTIONS

The 2016 presidential election was indeed historic, as it marked only the fourth time that a presidential candidate won the election by way of electoral college vote while not winning the popular vote.[4] Based on the politics of the previous eight years, the Republican electorate seemed primed for a candidate like Donald Trump to emerge. In 2008, presidential candidate John McCain selected Alaskan governor Sarah Palin as his running mate. Initial skepticism, intrigue, and a brief burst of enthusiasm would soon give way to regret and embarrassment for many Republicans. Palin's glaring deficiencies as a candidate, her policy positions, and her aggressive counter-establishment rhetoric were appealing for a moment, but the shine quickly wore away for GOP elites.[5] Palin thrust populism to the front lines and instilled within some Republican voters the notion that there was a real separation between rank and file voters and the political elites (i.e., elected officials and members of the establishment).[6] The rise in the levels of party polarization (or elite polarization) that began in the 1980s, which were exacerbated during the 2008 presidential election and President Obama's two terms, coupled with negative effects of the Great Recession and the growing perception that public officials were out of touch with the concerns of "real people," compelled many voters to embrace a growing populist movement.[7] Indeed, Alan Abramowitz argues that polarization does not only occur at the elite level and that "its causes can be found in dramatic changes in American society and culture that have divided the public into opposing camps—those who welcome those changes and those who feel threatened by them."[8]

The Republican Party was at a crossroads. One road would allow the party to better diversify in terms of its platform and electoral outreach and appeal, thus becoming more of a party of inclusion. The other road would lead the party toward a more populist message, rooted in grievances, and "status threat," thereby increasing a pattern of exclusion.[9] Populism, and the xenophobia that generally accompanies it, was not instilled in the Republican Party in 2008; it was something that lurked below the surface of the party's ranks long before. Additionally, as Tim Alberta claims, "Although racism was alive and well, and fears of ethnic targeting spiked after 9/11, xenophobia did not dominate the national political environment."[10] This shifts in the 2004 presidential election and fully takes its hold on the party in 2008. Ultimately, the Republicans would lose the 2008 election and would slowly allow more extreme candidates to dictate the party's message.

Since the 2008 election, we have seen a dramatic increase in the polarization within the American electorate and between the parties, due in large part to an increase in negative partisanship.[11] Negative partisanship refers to the notion that voters have become more ideologically homogeneous

within their own political parties; they tend to harbor increasingly negative feelings toward the opposing party.[12] Basically, the two parties have
moved further away from one another ideologically, and voters have started
to view the opposition party more negatively. Out of this environment,
insurgent oriented candidacies for local, state, and congressional offices
sprung up, and were promoted by the Tea Party movement, which began
in 2010 and corresponded with a populist moment within the Republican
Party.[13] The prevailing message of the movement revolved around concern
about "Washington elites" who were "perceived as Wall Street, the Obama
administration and Democrats who want to increase the size of government."[14] In 2010, there were a total of 138 Republican congressional candidates who were either Tea Party candidates or strongly supported by the
Tea Party movement.[15]

It was clear a decade ago that there was a disturbance within the Republican
Party, where this new batch of candidates were more conservative than most
of the Republican incumbents and provided a different message, primarily one that was much more fiscally conservative (i.e., concerned with the
nation's debt and deficient spending) and against the Affordable Health Care
Act.[16] In the 2010 midterm elections, Republicans were able to pick up seats
in the Senate and gain majority control of the House and many state legislatures and governorships.

Two years later, the Tea Party once again dominated the Republican
landscape. According to the 2012 American National Election Survey
(ANES), 52 percent of Republican voters identified as Tea Party supporters.[17]
Additionally, "Tea Party supporters were much more conservative than the
American public on social as well as economic issues, more religious and
much, much more negative in their opinions of Barack Obama."[18] It is clear
that the small government, anti-elitist/anti-establishment ideals expressed by
the Tea Party movement and its particular brand of populism had taken hold
within a large segment of the Republican electorate. Early unease between
the Tea Party and the Republican establishment subsided as, ultimately, the
GOP absorbed the Tea Party movement, thereby taking on some of its identity. In 2012, the Republicans lost the bid for the presidency but were able
to maintain control of the House.[19] The Tea Party effort was by and large a
success and paved the way for the populist message, which elevates concerns
and anxieties of "ordinary people" and positions those against goals and
motivations of the political elite. Additionally, as it pertains to the Trump's
rhetoric, populism has further amplified the "us versus them" message and
even treaded toward white nationalist appeals, which appear to have gained
a foothold in elements of the Republican Party. Ultimately, these dynamics
paved the way for Donald Trump to secure the vote of the Republican electorate in 2016.

Donald Trump's presidential campaign began when he announced his candidacy in June of 2015. From that point on, we witnessed a campaign that included contentious debates and countless number of hours of news coverage. Through each stage of the process, it appeared that Trump continued to lose support from the Republican elites (i.e., elected officials), only to gain a stronger foothold with Republican primary voters. As Trump began collecting convention delegates through caucuses and primaries, different tactics were deployed by #NeverTrump members of the GOP establishment in order to try to prevent Trump from winning the party's nomination. A group of Republican Party leaders, including a former adviser to President George W. Bush, met and discussed ways to stop the nomination of Trump through the use of a "unity" ticket or a third-party bid.[20] However, Trump was able to latch on to the populist sentiment which gained a foothold in the Republican Party and entice enough voters to the polls; on May 26, 2016, it was over, as he had enough bound delegates to mathematically secure the Republican nomination for the presidency. Out of a total of fifty-six caucus and primary contests, from all of the states (including DC) and territories, Trump won a total of forty-one. The number of states in which Trump won primary election contests is especially impressive given the amount of opposition that he received from the Republican Party establishment.[21]

Another plan to prevent the nomination of Trump was hatched by delegates to the Republican National Committee (RNC), which was wary of having Trump atop the ticket.[22] Certain Republican delegates, namely Kendal Unruh, attempted to stymie the nomination by adopting a "conscience clause" which would allow the bound delegates (those that are obligated to support whichever candidate wins their states primary contest) to vote against Trump if they saw fit.[23]

Incredibly, out of all living GOP presidents or presidential nominees, Bob Dole was the only one to formally endorse the Trump candidacy stating, "The voters of our country have turned out in record number to support Mr. Trump. It is important that their votes be honored, and it is time that we support the party's presumptive nominee."[24] Conversely, many prominent Republican figures, notably presidents George H. W. Bush and George W. Bush and former speaker of the House Paul Ryan (R-WI), were reluctant to endorse. George W. Bush went on to caution, "We do not need someone in the Oval Office who mirrors and inflames our anger and frustration."[25] Nonetheless, in November of 2016, then candidate Donald Trump defeated Hillary Clinton in the presidential election. Throughout the entire 2016 election cycle, and continuing through his entire first term, Donald Trump has received intense opposition from some members of the Republican Party establishment. A better understanding of those that opposed Trump, and their reasoning, is needed to understand the #NeverTrump movement.

THE OPPOSITION FROM THE REPUBLICAN
PARTY ESTABLISHMENT

Why did Donald Trump engender such opposition from the Republican Party establishment? After all, he is a Republican (even if only in title) who won the party's nomination for president, and was popular enough with the voting public to propel the party back into the White House after Obama's eight-year tenure. Additionally, his "take no prisoners" posture and apparent comfort with attacking opponents and driving up negative partisanship, resonated with the party's base and others within the electorate, thus projecting a sense of political strength party figures would seem to appreciate.[26] Early on, candidate Trump tried to convince the voting public that he was the lone voice of the people, the "forgotten man," an advocate for the masses who could get things accomplished, and that he alone would be able to solve the country's problems. Further building on the populist message and insurgency campaigns of the Palin and the Tea Party movement, Trump latched onto the rhetoric of "us" versus "them."[27]

It was not lost on some conservative elites that Trump included the Republican establishment as part of the "them" camp. Trump received scrutiny from the Republican Party establishment based on the fact that his campaign and subsequent presidency stood at odds with the platform and values of the GOP, and the party brand they had been trying to project. This sentiment was expressed by former senator John Danforth (R-MO) who asserted, "I think for our party to survive, it has to be bigger than any one person."[28] The GOP brand, which has been cultivated over decades is not reflected in a single figure but rather rooted in norms and policy goals, and Trump's dearth of overall social etiquette placed its future on a dangerous path, they believed.

A key difference between President Trump and establishment Republicans is with respect to their views for the direction of the party in the future. President Trump's primary campaign slogan ("Make American Great Again[29]") implies that the way to fix things is to revert back to how the party and country used to handle things. Generally, this campaign message emphasized that political elites, political correctness, and globalism (including immigration) were the source of voters' problems. By contrast, the Republican Party establishment had future goals that would propel the party forward, by learning from the election defeats in 2008 and 2012. Recall that the insurgency from the conservative right (the Tea Party movement) was fanned by the nomination of Sarah Palin for vice president. The Tea Party movement subsequently commandeered the Republican Party, basically refusing to negotiate with those outside their sphere.[30] With this push from the conservative right, Republicans found success in the House and state contests, but they were unsuccessful in their bid for the presidency in 2012, which prompted the Republican leadership to rethink their strategy for the party moving forward.

For instance, after Obama's reelection, then chairman of the RNC Reince Priebus, created the Growth and Opportunity Project task force. The reason that there needed to be a task force was to examine the lessons of the previous decade and formulate a strategy and message for the future. The focus of the task force was to reach out to the party leaders and activists across the country to determine an effective strategy that would allow the Republican Party to grow and ultimately regain the White House.[31] Two of the largest recommendations that the task force brought back to the RNC focused on the messages that the party sends to the public and the ever changing demographics of the American public. In essence, the Growth and Opportunity Project report (GOPR) argues that most people felt that the Republican Party did not care about much of the population and that the party needed to do a better job at targeting racial minorities as potential source of voters.[32] Out of the GOPR, the RNC utilized the information in a manner with the goal of making the Republican Party more successful at the national level. To do this, the GOPR recommended a shift in how members of the party approached people, policies, and overall campaign strategies. Trump's candidacy thwarted these plans, and rancorous undercurrents of intra-party conflict would eventually surface as the RNC found itself in a battle for the future of the party. Either they could allow the populist movement to fully take hold and steer the party in an inadvisable direction or they could fight to bring the party into the future. Ultimately, Trump took over the RNC, and most GOP elites fell in line. Only a few, the #NeverTrumpers, continue the fight.

The change that was occurring in the Republican Party, based on the defeats in 2008 and 2012, provide insight into why the Republican establishment and Donald Trump have been at odds with one another. It is clear from his initial campaign messages that Donald Trump had no intention of following along with the new approach that the Republican Party establishment wanted to implement. Trump presented messages that were in complete opposition to the one the GOPR recommended. Moreover, Trump often made disparaging remarks about minorities, which does not provide the inclusive environment that the Republican establishment wanted to create moving forward.

As described below, it is clear that establishment Republicans were concerned with the overall effect that Trump would have on the party. Based on the recommendations by the task force, the party was supposed to move toward being more inclusive and provide a way forward with respect to immigration. Instead of following this recommendation, it is clear that Trump accentuated concerns and exacerbated anxieties relating to immigration which incited crowds by playing toward their emotions and fears.

Conservative elites feared that Trump's tactics and candidacy would realign the base of support for each party in ways that would advantage the Democrats for a generation.[33] The fears of realignment, with respect to a Donald Trump presidency, was that voters would leave the Republican Party and join the ranks of the Democratic Party. In the short term, they were clearly mistaken. But if the GOPR is correct, Republicans may not benefit from the continued evidence that that American politics appears to be headed back toward party-centered elections, similar to those experienced in the nineteenth century.[34] It appears that voters' attention is being drawn toward national level events, which shifts the focus of the voter from the individual candidates and more toward the party itself.[35] The electorate elevates national offices (such as the president) in their voting calculus, which makes it unlikely that they will vote for any members of the opposition party.[36] Additionally, over the past few elections, split ticket voting has steadily declined, indicating that the individual characteristics of candidates are providing voters with less cues than the party they are associated with.[37] Therefore, based on recent electoral data, it would appear, due to the Trump phenomenon, that realignment will only take place in the future, as long as demographic trends continue to break Democrat's way.

ESTABLISHMENT OPPONENTS OF TRUMP

Former Presidents

One would expect that Democratic presidents—Presidents Obama, Clinton, and Carter—would speak out against Donald Trump, if for no other reason than their partisan differences. The intriguing aspect of the 2016 presidential election cycle was the harsh criticism that came from former Republican presidents. One aspect of the opposition to a Donald Trump presidency revolved around the perspective of what he and his personality would do to the office of the president, the overall political landscape, and the future of the Republican Party. All five living former presidents, including two Republicans, opposed the nomination of Donald Trump.

The Bush Family

One of the political families that is synonymous with the GOP is the Bush family. Therefore, it was virtually unfathomable when both former presidents George H.W. Bush and George W. Bush asserted that they did not think that Donald Trump was fit to be president. Both of the former presidents were publically critical of the nomination of Donald Trump. President George H.W. Bush commented, "I don't like him. I don't know much about him, but

I know he's a blowhard. And I'm not too excited about him being a leader."[38] Additionally, it was made public that President George H.W. Bush voted for Hillary Clinton instead of voting for the Republican nominee Donald Trump, which shows just how much the former president opposed Trump. Similar to his father, President George W. Bush had misgivings about the presumptuous Republican nominee, proclaiming "Wow, this guy doesn't know what it means to be president."[39] He also refused to vote for Donald Trump for president.[40]

Other members of the Bush family were also highly critical of then candidate Trump. Jeb Bush, former governor of Florida and 2016 presidential candidate, stated that he would not vote for Trump (even after signing a pledge stating he would vote for the eventual GOP nominee) based primarily on the fact that Trump "has not demonstrated that temperament or strength of character. He has not displayed a respect for the Constitution. And, he is not a consistent conservative. These are all the reasons why I cannot support his candidacy."[41] Recall, that during the 2016 primary season, Trump and Jeb Bush had a contentious relationship that ultimately ended with negative attack ads against each other and, ultimately, the decision of Jeb Bush to withdraw from the contest. One final member of the Bush family that disapproved of Trump was the matriarch and female face of the GOP for the last twenty-five years, Barbara Bush. She was known to be very critical of the candidacy and nomination of Trump. She was adamant that she would not vote for Trump, could not see any reason that other woman voters would vote for Trump, and even blamed her health concerns that plagued her at the end of her life on Trump.[42]

Indeed, it would be appropriate to note that it appears that nearly the entire Bush family was against the nomination of Donald Trump.[43] It should be eye-opening to experience one of the most prominent Republican Party families to disavow Trump in such a public manner. Their main opposition is based on the belief that Trump would do long lasting damage to the office of the Presidency, and the future of the Republican Party, to which they had committed their lives for a half century. Therefore, they did not want to see the party negatively impacted. In many ways, the Bush family represents the kinder, gentler, and more aristocratic version of the GOP, which is a direct contrast to Donald Trump's style and vision.

Others Who Opposed Trump

Others within the establishment wing of the Republican Party also opposed the nomination of Donald Trump and his presidency. These include members of the GOP leadership and other prominent party figures such as John McCain (R-AZ) and Mitt Romney (R-UT), and also those who do have the same reelection insecurities that members of Congress have such as former RNC chairman Michael Steele, and political strategist Rick Wilson. Therefore, they have tended to be more outspoken in their opposition to Trump and have generally maintained their disapproval. The common thread is that they have supported Republican ideals and candidates for many years while actively participating in politics as registered Republicans, but this all changed with the nomination of insurgent Donald Trump

Senator John McCain (R-AZ), a Republican member of Congress from 1983 until his death in 2018 (four years in the House and thirty-one years in the Senate), battled with the decision to back the party but not the candidacy of Donald Trump. McCain ran unsuccessfully for the GOP nomination in 2000, and secured the nomination in 2008. He had also built a reputation as a political "maverick" willing to cross party lines and ensure that what he saw as quality public policy was not sacrificed due to partisanship. Few questioned that he had the Republican Party's best interests at heart. As a long-standing legislator, John McCain was a conservative through and through and promoted those values. His willingness to engage in bipartisan alliances should not take away from his loyalty to the GOP brand and the policy goals of the party. To no surprise, his admonishment of Trump created massive waves within the Republican Party. Initially, after it had become clear Trump would be the nominee, McCain supported his nomination in order to help unite the party behind its standard-bearer. Eventually, however, he withdrew support after the recordings of Trump's vulgar language relating to women was released.[44] McCain went on to say, "There are no excuses for Donald Trump's offensive and demeaning comments in the just released video; no woman should ever be victimized by this kind of inappropriate behavior. He alone bears the burden of his conduct and alone should suffer the consequences."[45] This started a back and forth war of words between McCain and Trump, which would not end even after McCain's death. In the end, McCain, after observing the conduct of Trump, had decided that the Republican Party and country needed better out of its commander in chief.

Senator Mitt Romney (R-UT), former Republican governor of Massachusetts and the 2012 GOP presidential nominee has also been an outspoken voice since the beginning. For many years, Romney was seen as the standard-bearer of the party and was involved in shaping the future for the Republicans. When Trump started to gain momentum in the primary stage of the 2016 presidential elections, Romney was one of the first prominent members to speak out against him. In March of 2016, he delivered a speech for the Hinckley Institute of Politics, in which he used his time to publicly denounce Trump, stating, "I believe with all my heart and soul that we face another time for choosing, one that will have profound consequences for the Republican Party and more importantly, for the country."[46] He would go on to admonish Trump for his business dealings and his flawed moral character. In his speech, Romney showcased what others in the GOP were thinking but were afraid to voice. In a moment, Romney appeared to put the well-being of the party and country above his own personal ambitions. Even with the full understanding that he would be publicly attacked by the presidential candidate, Romney noted, "I wanted my grandkids to see that I simply couldn't ignore what Mr. Trump was saying and doing, which revealed a character and temperament unfit for the leader of the free world."[47] He expressed grave concerns about the future of not only the Republican Party but also the country, and in the end announced that he could not in good faith endorse the Trump candidacy.

Other "High Profile Others" also spoke out against the Trump candidacy. Over the course of the presidential campaign, and even after his election, they have placed their reputations on the line in order to voice opinions as it related to his potential presidency and his governing priorities, style, and personal failings. For instance, former Senators Jeff Flake (R-AZ) and Bob Inglis (R-SC), former speaker of the House Paul Ryan (R-WI), Representative Justin Amash (I-MI), and former Governor John Kasich (R-OH) have all spoken out against the nomination and presidency of Donald Trump. This group of individuals have disagreed with the rhetoric, policy objectives, and perceived direction of the GOP that would occur under a Trump presidency.

Rank and File "Others"

Former RNC chairman and former Lieutenant Governor of Maryland Michael Steele also refused to endorse the GOP nominee, Donald Trump, even indicating that he would not vote for Donald Trump in the general election, because of what he saw as the blatantly racist messages Trump promoted during his campaign.[48] Steele has maintained his disdain and doubled down on his belief that Trump was a racist, after Trump's comments relating to certain "shithole" countries where immigrants arrive from.[49] Similarly, Rick Wilson, a longtime Republican political strategist who helped craft the GOP messaging efforts against Obama in 2008, has been at the forefront of the #NeverTrump movement. Wilson disagreed with Trump on the most basic of political levels and did not want him destroying the party.[50] Wilson has strived to convince others within the establishment and also the American public that Trump is bad for the overall success of the party. Lastly, after endorsing the Republican nominee for 128 years, the Harvard Republican Club refused to endorse Trump in 2016, announcing that he "holds views that are antithetical to our values not only as Republicans, but as Americans. The rhetoric he espouses—from racist slander to misogynistic taunts—is not consistent with our conservative principles."[51]

It is clear from the evidence above that many prominent individuals and groups which had been inextricably connected with the GOP brand expressed strong reservations about Donald Trump from the outset. They took a stand guided by their interests in the preservation of the party, and many have maintained their opposition. Additionally, it is clear that those that stood in opposition to the nomination, and eventual presidency of Donald Trump, were concerned with not only the party itself but also with the potential dangers that Trump's rhetoric and actions would have within the population. During the election and the first term of the Trump administration, it is not difficult to notice discernable shifts within the tone and tenor of politics, and indeed the norms of society. It is clear that common civility and respect are no longer a priority as it pertains to American politics. Many of those that stood in opposition to Trump foresaw these developments. The 2016 election was a culmination of events that started with the insurgent campaigns of the Tea Party and continued with the overtaking of the Republican Party by a populist movement, which many within the establishment wanted to stop. Even after the 2016 election was over, it was clear that there were issues that remained between the factions. President Trump selected many polarizing figures to be a part of his White House staff and confidants. Many of these figures did not get along and this caused disruptions within the White House. For the most part, it is clear that President Trump has not made any efforts to smooth the relationship with the establishment since his election. President Trump appears to operate under the "take it or leave it" mentality of politics and business, which does not usually produce favorable results. Additionally, his presidency has been marred by corruption and Trump, though acquitted, became only the third U.S. president to be impeached by the House of Representatives.

CONCLUSION AND IMPLICATIONS

A candidate like Donald Trump—so disconnected from his party's principles and institutions—has never been elected to the presidency. Therefore, there were considerable moments of shock and disbelief from both Democrats and Republicans after the nomination and eventual election of Trump as president. It is clear that the GOPR, which embraced vision of inclusivity and modernization, is no longer an influence in Trump's GOP. Based on the comments made by members of the Republican Party highlighted above who opposed the nomination and eventual presidency of Donald Trump, it would appear that their main issue was the concern the party members had for the future of the party. It does not appear that Republican voters shared the concerns that motivated these conservative elites. Based on the nationalization of elections that has been occurring over the past few election cycles, it would appear that the bulk of the conservative voters have embraced Trumpism. As long as they continue winning, we can expect some establishment conservatives like the Bushes and Romneys of the world, motivated by noblesse oblige, to reject the ignoble and corrupt politics of Trumpism.

NOTES

1. Andrew Mercer, Claudia Deane, and Kyley McGeeney, "Why 2016 Election Polls Missed Their Mark," *Pew Research Center*, November 9, 2016, https://www.pewresearch.org/fact-tank/2016/11/09/why-2016-election-polls-missed-their-mark/.

2. Megan McArdle, "If #NeverTrumpers Don't Have an Endgame Maybe It's Because to Them Politics Isn't a Game," *The Washington Post*, March 1, 2019, https://www.washingtonpost.com/opinions/2019/03/01/if-nevertrumpers-dont-have-an-endgame-maybe-its-because-them-politics-isnt-game/.

3. Eli Yokley and Joanna Piacenza, "Is Trumpism Permanent?" *Morning Consult*, November 7, 2019, https://morningconsult.com/2019/11/07/state-of-the-republican-party-is-trumpism-permanent/.

4. "Electoral College Fast Facts," accessed November 22, 2019, https://history.house.gov/Institution/Electoral-College/Electoral-College/.

5. Tim Alberta, *American Carnage: On the Front Lines of the Republican Civil War and the Rise of President Trump* (New York: Harper Collins, 2019).

6. Alan Abramowitz, *The Great Alignment: Race, Party Transformation, and the Rise of Donald Trump* (New Haven: Yale University Press, 2018); Alberta, *American Carnage*.

7. https://voteview.com/parties/all, accessed January 28, 2020; Alan I. Abramowitz and Kyle L. Saunders, "Is Polarization a Myth?," *The Journal of Politics*, 70, no. 2 (2008): 542–55.

8. Abramowitz, *The Great Alignment*.

9. Diana C. Mutz, "Status Threat, Not Economic Hardship, Explains the 2016 Presidential Vote," *Proceedings of the National Academy of Sciences*, 115, no. 19 (2018): E4330–E4339; Alberta, *American Carnage*.

10. Alberta, *American Carnage*.

11. Gary C. Jacobson, "Polarization, Gridlock, and Presidential Campaign Politics in 2016," *The ANALS of the American Academy of Political and Social Science*, 667, no. 1 (September 2016): 226–46; Abramowitz, *The Great Alignment*.

12. Alan Abramowitz and Steven Webster, "The Rise of Negative Partisanship and the Nationalization of U.S. Elections in the 21st Century," *Electoral Studies*, 41, no. 1 (March 2016): 12–22.

13. Ilya Somin, "The Tea Party Movement and Popular Constitutionalism," *Northwestern University Law Review Colloquy*, 105, no. 300 (2011): 300–314.

14. Liz Halloran, "What's Behind the New Populism?" *National Public Radio (NPR), The Tea Party in America*, February 5, 2010, https://www.npr.org/templates/story/story.php?storyId=123137382.

15. Kate Zerinki, "Tea Party Set to Win Enough Races for Wide Influence," *The New York Times*, October 14, 2010, https://www.nytimes.com/2010/10/15/us/politics/15teaparty.html?_r=1&hp.

16. Alan I. Abramowitz, "Not Their Cup of Tea: The Republican Establishment Versus the Tea Party," *Sabato's Crystal Ball*, November 14, 2013, http://www.centerforpolitics.org/crystalball/articles/not-their-cup-of-tea-the-republican-establishment-versus-the-tea-party/.

17. Abramowitz, "Not Their Cup of Tea."

18. Abramowitz, "Not Their Cup of Tea."

19. Leigh A. Bradberry and Gary C. Jacobson, "The Tea Party and the 2012 Presidential Election," *Electoral Studies*, 40, no. 4 (December 2015): 500–508.

20. Shane Goldmacher and Nolan D. McCaskill, "Conservatives Call for 'Unity Ticket' to Stop Trump," *Politico*, March 17, 2016, https://www.politico.com/blogs/2016-gop-primary-live-updates-and-results/2016/03/erick-erickson-anti-trump-gop-unity-ticket-220933.

21. For comparison, Hillary Clinton won 34 states in 2016 and Mitt Romney won 42 states in 2012, with both candidates receiving wide party support in both election years (see https://www.thegreenpapers.com/P16/; https://www.realclearpolitics.com/epolls/2012/president/republican_delegate_count.html.

22. Tom LoBianco and Tal Kopan, "RNC Delegates Launch 'Anybody but Trump' Drive," *CNN*, June 17, 2016, https://www.cnn.com/2016/06/17/politics/delegate-unbinding-effort-organized/.

23. LoBianco and Kopan, "RNC Delegates Launch."

24. Jeremy Diamond, "Bob Dole Endorses Donald Trump," *CNN, May* 6, 2016, https://www.cnn.com/2016/05/06/politics/bob-dole-endorses-donald-trump/index.html.

25. "Former Republican Presidents Will Not Endorse Trump," *BBC News*, May 5, 2016, https://www.bbc.com/news/election-us-2016-36214738.

26. Abramowitz, *The Great Alignment.*

27. Alberta, *American Carnage.*

28. Yokley and Piacenza, "Is Trumpism Permanent?"

29. https://www.donaldjtrump.com.

30. Alberta, *American Carnage.*

31. Henry Barbour, Sally Bradshaw, Ari Fleischer, Zori Fonalledas, and Glenn McCall, "Growth & Opportunity Project," *The Wall Street Journal*, March 18, 2013, https://online.wsj.com/public/resources/documents/RNCreport03182013.pdf.

32. Barbour et al., "Growth & Opportunity Project."

33. Russell J. Dalton, *Dealignment and Changing Electoral Politics* (Thousand Oaks: CQ Press, 2013); Edward G. Carmines, John P. McIver, and James A. Stimson, "Unrealized Partisanship: A Theory of Dealignment," *Journal of Politics*, 49, no. 2 (1987): 376–400.

34. Morris P. Fiorina, "The (Re)Nationalization of Congressional Elections," *A Hoover Institution Essay on Contemporary American Politics*, 2016, https://ww

w.hoover.org/sites/default/files/research/docs/fiorina_renationalizationofcongression alelections_7.pdf; Gary C. Jacobson, "It's Nothing Personal: The Decline of the Incumbency Advantage in U.S. House Elections," *Journal of Politics*, 77, no. 3 (July 2015): 861–73; Jamie L. Carson and Jason Roberts, *Ambition, Competition, and Electoral Reform: The Politics of Congressional Elections Across Time* (Ann Arbor: University of Michigan Press, 2013).

35. Jacobson, "It's Nothing Personal"; Daniel J. Hopkins, *The Increasingly United States: How and Why American Political Behavior Nationalized* (Chicago: University of Chicago Press, 2018).

36. Abramowitz and Webster, "The Rise of Negative Partisanship"; Fiorina, "The (Re)Nationalization of Congressional Elections"; Joel Sievert and Seth C. McKee, "Nationalization in U.S. Senate and Gubernatorial Elections," *American Politics Research*, 47, no. 5 (September 2019): 1055–80.

37. Jacobson, "It's Nothing Personal."

38. Alicia Cohn, "George W. Bush: 'I'm Worried That I Will Be the Last Republican President,'" *The Hill*, November 4, 2017, https://thehill.com/blogs/blog -briefing-room/news/358745-george-w-bush-im-worried-that-i-will-be-the-last-repu blican.

39. Cohn, "George W. Bush."

40. Frank McGurty, "Neither George Bush Voted for Trump, Book Author Tells New York Times," *Reuters*, November 4, 2017, https://www.reuters.com/article/us-trump-bush-book/neither-george-bush-voted-for-trump-book-author-tells-new-york-t imes-idUSKBN1D40TP.

41. Jessica Taylor and Domenico Montanaro, "Jeb Bush Won't Vote for Trump: 'I Cannot Support His Candidacy,'" *National Public Radio (NPR)*, May 6, 2016, https ://www.npr.org/2016/05/06/477077226/jeb-bush-wont-vote-for-trump-i-cannot-supp ort-his-candidacy.

42. Allan Smith, "Barbara Bush Said 'Angst' over Trump Caused Heart Problems, New Book Reveals," *NBC News*, March 27, 2019, https://www.nbc news.com/politics/donald-trump/new-barbara-bush-biography-details-dislike-t rump-n987816.

43. Only Jeb Bush's son George P. Bush eventually supported Trump's election in November 2016. See Colby Itkowitz, "Trump Introduces George P. Bush as 'The Only Bush Who Got It Right,'" *The Washington Post*, April 10, 2019, https://www .washingtonpost.com/politics/trump-introduces-george-p-bush-as-the-only-bush-wh o-got-it-right/2019/04/10/69d9b538-5bd8-11e9-842d-7d3ed7eb3957_story.html.

44. Alan Rappeport, "John McCain Withdraws Support for Donald Trump After Disclosure of Recording," *The New York Times*, October 8, 2016, https://www.nyt imes.com/2016/10/08/us/politics/presidential-election.html.

45. Paul Kane, "John McCain Abandons His Support of Donald Trump," *The Washington Post*, October 8, 2016, https://www.washingtonpost.com/news/powe rpost/wp/2016/10/08/john-mccain-abandons-his-support-of-donald-trump/.

46. Leigh Ann Caldwell, "Mitt Romney Lays Out Scathing Critique of Donald Trump," *NBC NEWS*, March 3, 2016, https://www.nbcnews.com/politics/2016-el ection/mitt-romney-eviscerate-donald-trump-phony-fraud-n530877.

47. Monica Langley, "Behind Mitt Romney's Increasingly Lonely Challenge to Donald Trump," *The Wall Street Journal*, May 28, 2016, https://www.wsj.com/ articles/behind-mitt-romneys-increasingly-lonely-challenge-to-donald-trump-14643 54734.

48. Tessa Berenson, "Former RNC Head Michael Steel Won't Vote for Donald Trump," *Time*, October 21, 2016, https://time.com/4540209/rnc-michael-steele-d onald-trump/.

49. Kate Samuelson, "'The Evidence Is Incontrovertible.' The RNC's First Black Chairman Says Trump Is Racist," *Time*, January 12, 2018, https://time.com/5101077/ donald-trump-racist-michael-steele-shithole-countries/.

50. Rex Huppke, "GOP Strategist Grinds Trump into Hamburger in New Book, 'Everything Trump Touches Dies,'" *Chicago Tribune*, August 6, 2018, https://ww w.chicagotribune.com/columns/rex-huppke/ct-met-trump-rick-wilson-huppke-201 80806-story.html.

51. Fortune Staff, "Read the Harvard Republican Club's Letter Blasting Donald Trump," *Fortune*, August 5, 2016, https://fortune.com/2016/08/05/harvard-republ ican-club-trump/.

Part II

WHY #NEVERTRUMP?

Chapter 7

The Art of the Deal?

#NeverTrumpers and the Struggle for GOP Foreign Policy

Wesley B. Renfro

Despite vocal opposition from many prominent Republicans, Donald J. Trump skillfully capitalized on his celebrity and developed a significant political following among the base in the Republican Party.[1] Their fervent support helped propel Trump, an unlikely candidate and an unconventional Republican, to victory in the 2016 election. One defining feature of Trump's presidency is the degree to which his base has remained loyal despite scandals and criticism from high-profile Republicans. While his political ascent has been unusual in many ways, his strained relationship with conservative elites and establishment figures in the GOP is of special note. In the early stages of Trump's 2016 campaign, many conservatives either dismissed Trump's candidacy or openly criticized him.[2] While objections varied, oft repeated ones included Trump's lack of experience, opposition to his policy goals, and objections to his personal style, rhetoric, and character. Part of this opposition, which included both living former Republican presidents and scores of former elected officials and high-ranking policymakers, evolved into the #NeverTrump movement.[3] The elites opposed to Trump had impressive conservative bona fides and represented a broad swathe of Republican orthodoxy. Elites from the national security and foreign policy establishment were, however, especially plentiful in this movement and this chapter will focus on them because they are both abundant and historically well-respected in conservative circles.

Some of the initial opposition to Trump lessened when it became clear that he was going to be the GOP standard-bearer and further faded, at least for some, when Trump won the 2016 presidential election. However, there remains a vigorous #NeverTrump movement. This group includes many prominent neoconservatives, former elected officials, and thinkers, writers, pundits, academics, and former policymakers. In the pre-Trump Republican order, one would have easily supposed that collectively these individuals *were* the Republican Party. Trump's election and his remaking of the GOP dispelled this notion as his ascent quickly made plain the degree to which these elites differed from base Republicans in their support for Trump. The continued existence, even in its current form, of a #NeverTrump movement—a schism between conservative elites and masses—is truly unusual and warrants attention, as there is no escaping the conclusion that Trump has totally remade the party in his own image.[4] It may be tempting to downplay the structural aspects of these divides by suggesting that these divisions are simply knock-on effects caused by electing an unconventional president into the White House. This sort of analysis misses deeper divisions which were quietly brewing before Trump's rise as a politician and fails to contend with forces that may remake the Republican Party and, perhaps, the future of American politics.

This chapter proceeds by exploring the origins, the development, and the consequences of the #NeverTrump movement through the lens of national security and foreign policy elites. It pays special attention to the divides between neoconservative elites and Trump supporters, the sources of the tension, and the possible consequences of these divides. The chapter will chronicle an unusual and interesting story in contemporary American politics, one which has not gained wide traction. Given the tumult associated with an administration and news media that has careened from breaking story to breaking story with breakneck speed, even by Washington's fast baseline, this is perhaps unsurprising. Capturing this chronology and describing the divide between Donald Trump and many in the national security and foreign policy establishment is, therefore, valuable on its own. This work is also useful as it opens the possibility of a more analytical, forward-thinking discussion of what these divisions and trends signal for post-Trump GOP foreign policy.

NATIONAL SECURITY, FOREIGN POLICY, AND NEOCONSERVATIVE ELITES IN THE #NEVERTRUMP MOVEMENT

There is no single event or policy that fully explains the how and why of all elite opposition to Trump. Among members of the foreign policy and national security elite several public documents help shed light on the motivations and concerns of many former policymakers, elected officials, pundits, and academics. Most famously, on August 8, 2016, a group of fifty prominent Republican members of what might generally be understood as the foreign policy and national security establishment published a public letter stating their opposition to Trump.[5] This sort of statement from former policymakers is highly unusual but this letter merits special attention because its signatories are all Republicans and because they are so forceful, clear, and articulate in their opposition to the Republican nominee, Donald Trump.

The list of signatories is impressive and contains many individuals who would normally be seeking to curry favor with any Republican with a non-trivial chance of securing the White House. After all, many of these individuals would have presumably liked to return in public life in a Republican administration.

Some of this highest profile names include the following:

Michael Chertoff, Former Secretary of Homeland Security
Eliot Cohen, Former Counselor at the Department of State
Peter Feaver, Senior Director for Strategic Planning at the National Security Council
David Gordon, Former Director of Policy Planning at the Department of State
Michael Hayden, Former Director of both the Central Intelligence Agency and the National Security Agency
John Negroponte, Former Director of National Intelligence
Tom Ridge, Former Secretary of Homeland Security
Philip Zelikow, Former Counselor at the Department of State

This prominent group of former officials was blunt in their assessment of Donald J. Trump. They opined:

> From a foreign policy perspective, Donald Trump is not qualified to be President and Commander-in-Chief. Indeed, we are convinced that he would be a dangerous President and would put at risk our country's national security and well-being. Most fundamentally, Mr. Trump lacks the character, values, and experience to be President. He weakens U.S. moral authority as the leader of the free world. He appears to lack basic knowledge about and belief in the U.S. Constitution, U.S. laws, and U.S. institutions, including religious tolerance, freedom of the press, and an independent judiciary.[6]

They further spotlight a number of specific concerns, including Trump's basic character and his values, his lack of knowledge and his fundamental unwillingness to learn the mechanisms of the U.S. government and nuances of global affairs, and his use of false statements.

It is important to note that while this is perhaps the best exemplar and most well-known public statement from foreign policy and national security elites, it is not the only such public declaration of conservative foreign policy opposition to Trump. An earlier letter dated March 2, 2016, organized by Eliot Cohen and Bryan McGrath, was signed by a group of 122 policymakers and academics. This letter outlined an array of issues that largely foreshadowed the complaints enumerated in the August 8 declaration.[7] They wrote:

> Mr. Trump's own statements lead us to conclude that as president, he would use the authority of his office to act in ways that make America less safe, and which would diminish our standing in the world. Furthermore, his expansive view of how presidential power should be wielded against his detractors poses a distinct threat to civil liberty in the United States. Therefore, as committed and loyal Republicans, we are unable to support a Party ticket with Mr. Trump at its head. We commit ourselves to working energetically to prevent the election of someone so utterly unfitted to the office.

In the broader public landscape of #NeverTrump, there are bountiful examples of elite members of the GOP who only eventually, and perhaps with some teeth gnashing, agreed to support or serve President Trump. South Carolina Senator Lindsay Graham (R-SC), known for his interest and expertise in national security matters, exemplifies this pattern. Once a skeptic of Trump, he morphed into an ardent supporter.[8] Senator Graham, despite occasional breaks with Trump over specific policies, eventually announced himself a convert.[9] Discussing his belated support for Trump, Graham said, "I stepped up and I'm getting rewarded for it by conservatives, the liberals are all upset."[10] Conversely, the individuals who signed these letters generally did not convert. As Nakamura reports, "Their transgression was signing one or both of two public #NeverTrump letters during the campaign, declaring they would not vote for Trump and calling his candidacy a danger to the nation."[11] While the next section will more fully explore the issue areas that produced an estrangement between so many GOP foreign policy and national security hands and the Trump administration, this section must first contend with the saga of Eliot Cohen and the ideology that he represents.

ELIOT COHEN AND THE NEOCONSERVATIVE #NEVERTRUMPERS

While the signatories of both letters are not a monolith, a close examination reveals the presence of various strains of conservative thinking, including neoconservatism. Although its origins predate the September 11, 2001, attacks by a generation, neoconservatism became widely known and widely associated with the George W. Bush presidency—especially his first term. As an ideology, neoconservatism stresses that it is sometimes necessary and desirable to engage in foreign intervention to secure vital American objectives.[12] Rooted in Washington's twentieth-century experiences with the USSR and other autocratic regimes, neoconservatives have a reflexive objection to non-democracies. This position places neoconservatives at odds with more traditional realpolitik approaches to foreign policy. It is also worth noting that American neoconservatives have inconsistently practiced this in their own foreign policy. For example, few have objected to Washington's long-standing alliance with the al-Saud family. Neoconservatives also place unusual emphasis on protecting American sovereignty in a world that increasingly includes institutions and other mechanisms that may reduce national sovereignty.

Eliot Cohen is an academic turned practitioner turned Dean of the prestigious School of Advanced International Studies at Johns Hopkins. As a scholar-practitioner, Cohen enjoys influence in both communities and has unquestionable neoconservative credentials. He was a signatory to the Project for a New American Century's Statement of Principles in 1997.[13] An ardent champion of the 2003 invasion of Iraq, he served in several roles, including stints at the Pentagon, the Department of State, and as an advisor to Condoleezza Rice, in the George W. Bush presidency.[14] While many, and perhaps most, foreign policy experts now view the Iraq War and this kind of application of neoconservatism as a failed experiment, Cohen's recent work strongly suggests that he very much supports interventionist (read neoconservative) foreign policies.[15] Certainly not every member of the Republican Party espouses neoconservative principles, but it is fair to conclude that neoconservatism is well represented in GOP orthodoxy and that there is no shortage of neocons in the elite ranks of the modern conservative movement, including Cohen.

Therefore, it is not surprising that Cohen helped draft the March 2, 2016, anti-Trump missive. Many political leaders, presidents included, are often inconsistent in the application of their professed ideologies. It is not clear, however, if Donald Trump has any internally consistent set of principles that might constitute a foreign policy. An anonymous senior member of the Trump administration summarizes Trump's lack of ideological coherence when, in an op-ed in *The New York Times*, they conclude, "Anyone who works with him knows he is not moored to any discernable first principles that guide his decision-making."[16] Much is made of "Make America Great Again" but as an ideology it remains largely undeveloped. It functions less as an ideology than as a slogan or clever rhetorical device. Trump's past public statements strongly suggest an aversion to large-scale intervention a la the Iraq invasion. As president, Trump has shifted from some of his past statements and likes to invoke the specter of massive American military power as a potential stick. This might simply be part of Trump's instinctive bluster or it may represent an evolution in his own thinking about the proper role of American power in the global system. In early 2016, however, most neocons were deeply skeptical of candidate Trump because of his opposition to intervention and, perhaps, because of his unconventional background and somewhat checkered past.

As earlier described, the tide often turns. Despite helping lead a public and blunt critique of then candidate Trump, Cohen eventually went on to suggest in November 2016, with caveats and qualifications, that Republicans should consider working in the Trump administration.[17] He writes, "Whether you agree with that assessment [the contents of the August 8, 2016, letter] does not matter, though, because he won. I can think of three reasons why that may not be as awful as we think." He then explains that "buffers and restraints are built into the system" and that "Trump may be better than we think." Finally, he concludes that "part of the magic of America is its ability to regenerate itself."[18] Cohen goes on to appeal to the professionalism of the staffers and the enduring nature of the system rather than the traits of the current president when he claims:

> It goes without saying that friends in military, diplomatic, or intelligence ser-vice—the career people who keep our country strong and safe—should continue to do their jobs. If anything, having professionals serve who remember that their oath is to support and defend the Constitution—and not to truckle to an individual or his clique—will be more important than ever.[19]

This hardly sounds like an enthusiastic endorsement of Trump or his likely governing style and Cohen's tepid peace with Trump would prove short lived as Cohen recanted in public fashion in only a few days.[20]

The previously cited anonymous op-ed in *The New York Times*, however, does seem to confirm that administration officials, even quite senior appoin-tees, are working in ways that Cohen predicted. Its author writes, "That [a desire to make America more safe and prosperous] is why many Trump appointees have vowed to do what we can to preserve our democratic institu-tions while thwarting Mr. Trump's more misguided impulses until he is out of office."[21] Other critics, however, did eventually come around to supporting Donald Trump. While it is impossible, at least at this juncture, to divine their motives, it is likely that some are not true converts to Trumpism but support the president for instrumental reasons.

Trump's pre-presidential statements about the merits of foreign policy interventions and his fondness for autocratic leaders is apostasy for neocon-servatives. Trump's approach to foreign policy suggests that he is inherently suspicious of international institutions and globalism. Moreover, he empha-sizes and valorizes American sovereignty.[22] While many neoconservatives probably have some degree of trepidation vis-à-vis Trump, they are very likely to support these latter positions as they are wholly compatible with neoconservative thinking. This also spotlights another area of divergence between both conservatives cut from a realist cloth and neocons and Trump's newer cadre of foreign policy hands: the former believe in growing American power and marshalling it judiciously on the global stage but the latter seem much more isolationist and unwilling to project power.

This area of overlap created a bridge between some neocons and the president. They further bonded over nationalistic rhetoric, support for some Trump policies such as immigration, and a deeply held belief that the United States would produce the most good for itself, and perhaps by extension the rest of the world, when it was acting alone. Stephen Wertheim, summarizing this reversal, notes:

> Even allowing for Trump's opportunism and inconsistencies, his election victory appeared to deal a double blow to the neoconservative persuasion. It not only broke the neocons' hold on the Republican Party, but also, in the same stroke, revealed that they lacked a popular constituency. . . . Today, neoconservatives are riding high once more, in the White House, on Capitol Hill, and in the most prominent organs of opinion. . . . A new configuration of right-wing foreign policy is coming into view, and the neocons are in the lead once more.[23]

Wertheim's analysis is cogent and moving but it is not yet clear if neoconservatism is a coherent whole. Many formerly prominent neocons, including Cohen, remain opposed to Trumpism. On the other hand, a new breed of conservatives, often referred to as the alt-right, has become more of a force in Trump's GOP. Trump has certainly remade the GOP in his own image and he may be simultaneously remaking neoconservative thinking in a similar fashion. The neocons who converted to Trumpism, regardless of sincerity, now tend to focus on anti-globalism and seem content to ignore Trump's fondness for dictators, his apparent unwillingness to endorse the necessity of large-scale military intervention as a means to secure American interests, and his personal foibles. In this regard, it is becoming somewhat difficult to distinguish some of these individuals from garden variety members of the alt-right. They may have detached "neoconservatism" as traditionally and conventionally understood, from the evolving ideology of neoconservatives themselves.

Cohen, ever a principled neocon, found that he could not hold his nose and endorse Trumpism. Within a matter of days of publishing his call for conservatives to work for Trump, Cohen made a stunning about face. In a November 15, 2016, opinion piece in *The Washington Post*, he recounted how an exchange with a friend involved in the Trump transition convinced him that his earlier call to serve Trump, even with reservations and gritted teeth, was wrong.[24] Cohen, describing his friend involved in the transition, writes, "He is in the midst of a transition team that was never well-prepared to begin with and is now torn by acrimony, resignations and palace coups. And then there are the pent-up resentments against a liberal intellectual and media establishment that scorned his ilk for years." He then goes on to explain the danger not only of Trump but of many in his inner circle. Cohen concludes by noting:

> My bottom line: Conservative political types should not volunteer to serve in this administration, at least for now. They would probably have to make excuses for things that are inexcusable and defend people who are indefensible. At the very least, they should wait to see who gets the top jobs. Until then, let the Trump team fill the deputy assistant secretary and assistant secretary jobs with civil servants, retired military officers and diplomats, or the large supply of loyal or obsequious second-raters who will be eager to serve. The administration may shake itself out in a year or two and reach out to others who have been worried about Trump. Or maybe not.[25]

It is important to stress that Eliot Cohen is, by all conventional litmus tests, an academic and practitioner with unwavering loyalty for to the traditional conservative cause. Like any good professor talking about future events, Cohen appropriately qualifies his conclusions. However, years later, his comments seem prescient. After all, this White House has seen unusual levels of turnover in all areas of staffing, including foreign policy and national security. Numerous former staffers have made their dissatisfaction with the Trump administration plain, and many positions, formerly assumed to be critical, remain unfilled.[26] The latter consequence is surely a function of Trump summarily rejecting individuals who were, at least for a brief but critical period, publicly involved with the #NeverTrump movement.

Cohen, for his part, has emerged as a loud and very public critic of all things Trump, despite the fact that it might have prevented his appointment to prominent foreign policy positions in the Trump administration. His writings and commentary have gained some note and have critiqued the president and his counselors on matters of substance in foreign policy and national security, especially regarding Trump's practice of revoking security clearances from those who criticize him, and Trump's hostility toward liberalism as an ordering principle in global affairs. He has set an example for those foreign policy conservatives who have chosen principles over power and party.

FOREIGN POLICY DIVISIONS IN
THE TRUMP-ERA GOP

Although there is much thoughtful analysis indicating that he has remade the GOP, Trump's grip is not absolute. There remain important individuals at the elite level who remain opposed to him and his presidency. While this number is relatively small, they do exist, an anomaly in for any administration. Support for Trump by members of his own party also varies by issue. In early 2020, for example, Trump authorized a military strike which killed Iran's Major General Qassim Suleimani. Although the story shifted several times, it quickly became clear that Trump's policy had largely sidelined Congress, including congressional Republicans. As a result, several Republicans signaled that they would support invoking the War Powers Act in a bid to curtail Trump's foreign policy.[27] While it is clear that Trump is fully in charge of the GOP, it is noteworthy that some members are willing to disagree and even rebuke the president. Moreover, it is also possible that there exists a sizeable number of Republicans who publicly support Trump for opportunistic reasons but might be quite happy to reject Trumpism once he is out of office. It is also worth pointing out that Trump's foreign policy and national security apparatus, like most other areas of his administration, are understaffed and are often led by individuals with weak resumes in their areas of responsibility. This became particularly true following his impeachment acquittal, when he began purging appointees seen as insufficiently loyal. While there are numerous causes of this, the schism between the individuals who signed these letters and the Trump administration is relevant. Although these letters and subsequent controversy are illustrative of a certain level of chaos and division in GOP politics during the Trump age, they do not signal much about the specific policy objections that separate Donald Trump and his advisors from conservative orthodoxy. The following section will provide an overview of some of the specific national security and foreign policy issues that inspired the #NeverTrump crowd to publicly disavow the head of their party and the sitting president.

Unconventional is a word that is often applied to the Trump administration. For many members of the GOP base, Trump's unorthodox approach to the presidency and policymaking is a welcome antidote to a conservative party that no longer represents their preferences. Moreover, many in the base seem to love the president not only for his policies but also for his bombast and vitriol. Railing against elites, sometimes in public and sometimes in private, has long been a pastime of some presidents, including both Nixon and Kennedy. However, Trump's comments are downright inflammatory in comparison. As indicated above, the written statements that formed the core of the #NeverTrump movement among national security and foreign policy elites strongly suggests their disdain for Trump's rudeness and reflexive bellicosity.

The biggest objections of conservative foreign policy experts revolve around Trump's lack of commitment to an American-led liberal world order and the associated institutions, especially NATO, that undergird this arrangement. To be sure, other differences exist, including Trump's willingness to praise authoritarian leaders and his lack of support for free trade. However, the NATO issue is especially salient and national security and foreign policy experts bemoan Trump's general aversion to the alliance, his skepticism about the innate value of American leadership in the global arena, and his break with European allies, who they believe to be essential, on a number of issues, including the Iran nuclear deal.[28]

In an op-ed that that coincided with the 70th anniversary of the founding of the NATO alliance, Nicholas Burns, an academic and former ambassador to NATO in the George W. Bush administration, and Douglas Lute, a former ambassador to NATO during the Obama and Trump administrations, summarize some of the more common critiques of Trump's approach to NATO. According to Burns and Lute, "NATO is still the world's strongest military alliance. But its single greatest danger is the absence of strong, principled American presidential leadership for the first time in its history. Starting with NATO's founding father, President Harry S. Truman, each of our presidents has considered NATO a vital American interest. President Trump has taken a dramatically different path."[29] Although they believe that there are myriad issues with Trump and the NATO alliance, they spotlight his questioning of Article Five, the crucial part of the alliance that means that an attack on any single member state will be considered an attack on all the member states, and his willingness to support Vladimir Putin. Their conclusions are based on their own experiences as policymakers working with NATO and a recent research project that suggests that the leaders of NATO members view Trump as a serious threat to the alliance.[30]

Among the #NeverTrump crowd, American commitment to NATO, and the things that NATO represents, is a bedrock principle. It is a defining part of the global order that has shaped international politics since the end of World War II and it is crucial for American success and helps promote causes, like freedom and capitalism, that have long been considered grace notes of the United States. Trump's disregard for the institution, including reports that he privately contemplated that the United States leave the organization, is nothing short of apostasy.[31]

The preceding sections outlined some of the sources of opposition that fuel the #NeverTrump movement among national security and foreign policy elites and provides some examples of responses and policymakers. These examples, however, do not represent the entire list of grievances and differences that have split Trump from some elites in his own party. While this chapter cannot fully grapple with all other areas of divergence, I briefly explore a few others below.

Trump's willingness to deal with North Korea, and its dictator, in normalized and perhaps even laudatory ways has given more conventional voices in conservative politics pause. Most policymakers and diplomats, in the United States and elsewhere, view North Korea as a pariah state. With its deplorable record of human rights abuses and its secretive and despotic regime, there is much cause to condemn North Korea and Kim Jong-un. Trump, however, has shown an unusual willingness to praise the autocrat.[32] Bucking convention, Trump has met with the dictator multiple times, even going so far as to cross the border into North Korea to shake hands with Kim, the first president to ever do so. While some consider this boldness a much-needed interjection of energy into a stalemated relationship a la Nixon's visit to China, most conservative foreign policy experts reject this interpretation. Several years into this relationship, Trump's policy shift has not produced visible policy gains (and in fact may have emboldened Kim's position) but has led to further criticism from Democrats and #NeverTrumpers. Foreshadowing a later rift, John Bolton was critical of Trump's diplomatic overtures toward North Korea.[33]

Other sections in this book more fully grapple with trade issues, but it is important to note that Trump's trade war with China and his use of tariffs (and the accompanying disavowal of free trade) puts him at stark odds with conventional conservative ideology.[34] It is also true that some in the #NeverTrump movement applaud the administration's willingness to confront Beijing and many have considered Washington's policies vis-à-vis a rising China feckless. Despite supporting a firmer line against China, however, most conservative foreign policy experts deplore the methods and many believe that they are counterproductive. Orthodox conservative thinking is firmly wedded to free(r) trade as a policy instrument that both bolsters the American economy and reinforces a liberal order that rests on mutual dependence.

Although other chapters consider the question of Russia, one aspect of this relationship does merit attention here. Trump has often expressed admiration for (or even envy of) authoritarian leaders, including Vladimir Putin, and has repeatedly made statements that make some policymakers, both conservative and otherwise, wonder how committed he is to democracy. This attitude, coupled with the fact that Trump's campaign was likely bolstered by Russian interference in the 2016 election, worries many. To be sure, the United States has long had a messy and flawed democracy in which not all citizens have enjoyed identical rights and freedoms. Despite, or perhaps in spite of, this complicated history, American presidential rhetoric has long been characterized by a deep and sustained support of democracy and a championing of democratic norms at home and abroad. Trump's violation of this presidential norm is deeply offensive, and worrying to some. Wright sums many of these concerns when he writes:

> Although Trump has changed his mind on many issues, he has clear, consistent, visceral foreign policy instincts that date back three decades. He has long rejected the United States' security alliances as unfair to the taxpayer and accused allies of conning Washington into defending them for free. . . . And he has a history of expressing admiration for strongmen around the world: in 1990, for example, he lamented in an interview that Soviet Leader Mikhail Gorbachev had not cracked down on demonstrators as Beijing had in Tiananmen Square one year before.[35]

Trump's repeated praise of dictators and his willingness to engage with them offends many in the national security community. While there is some measure of hypocrisy in their outrage given that the United States has long-standing relationships with many authoritarian regimes with appalling records vis-à-vis human rights, two factors seem to set Trump apart from his predecessors in terms of dealing with authoritarian leaders. First, unlike previous presidents who were often willing to work quietly with dictators, Trump revels in their company and is not shy about praising their virtues. Second, President Trump seems occasionally so enamored with dictatorial arrangements that some question his commitment to a constitutionally constrained presidency in the United States.[36]

IGNORING DIPLOMATIC NORMS

This chapter has, thus far, mostly discussed issues of policy and substance. However, even a cursory examination of the reasons underpinning the #NeverTrump movement indicates that while real and meaningful policy differences are necessary to understand the movement, they are also insufficient. There are also staunch objections to Trump's character, rhetoric, and tone. This is rooted both in the belief that diplomacy is partially predicated on measured speech and a more general sense that Trump's impulsive and bombastic style weakens American strategic position in the world. Max Boot, for example, professes to dislike ideological labels but was, nonetheless, an influential thinker and writer in conservative, and especially neoconservative, foreign policy circles. He has consistently and publicly objected to Trump on policy grounds, in that he does not think Trump is effective in any policy sense. Additionally, he finds the forty-fifth president personally offensive. A signatory to Eliot Cohen's statement and an original #NeverTrump pundit, he argues that it "is too early to conclude that Donald Trump is the worst president ever." He adds quickly, "But it's not too early to conclude that he is the worst person ever to be president. . . . Beyond Trump's reported violations of the law, there are his regular violations of the norms of human decency."[37]

Although there are many instances in which Donald Trump flouted the norms that typically regulate national security and foreign policy security policymaking, his revocation of former CIA Director John Brennan's security clearance in 2018 illustrates what is at stake. While this action was entirely legal, it is also highly unorthodox. Not surprisingly, it provoked a strong response from those affiliated with the #NeverTrump movement. This incident created its own cottage industry of commentary, analysis, and sound bites and this chapter cannot chronicle them all. However, the response from Michael Hayden, a retired four-star general who directed the Central Intelligence Agency, is illustrative. Hayden, in an interview, noted that security clearances should not be revoked based on political allegiance. He noted that "if his [Trump's] not revoking my clearance gave the impression that I somehow moved my commentary in a direction more acceptable to the White House, I would find that very disappointing and frankly unacceptable."[38]

This trading of barbs between a seated president and a highly respected general and policymaker is noteworthy on its own. It is also worth considering how this exchange demonstrates another unusual dynamic that characterizes the #NeverTrump movement. Trump largely "blacklisted" the conservative policymakers, think tankers, and academics who opposed his candidacy.[39] As it has become clear that they have no forthcoming offers of service, they in turn have hardened in their opposition to Trump and are vocally critical of the president in ways that would have otherwise been unimaginable. There is no real precedent for their professional and personal scorn for the forty-fifth president and the degree to which they have gone public with their concerns is nothing short of remarkable. Despite their seemingly unimpeachable credentials and their unusually public criticism of Trump, this group has no discernable impact on GOP politics. No amount of criticism from fellow conservatives, including conservatives with usually venerated military backgrounds, seems to have hurt the president.

National security and foreign affairs elites have had a difficult time maintaining their currency in the media, and their popular appeal is limited, which helps explain why their overt criticism has not hurt the president. Donald J. Trump shows considerable, even savant-like, ability to manipulate and control the media narrative. Some of this is because he receives often sycophantic praise from conservative media outlets like Fox News. He is also unusually skilled at social media and his team is formidable in their ability to engineer national conversations in ways that benefit the president. Against this juggernaut and without their own media platforms, his impressively credentialed but less bombastic foes do not stand a chance. As Wertheim points out, many of these conservative elite Trump critics are more readily found on left leaning news outlets.[40] In an era where the web, cable television, and conservative radio are the three legs that support conservative media, op-eds in outlets like the now defunct *The Weekly Standard* are unlikely to gain traction. Even more tellingly, prominent GOP critics, including Ron Paul (R-TX), the late John McCain (R-AZ), and John Bolton after his 2019 fracture with Trump, are largely silenced and sidelined by their comparative lack of skill in commandeering public and media attention.

IMPLICATIONS FOR THE FUTURE GOP

The rise of Donald Trump has bucked conventional wisdom about American party politics and has confounded political scientists and analysts of all areas of expertise levels of experience. It remains unknown if Trump is sui generis and the GOP will revert to a pre-Trump mean when his time in the Oval Office concludes. This is the last hope for folks like Max Boot, Bill Kristol, and Eliot Cohen. They want a president who speaks in more conventional ways, who does not flout long-standing norms and policies, and who seeks advice and counsel from individuals with established conservative credentials. While it does seem safe to assume that the next inhabitant of the Oval Office will not be a replica of Donald Trump, it is also less clear if the GOP will revert to pre-Trump practices. Trump has dramatically remade the party, and perhaps more importantly its voters, in many ways, and even many of those who were initially opposed to his candidacy have become full-throated supporters. Others have remained stubbornly resistant to Trump and Trumpism, including important members of the usually staid national security and foreign policy communities. This arrangement is, without question, a case of misalignment between Republican foreign policy elites and the Republican voters and elected officials who represent those voters.

It also reflects a growing schism between conservatism and the Republican Party. On this, George Will has written and spoken about a growing, and perhaps unreconcilable, divide between pre-Trumpian conservative thinking and Trump's Republican Party.[41] Echoing Will, a group of GOP strategists published an opinion piece in *The New York Times* that made plain some of the critical divides between the Republican Party that they joined and a Republican Party branded in Trump's image. They write, "Mr. Trump and his enablers [congressional Republicans] have abandoned conservatism and long-standing Republican principles and replaced them with Trumpism, an empty faith led by a failed prophet."[42]

Although the discord discussed in this chapter and elsewhere in this book have become more prominent since Trump announced his candidacy in 2015, it predates the rise of Trump as a serious force in American political life. The exact sources and dates vary but it is clear that the rise of the Tea Party helped set the stage for the rise of Trump and the decline of more well-established voices in conservative politics. Dissatisfied with the policies of the George W. Bush and Obama administrations and moved by a deeply held sense of grievance, this populist political movement largely rejects interventionism (such as the war in Iraq), desires a smaller government, and explicitly disdains the political class. Such animosity may not leave a place in the GOP for elite foreign policy thinkers tied to traditional norms of diplomacy and U.S. leadership abroad.

One important question remains unanswered. Has the #NeverTrump movement in the national security and foreign policy communities had a meaningful impact on American politics? Though this chapter has mostly focused on academics and policymakers who objected to Trump from the beginning of his candidacy and who did not join the Trump administration, it is important to remember that that other permutations exist. There are those who were initially part of the #NeverTrump movement who eventually warmed and reversed position on Trump either because of self-interest or genuine conviction. There are yet others who were either supportive or perhaps neutral on Trump at the onset, then joined the administration but subsequently left and have gone public with their objections and concerns.

One of the latter is James Mattis, who served as Trump's Secretary of Defense from his inauguration until late 2018. He left his position due to serious policy differences with Trump, especially regarding NATO. In his public resignation letter, he wrote:

> My views on treating allies with respect and also being clear-eyed about both malign actors and strategic competitors are strongly held and informed by over four decades of immersion in these issues. We must do everything possible to advance an international order that is most conducive to our security, prosperity and values, and we are strengthened in this effort by the solidarity of our alliances. Because you have the right to have a Secretary of Defense whose views are better aligned with yours on these and other subjects, I believe it is right for me to step down from my position.[43]

More recently, John Bolton, resigned as Trump's National Security Advisor over serious policy differences with the forty-fifth president. Although it appears that there were multiple schisms between Trump and Bolton, the most serious issue was Trump's plan to bring members of the Taliban to Camp David in an effort to end American involvement in Afghanistan.

Bolton was widely regarded as having compatible views with the president and his departure signals something of a wider split between some in the GOP over this issues and others. Catie Edmondson, writing in *The New York Times*, notes:

> It is the latest sign of the divide among Republican lawmakers on national security, pitting a camp of hawkish conservatives including Representative Liz Cheney, the House's third-ranking Republican, and Senator Mitt Romney, the 2012 GOP nominee, against a newer; anti-establishment group aligned with Mr. Trump's impulses to put an end to the nation's intractable military conflicts.[44]

Between the original #NeverTrump crowd and the growing universe of former policymakers who seem burned by their tenure in the Trump administration, it is worth contemplating who is left to support and execute Trump's foreign and national security policies and what does this unusual state of affairs have on the GOP, American politics, and the United States' presence in the world? This, perhaps, is the central impact of the #NeverTrump movement. Trump was denied, if he ever wanted, the counsel of Republican experts. This includes not only high-level officials but also mid-level officials who serve in routine but critical agencies and departments related to national security and foreign policy. Indeed, one of the more striking features of Trump's administration is the degree to which positions either go unfilled or are subject to unusually high turnover.

The chronic understaffing of diplomatic and security agencies, most notably the Department of State, has consequences. Daniel Drezner shows that Trump's approach reduced the number of career staffers, diminished their influence, and produced working conditions that further led to a thinning of the ranks. This made it more possible for Trump to pursue unconventional policies, including meeting with North Korean dictator Kim Jong-un.[45] While a counterfactual, it is interesting to ponder if Trump's lack of advice from career diplomats helped lead him to the withholding of aid to Ukraine in 2019. In other words, in the absence of a more conventional national security and foreign policy apparatus—did Trump make decisions, including in the Ukraine case, that he would not have done otherwise? This decision, of course, is of enormous importance, as it caused a quid pro quo scandal that led to Trump's impeachment by the House of Representatives.

President Trump's commentary on his own foreign policy largely mirrors the rest of his rhetoric. He frequently engages in self-aggrandizing sentiment, is prone to telling easily disproved lies, and is ceaseless and intense in his personal attacks directed at real or perceived foes (recall his campaign attacks on a Gold Star family). His bombast seems to not have hurt him with his base and has probably helped him. In a counterfactual exercise, it is difficult to imagine any former president engaging in such vitriolic behavior toward fellow conservatives and not being chastened by members of the base. Trump's support among Republicans is unflaggingly high and when he engages in uncouth statements toward other conservatives, his base seems unfazed. One plausible interpretation is that they view the objects of Trump's ire as elites and therefore in a different category that populist Trump supporters therefore making Trump's rage warranted.

All of this highlights a key takeaway from any study of the Trump candidacy and presidency: Donald Trump doesn't think or behave in ways that are compatible with orthodox conservatism. Moreover, he has been wildly successful in convincing his supporters and some former critics to rally to his cause despite their previous ideological differences. Despite his impeachment and the general tumult associated with his tenure in the Oval Office, it is possible that Trump will win a second term. This would be a powerful vindication for Trump and Trumpism and an equally potent rebuke of the #NeverTrump movement. It would likely be the death knell for most organized forms of conservative resistance to the president and would probably incentivize others to emulate Trump's tactics and rhetoric in their own campaigns. Should Trump lose, especially if he loses badly, members of the #NeverTrump movement will be at least partially vindicated. However, that may not automatically involve being welcomed back into the GOP fold. Whether it is in January 2021 or January 2025, Republicans will have to contend with their future sans Trump.

One distinct possibility is that the GOP reverts to the mean and Trumpism is sidelined or forgotten, especially if his non-traditional foreign policy proves disastrous. In this scenario, members of the #NeverTrump movement and their allies would be once again be welcome in government and would once again be opinion leaders in conservative politics. In practical terms, this would mean that Republicans would support free(r) trade, push hardline and not accommodationist policies vis-à-vis unfriendly autocrats, and champion Washington's leadership of NATO and other institutions key to a liberal vision of global affairs. This outcome, however, seems unlikely because it is so divorced from the current preferences and wishes of Republican voters.

There has been much chicken and egg style debate that ponders if Donald Trump is the cause of the set of policies, ideologies, and grievances that we might call Trumpism or if he is simply channeling the thinking of so many citizens that were formerly understood to be conservatives. In an academic sense, this is a question of enormous import. In terms of the future of politics in the GOP, the United States, and the globe—it is less salient. Whether Donald Trump is a cause or a consequence, or more likely some sort of feedback loop, his sometimes inconsistent policy preferences seems to have been widely and deeply adopted by his base. At present they do not seem to have much appetite for a reversion to the ideological mean. Gideon Rose, pondering a post-Trump foreign policy, writes:

> That would be a huge mistake. For by the time Trump leaves office, the dial on U.S. foreign policy will have moved from supporting the order to undermining it [a liberal world order]. During Trump's tenure, the United States will have broken the bonds of trust needed to keep the common project moving forward, and without trust, the order will gradually start to come apart. Unless there is a major change in course, other countries will follow Washington's lead and chase after hares, and nobody will get to eat venison for a long time.[46]

Rose's analysis may prove prescient but that doesn't mean that the GOP base will heed his call. To many in the base, Rose is nothing more than another effete intellectual who does not understand their version of America. This, too, is evidence of misalignment between elites and masses in the GOP. But where does this leave the Republican Party? In Trump's eventual absence, who will assume leadership of the party? It does seem at least plausible to conclude that a Trump-style party without Trump might struggle to win elections. Trump's base is both aged and, in purely demographic terms, a shrinking slice of the electorate nationally. Should the party find itself unable to remain electorally competitive, it is likely that it will either disappear and quickly be replaced by another version of right of center politics, or rebrand its policies and messaging in a bid to win more elections. It is not clear if either outcome will produce rapprochement between old guard elites in the party (should there be any left active in political life) and the masses.

As this chapter concludes, it is worth noting that while this work has tried to grapple with a particular instance of mass and elite division in a single political party, there has been a sustained upswing in politics of all persuasions that rejects expertise and evinces considerable contempt and distain for experts and elites. A cursory examination of the state of the Democratic Party reveals similar dynamics. This process of resisting expertise and decrying elites, moreover, is not confined to American politics and is playing out in important politics contests in many parts of the world, especially in Europe. Donald J. Trump did not create these rifts but he has masterfully capitalized on them to his own advantage. It is less clear if exploiting these divisions will continue to benefit the GOP or the country when Trump is no longer president.

NOTES

1. Marc Fisher, "Master of Celebrity: How Trump Uses—And Bashes—The Famous to Boost Himself," *The Washington Post*, June 21, 2018, https://www.was

hingtonpost.com/lifestyle/style/master-of-celebrity-how-trump-uses--and-bashes--
the-famous-to-boost-himself/2018/06/20/fef51c98-6b33-11e8-bf8c-f9ed2e672adf
_story.html.

2. Jonathan Marin and Alexander Burns, "As Donald Trump Incites Feuds, Other
G.O.P. Candidates Flee His Shadow," *The New York Times*, August 6, 2016, https://
www.nytimes.com/2016/08/07/us/politics/donald-trump-gop.html.

3. Quint Forgey, Daniel Lippman, Andrew Restuccia, and Brent D. Griffiths,
"Trump vs. the Bushes: A Political Rivalry of Its Time," *Politico*, December 1, 2018,
https://www.politico.com/story/2018/12/01/trump-bush-rivalry-1037143.

4. Larry M. Bartels, "Partisanship in the Trump Era," *The Journal of Politics*, 80,
no. 4 (October 2018): 1483–94.

5. David E. Sanger and Maggie Haberman, "50 G.O.P. Officials Warn Donald
Trump Would Put Nation's Security 'at Risk,'" *The New York Times*, August 8, 2016,
https://www.nytimes.com/2016/08/09/us/politics/national-security-gop-donald-trum
p.html.

6. Sanger and Haberman, "50 G.O.P."

7. "Open Letter on Trump from GOP National Security Leaders," *War on the
Rocks*, March 2, 2016, https://warontherocks.com/2016/03/open-letter-on-donald
-trump-from-gop-national-security-leaders/.

8. Mark Leibovich, "How Lindsey Graham Went from Trump Skeptic to Trump
Sidekick," *The New York Times*, February 25, 2019, https://www.nytimes.com/2019
/02/25/magazine/lindsey-graham-what-happened-trump.html.

9. Leibovich, "How Lindsey Graham."

10. Sheryl Gay Stolberg, "What Happened to Lindsey Graham? He's Become a
Conservative Rock Star," *The New York Times*, November 8, 2018, https://www.nyt
imes.com/2018/11/02/us/politics/lindsey-graham-trump-midterms.html.

11. David Nakamura, "'Never Trump' National-Security Republicans Fear They
Have Been Blacklisted," *The Washington Post*, January 16, 2017, https://www.was
hingtonpost.com/politics/never-trump-national-security-republicans-fear-they-have
-been-blacklisted/2017/01/16/a2fadf54-d9a3-11e6-b8b2-cb5164beba6b_story.html.

12. Gary Dorrien, *Imperial Designs: Neoconservatism and the New Pax Americana*
(New York: Routledge, 2004). See also Danny Cooper, *Neoconservatism and
American Foreign Policy: A Critical Analysis* (New York: Routledge, 2011). Cooper
is clear that there is not necessarily consensus on the term. Stephen Wertheim,
"Return of the Neocons," *The New York Review of Books*, January 2, 2019, https://
www.nybooks.com/daily/2019/01/02/return-of-the-neocons/ provides a clear set of
bedrock neoconservative principles.

13. Project for a New American Century, "Statement of Principles," last modified
June 3, 1997, https://www.rrojasdatabank.info/pfpc/PNAC---statement%20of%2
0principles.pdf.

14. Johns Hopkins, "Eliot A. Cohen Named Ninth Dean of Johns Hopkins SAIS,"
July 8, 2019, https://sais.jhu.edu/news-press/eliot-cohen-named-ninth-dean-johns
-hopkins-sais.

15. Eliot A. Cohen, *The Big Stick: The Limits of Soft Power and the Necessity of
Military Force* (New York: Basic Books, 2017).

16. Anonymous, "I Am Part of the Resistance Inside the Trump administration," *The New York Times*, September 5, 2018, https://www.nytimes.com/2018/09/05/opini on/trump-white-house-anonymous-resistance.html.

17. Eliot A. Cohen, "To an Anxious Friend...," *The American Interest*, November 10, 2016, https://www.the-american-interest.com/2016/11/10/to-an-anxious-friend/.

18. Cohen, "Anxious."

19. Cohen, "Anxious."

20. Eliot A. Cohen, "I Told Conservatives to Work for Trump. One Talk with His Team Changed My Mind," *The Washington Post*, November 15, 2016, https://ww w.washingtonpost.com/opinions/i-told-conservatives-to-work-for-trump-one-talk-wi th-his-team-changed-my-mind/2016/11/15/f02e1fac-ab7c-11e6-977a-1030f822fc35 _story.html.

21. Anonymous, "I Am."

22. Thomas G. Weiss, "The United Nations and Sovereignty in the Age of Trump," *Current History,* 117, no. 795 (January 2018): 10–15.

23. Wertheim, "Return."

24. Cohen, "I Told."

25. Cohen, "I Told."

26. Kathryn Dunn Tenpas, "Record-Setting White House Staff Turnover Continues with News of Counsel's Departure," *Brookings*, October 19, 2018, https://www.bro okings.edu/blog/fixgov/2018/10/19/record-setting-white-house-staff-turnover-cont inues-with-news-of-counsels-departure/.

27. Rachel Oswald, "Senate Could Vote to Curb Trump War Powers, but Timing Unclear," *Roll Call*, January 14, 2020, https://www.rollcall.com/2020/01/14/senate -could-vote-to-curb-trump-war-powers-but-timing-unclear/.

28. G. John Ikenberry, "The Plot Against American Foreign Policy: Can the Liberal Order Survive?" *Foreign Affairs,* 96, no. 3 (May/June 2017): 2–9.

29. Nicholas Burns and Douglas Lute, "NATO's Biggest Problem Is President Trump," *The Washington Post*, April 2, 2019, https://www.washingtonpost.com/ opinions/natos-biggest-problem-is-president-trump/2019/04/02/6991bc9c-5570-11e9 -9136-f8e636f1f6df_story.html.

30. Nicholas Burns and Douglas Lute, "NATO at Seventy: An Alliance in Crisis," *Belfer Center for Science and International Affairs*, February 2019, https://www .belfercenter.org/NATO70.

31. Lauren Stauffer, "How President Trump Shattered the Bond between Republicans and NATO," *The Washington Post*, April 4, 2019, https://www.was hingtonpost.com/outlook/2019/04/04/how-president-trump-shattered-bond-between -republicans-nato/; See also: Rebecca Kheel, "GOP Reasserts NATO Support after Report on Trump's Wavering," *The Hill*, January 16, 2019, https://thehill.com/policy /defense/425543-gop-reasserts-nato-support-after-report-on-trumps-wavering.

32. Philip Rucker, "Trump Praises Kim Jong Un's Authoritarian Rule, Says 'I Want My People to Do the Same,'" *The Chicago Tribune*, August 22, 2019, https:// www.chicagotribune.com/nation-world/ct-trump-kim-jong-un-20180615-story.html.

33. Simon Denyer and Ashley Parker, "Trump Appears to Contradict Bolton on North Korea, Expresses 'Confidence' in Kim," *The Washington Post*, May 25,

2019, https://www.washingtonpost.com/world/bolton-says-north-korea-is-violating -un-resolutions-and-refusing-talks/2019/05/25/b9541aa0-7e5a-11e9-b1f3-b233fe5 811ef_story.html.

34. Joshua Tait, "Will Conservatives Abandon the Free Market?" *The National Interest*, April 18, 2019, https://nationalinterest.org/feature/will-conservatives-aban don-free-market-53172. See also: Inu Manak, "Are Republicans Still the Party of Free Trade?" *The Cato Institute*, May 16, 2019, https://www.cato.org/blog/are-repub licans-still-party-free-trade.

35. Thomas Wright, "Trump's Foreign Policy Is No Longer Unpredictable," *Foreign Affairs* (January 18, 2018), https://www.foreignaffairs.com/articles/world /2019-01-18/trumps-foreign-policy-no-longer-unpredictable.

36. Edward-Isaac Dovere, "Donald Dreams of Dictators," *Politico*, June 15, 2018, https://www.politico.com/story/2018/06/15/trump-dictators-authoritarians-strongm en-649635.

37. Max Boot, "Donald Trump Is the Worst Person Ever to Be President," *The Salt Lake Tribune*, October 4, 2018, https://www.sltrib.com/opinion/commentary/201 8/10/04/max-boot-donald-trump-is/.

38. Maegan Vasquez, "Michael Hayden Says He, Too, Would Honored If Trump Revoked His Security Clearance," *CNN*, August 18, 2018, https://www.cnn .com/2018/08/19/politics/intelligence-chiefs-michael-hayden-john-brennan-cnntv/i ndex.html.

39. Nakamura, "'Never Trump.'"

40. Wertheim, "Return."

41. George Will, *The Conservative Sensibility* (New York: Hachette Books, 2019).

42. George T. Conway III, Steve Schmidt, John Weaver, and Rick Wilson, "We Are Republicans, and We Want Trump Defeated," *The New York Times*, December 17, 2019, https://www.nytimes.com/2019/12/17/opinion/lincoln-project.html.

43. Andrew Prokop, "Read: Defense Secretary James Mattis's Resignation Letter Laying out his Disagreements with Trump," *Vox*, December 20, 2018, https://www .vox.com/2018/12/20/18150826/james-mattis-resigns-letter-trump-read.

44. Catie Edmondson, "Bolton Ouster Underscores a G.O.P. Divided on Foreign Policy," *The New York Times*, September 11, 2019, https://www.nytimes.com/2019 /09/11/us/politics/trump-republicans-foreign-policy.html.

45. Daniel Drezner, "Present at the Destruction: The Trump administration and the Foreign Policy Bureaucracy," *The Journal of Politics,* 81, no. 2 (April 2019): 723–30.

46. Gideon Rose, "The Fourth Founding: The United States and the Liberal Order," *Foreign Affairs,* 98, no. 1 (January/February 2019): 10.

Chapter 8

Whose Conservatism?

Domestic Policy and #NeverTrump Opposition

Robert (Bo) Wood

Of the many reasons Republicans gave for resisting the candidacy of Donald Trump in the fall of 2015, few were based on opposition to his domestic policy agenda. This may seem puzzling to readers in 2020 but is easily understood when three contextual elements from the period leading up to the 2016 primary season are considered. First, Trump's candidacy was initially dismissed by both the media and Republican establishment as a simple publicity stunt calculated to boost his brand. Eleven other candidates were already in the race, including five current or former members of the U.S. Senate, four current or former governors, a neurosurgeon, and the CEO of a major corporation. Jeb Bush, a former Florida Governor and early favorite, had announced his own candidacy only a day earlier, joining a crowded field that would soon swell to sixteen before the Iowa caucuses convened in January. Serious Republicans invested no more time researching Trump's domestic policy positions than they did those of Bobby Jindal or George Pataki.

Second, Trump emphasized, intentionally or not, the malleability of his policy positions from the start. Having never before held public office, he had no public record of decisions that might reveal his policy positions. He had been an outspoken critic of many Obama administration policies, but had also supported multiple Democratic candidates including Hillary Clinton, Nancy Pelosi, and Harry Reid.[1] He had reportedly switched party affiliation five times since the late 1980s and identified as a Democrat as late as the mid-2000s.[2] From Trump's perspective, however, his independence from political ideology was a strength that allowed him to consider any deal on any issue at any time. This lack of concrete political principles was no doubt troubling to Republican leadership but was easily ignored or dismissed during the summer and autumn of 2015 with so many other qualified candidates in the race.

Third, Trump's position on key domestic issues remained vague, contradictory, or missing altogether for much of the primary cycle. Whether this was an intentional move to undercut potential opposition or because he simply viewed some issues as relatively less important than others, Trump's positions were most often articulated through unscripted remarks that confused more than they clarified. This practice was present from the very first moments of his candidacy, and his announcement speech contains key indicators of his domestic policy priorities that were added extemporaneously. The campaign's prepared remarks, as circulated before the speech, totaled less than 1,200 words and included a range of domestic issues traditionally embraced by GOP candidates, such as repealing and replacing Obamacare, tax reform, reducing the size of government, rebuilding our infrastructure, protecting veterans and their families, and protecting Social Security, Medicare, and Medicaid from cuts.[3] As delivered, Trump's speech totaled more than 6,300 words, and his additional 5,000 words both depart from and expand upon the themes of his written speech.[4] They provide the first glimpses of at least three important differences from the Republican establishment domestic policy positions that would define his campaign and fuel #NeverTrump sentiment in the months to come. Those differences are in trade policy, fiscal responsibility, and immigration.

TRADE POLICY

The first of these differences between Trump and #NeverTrump conservatives is trade. Straddling the line between the foreign and the domestic policy worlds, trade policies often have far reaching impacts on both the domestic and the global economy. For over half a century, Republicans have largely supported the reduction and removal of trade barriers through trade agreements, while Democrats have just as often opposed them, citing environmental, labor, and other concerns that create unfair competition. Given the climate of uncertainty surrounding Trump's political beliefs at the time of his announcement, his rhetoric on America's trade relationships at the beginning of his announcement speech might have raised a red flag for many free trade Republicans, had they not dismissed his candidacy. Much of the speech as delivered invoked the concepts of winning and losing. According to Trump, America had been losing on trade deals for far too long. Within the first thirty seconds of his remarks, his position was clear:

> Our country is in serious trouble. We don't have victories anymore. We used to
> have victories, but we don't have them. When was the last time anybody saw us

beating, let's say, China in a trade deal? They kill us. I beat China all the time. All the time. When did we beat Japan at anything? They send their cars over by the millions, and what do we do? When was the last time you saw a Chevrolet in Tokyo? It doesn't exist, folks. They beat us all the time. When do we beat Mexico at the border? They're laughing at us, at our stupidity. And now they're beating us economically. They are not our friend, believe me. But they're killing us economically.[5]

Trump was not the first Republican candidate to rail against trading partners for not living up to their agreements. Four years earlier, during the 2012 Republican Primary, Mitt Romney had surprised many with strong comments on China's trade practices and their impact on jobs and the economy in a South Carolina debate. Romney said "We can't just sit back and let China run all over us. People will say, well, you'll start a trade war. There's one going on right now, folks. They're stealing our jobs and we're going to stand up to China."[6]

Romney's comments were surprising for two reasons. First, he had a reputation as a wealthy business executive with a history of outsourcing jobs. Second, they openly challenged the largely uninterrupted commitment to free trade principles championed by the party. Romney got some applause with his statement but saw no appreciable bump in support and soon moved back to more traditional conservative positions. He was not however, wrong. China has repeatedly failed to fulfill the commitments made when admitted to the World Trade Organization in 2001. Both the Bush and Obama administrations filed and won multiple trade enforcement actions with the WTO. Yet both administrations also believed in the value of a global system of free trade and tended to work within the system to encourage China to normalize trade practices while avoiding the potential economic disruptions a trade war might bring.

Trump's approach would be different. In the private sector, transactions are often framed as zero sum and Trump was known for using whatever leverage was available to win. In his prepared remarks, Trump devotes two sentences to trade relationships generally. "It is time to stop sending jobs overseas through bad foreign trade deals. We will renegotiate our trade deals with the toughest negotiators our country has . . . the ones who have actually read *The Art of the Deal* and know how to make great deals for our country." Further down, an additional two sentences mention China more specifically: "It is time to get tough with the Chinese on currency manipulation and espionage. We will tax China for each bad act, and if they continue then we will tax them at an even higher level."[7]

These sentences make clear a willingness to use tariffs and other protectionist policies that sound more like a Democratic candidate than a Republican, but as delivered, the speech goes even further. To illustrate his thinking on how other countries are beating us in trade, he provides three examples. The first describes an unnamed friend who makes a (presumably American) product and cannot enter the Chinese market due to regulatory barriers. When he does overcome the trade barriers, he is charged a large tariff on his product. The second claims that China would not buy planes from Boeing unless they shared patent and other confidential information. The third details a hypothetical scenario where Ford considers building an auto plant in Mexico but reconsiders when Trump (as president) threatens to impose a 35 percent tax on cars coming to the United States from this plant.

Each of these examples has some basis in fact. China has manipulated its currency, blocked foreign firms from competing in its markets, required companies to share their technology in order to open factories, and consistently ignored intellectual property rights. Numerous automotive manufacturers have moved production to Mexico (and elsewhere) to reduce costs. Yet in taking this stance, Trump was positioning himself against more than half a century of settled opinion within the GOP establishment. In the modern era, the Republican Party has consistently identified itself as the party of business and commerce. In principle and in practice, the GOP has supported free and unencumbered market system policies whenever and wherever possible and has broadly embraced David Ricardo's theories of comparative advantage when considering trade relationships with other nations.[8] When NAFTA was approved by Congress in 1993, support from Republicans in both chambers of Congress was significantly higher than from Democrats, who were concerned about the loss of jobs to cheaper labor markets abroad.[9] From the GOP establishment perspective, society's net gain, both economically and diplomatically, from free trade policies is worth the disruptions they cause in impacted sectors of the economy.

The frustration Mr. Romney sensed among working-class voters in South Carolina in 2011 was, in hindsight, a harbinger of a growing wave of populist support that would propel Mr. Trump to the White House a few years later. These voters were frustrated with the outsourcing of their jobs and the perception that other countries were cheating at their expense. Yet, while an establishment Republican might respond to these concerns by attempting to explain the societal advantages of free trade, Trump's lack of ideological baggage allowed him to both recognize and respond to their concerns. "Nobody gave them hope," Trump says of these anxious Americans, enumerating the deficiencies of those three Republican standard-bearers who came before him. "I gave them hope."[10]

In the first three years of his presidency, Trump has demonstrated that his advocacy of "America First" trade policies was not simple campaign rhetoric. He has withdrawn the United States from proposed agreements such as the Trans-Pacific Partnership (TPP) and renegotiated existing deals such as NAFTA and KORUS. He has shown a distinct preference for bi-lateral trade deals over sweeping multilateral agreements with trading partners and has imposed (or threatened to impose) tariffs on a wide range of imports to secure concessions from trading partners. Heading into the 2020 election cycle, the ultimate success of these strategies is still very much in doubt, yet his support from these workers remains strong. Employment in manufacturing has increased, but has done so at essentially the same rate as employment across the economy generally.[11] Retaliatory tariffs on agricultural products have also inflicted serious harm on farmers and farming communities, yet these voters also continue to support the president.

It remains unclear whether this support stems from a pragmatic belief that Trump's trade policies will ultimately prove beneficial, from his positions on other issues they care about, or from personal loyalty to a president who fought for them when no one else would. It is reasonably clear however, that these voters reflect a growing misalignment between the positions of GOP elites and their voters. Respected voices at conservative think tanks such as the American Enterprise Institute and the Cato Institute continue to espouse the value of free markets and free trade.[12] Conservative outlets such as *National Review* and the now shuttered *The Weekly Standard* continue to warn of potentially dangerous consequences from the protectionist path we are taking. Max Boot, for example, refers to Trump as "the flim-flam man" for his remarkable capacity to create crises—particularly those related to foreign policy and trade—and then claim credit for resolving them regardless of whether the result is superior to the pre-crisis state.[13] The most striking thing, for Boot, is that both the president and the bulk of his supporters appear to view these interactions as a win for the president and for America. Republican members of Congress who believe in the principles of free trade are thus challenged to navigate a path that preserves the trade relationships built over the last seventy years without alienating the president.

FISCAL RESPONSIBILITY

A second area of concern for some establishment Republicans and conservatives was Trump's history of using other peoples' money wherever possible to manage his exposure to risk. As a businessman, Trump was well known for borrowing to finance his visionary projects, often with great success. In many ways, this aspect of his candidacy most strongly reflected a cherished ideal of the Right—the potential to harness the entrepreneurial instincts of the successful businessman to solve the seemingly intractable problems of government. Yet Trump's record of success was far from perfect, and some

Republicans worried that tactics Trump used in the private sector would prove disastrous if applied to government. In four separate instances, Trump companies filed for bankruptcy protection.[14] Stories of contractor payments delayed or withheld on his projects were widespread.[15] Lawsuits, liens, debt renegotiation, and other legal maneuvers were key tactics for Trump, and some saw more danger than potential in his approach to fiscal responsibility.

Republicans have long considered themselves the party of fiscal responsibility, particularly when the occupant of the White House is someone they might label a free-spending Democrat. Prior to the election of Ronald Reagan, this generally meant that Republicans opposed deficit spending and expected the nation to live within its means as would any home, business, or state. For many Republicans, this was a simple common-sense principle. Yet, to combat the corrosive effects of the 1982 recession, Reagan introduced tax reforms that substantially increased the nation's deficits. The military buildup over which he presided was also quite expensive, as was the expansion of Medicare. This misalignment between Republican fiscal theory and Republican fiscal behavior continued under George H. W. Bush, with deficits mounting from Operation Desert Storm, the Savings and Loan bailout, and a new recession in 1991.[16]

The emergence of Texas billionaire Ross Perot as an independent candidate in 1992 marks an important point of demarcation for Republicans on this topic. Perot built his candidacy on the need to reverse course and eliminate the debt accumulated under Reagan and Bush. He challenged all Americans, but especially Republicans, to prioritize fiscal responsibility. The "Contract with America" proposed by Republicans two years later included a proposed balanced budget amendment to the Constitution, even while the Clinton administration rolled out a plan for universal healthcare coverage with little discussion of how the ambitious programs would be funded. The resulting Republican majorities in both chambers brought fiscal responsibility to the forefront, forcing Clinton to abandon these proposals and focus instead on reforming the welfare system and streamlining the federal bureaucracy.

Under the presidency of George W. Bush, concern from Republicans over growth of the deficit was subdued, even while tax cuts and wars in Afghanistan and Iraq caused deficits to increase in every year of his presidency. The Great Recession however, proved to be another turning point for Republicans. The drastic measures taken by the Obama administration to stabilize the economy after 2008 alarmed many Republican voters and elected officials. The American Recovery and Reinvestment Act, the Troubled Asset Relief Program, and other stimulus measures produced a deficit of more than $1.5 trillion in FY2010.[17] Concern over the dramatic trajectory of government spending fueled the rise of the Tea Party in 2010. The elimination of deficits and paying down the national debt were among the most salient issues to these voters, yet by the end of the primary cycle in 2016, Trump enjoyed widespread support among Tea Party voters without ever committing to fiscal responsibility.[18] Ironically, three of his rivals for the nomination—Ted Cruz (R-TX), Rand Paul (R-KY), and Marco Rubio (R-FL)—were elected to their respective Senate seats as Tea Party champions, largely *because* of their support for fiscal responsibility.[19]

Trump accomplished this feat primarily though vague and often contradictory statements about his position on many policy issues and how they would be funded. His history in business suggested no inclination to avoid increasing the national debt, yet on many occasions he had publicly criticized the rising deficits under the Obama administration. He promised to eliminate annual deficits and pay off the national debt within eight years.[20] He espoused simplifying and reducing the tax burden of both individuals and corporations, while simultaneously promoting the construction of a wall across the southern border of the United States, repealing and replacing Obamacare with something that provided better coverage, and restoring military budget cuts imposed by the Sequester in 2013. For many deficit-hawk Republicans, this was a movie they had seen before and had no desire to repeat.

A number of fiscally conservative Super PACs raised and spent millions in Iowa, Florida, and other early primary states to paint Trump as a fiscal liberal.[21] The Club for Growth went so far as to deny congressional endorsements to candidates who supported Trump before the nomination was decided.[22] Speaker Paul Ryan (R-WI), who was for years considered an "intellectual leader among conservatives and the conscience of the GOP on fiscal issues" declared that he was "not ready" to endorse his party's presumptive nominee in May of 2016, citing doubts that Trump was a "true" conservative.[23] Ryan was a well-known champion of fiscal reform and the most prominent member of the majority party in the House of Representatives when he again distanced himself from Trump after the release of the "Access Hollywood" recording in October.[24] Yet none of these efforts proved effective at raising the salience of fiscal responsibility with Republican primary voters in 2016 and Trump was able to largely skirt the issue during the general election.

Many of the objections raised by #NeverTrump fiscal conservatives have proven prescient, although others who expressed concern have ended up supporting Trump's deficit-spending policies. By November 2017, Speaker Ryan, on behalf of the House majority, declared that "We're with Trump," signaling a full embrace of the president's agenda.[25] After promising as a candidate to both balance the federal budget and eliminate the national debt within eight years, President Trump instead introduced a massive tax reduction package and supported substantial increases in both defense and domestic spending.[26] This combination of reduced revenue and increased spending has increased the deficit in each of the first three years of the Trump presidency, reaching $960 billion for FY2019.[27] The CBO projects an average deficit of $1.2 trillion per year for the next ten years if existing patterns of taxing and spending remain unchanged, and under these assumptions, the federal debt would be equal to 95 percent of GDP by 2029.[28]

The stark reality of these numbers highlights a significant opportunity for Trump's critics in the upcoming 2020 cycle, though it will undoubtedly be difficult for the Democratic nominee to criticize his record on deficit spending while supporting the more ambitious public programs currently favored by Democratic primary voters. Many of the #NeverTrump conservatives who opposed him on fiscal grounds in 2016 have long since aligned themselves with Trump or exited the field, though some groups, such as the Concord Coalition and the Center for Responsible Federal Budget continue to push for fiscal reforms and discipline.[29] Ironically, Republicans concerned with ballooning deficits may see their hopes rekindled in a second Trump term. Speaking on this subject, Senator John Thune (R-SD) recently said, "It's going to take presidential leadership to do that, and it's going to take courage by the Congress to make some hard votes. We can't keep kicking the can down the road. I hope in a second term, he is interested. With his leadership, I think we could start dealing with that crisis. And it is a crisis."[30]

IMMIGRATION AND BORDER SECURITY

Of all the domestic policy issue positions taken by Trump, the most visible and central to his 2016 candidacy were those relating to immigration and border security. Although he was vague or noncommittal on many other domestic issues, Trump, from the beginning, maintained a strong and unwavering position on curtailing illegal (and legal) immigration and boosting border security that resonated with Republican primary voters. It was clear from the prepared remarks of his announcement speech that this would be a priority:

> It is way past time to build a massive wall to secure our southern border—and nobody can build a bigger and better wall than Donald Trump. A country without borders is, quite simply, not a country. Mexico is not our friend. They are beating us at the border and hurting us badly at economic development. They are sending people that they don't want—the United States is becoming a dumping ground for the world.[31]

When delivering the speech however, his extemporaneous and hyperbolic additions gave it a darker and more inflammatory attitude toward immigrants:

When Mexico sends its people, they're not sending their best. They're not sending you. They're not sending you. They're sending people that have lots of problems, and they're bringing those problems with us. They're bringing drugs. They're bringing crime. They're rapists. And some, I assume, are good people.[32]

This remarkable speech dominated news coverage of his announcement and, while it struck a responsive chord with many frustrated GOP voters, it set off alarm bells for others, including many establishment Republican leaders. In the "Conservatives Against Trump" issue of the *National Review*, many of the essays highlighted his racist positions and resulting policies on their list of disqualifying traits.[33] For example, David Boaz, executive vice-president of the Cato Institute, said "Not since George Wallace has there been a presidential candidate who made racial and religious scapegoating so central to his campaign." Conservative radio host Michael Medved added: "His much-heralded hard line on immigration discards pragmatic reform policies favored by the two most popular conservatives of the last half century, Ronald Reagan and George W. Bush." And of Trump's proposed "temporary" ban on all Muslims entering the country, Michael Mukasey noted:

Even assuming an infallible way to identify who is Muslim, the proposal is both under- and over-inclusive. It is under-inclusive because it does not address potential terrorists who have U.S. Passports or residents, or who are already here, or may threaten us abroad; it is over-inclusive because it bars the huge majority of Muslims who are not potential terrorists.[34]

Trump's rhetoric on immigration and border security was particularly troubling to establishment Republicans trying to broaden the party's base of support. In the wake of Republican losses during the 2012 election cycle, the Republican National Committee commissioned a task force to "dig deep to provide an honest review of the 2012 election cycle and a path forward for the Republican Party to ensure success in winning more elections."[35] During the first few months of 2013, the Growth and Opportunity Project Report (GOPR) gathered data from more than 52,000 Republicans of all types through a combination of surveys, conference calls, focus groups, listening sessions, interviews, and one-on-one meetings.[36] The final report, totaling nearly 100 pages, makes extensive recommendations across seven major content areas. The first two of these, "Messaging" and "Demographic Partners," articulate in stark terms a need to attract younger and more diverse members to the party.

The GOPR states: "The GOP today is a tale of two parties. One of them, the gubernatorial wing, is growing and successful. The other, the federal wing, is increasingly marginalizing itself, and unless changes are made, it will be increasingly difficult for Republicans to win another presidential election in the near future."[37] Moreover, the report argues that "America is changing demographically, and unless Republicans are able to grow our appeal the way GOP governors have done, the changes tilt the playing field even more in the Democratic direction."[38]

The report acknowledges the reality of the demographic shift taking place in America, and points out that while the policy preferences of many Hispanic Americans align closely with GOP positions on a wide range of other issues, Republicans have little chance of reaching these voters so long as the Party is perceived as hostile on immigration.

> If Hispanic Americans perceive that a GOP nominee or candidate does not want them in the United States, they will not pay attention to our next sentence. It does not matter what we say about education, jobs, or the economy; if Hispanics think we do not want them here, they will close their ears to our policies.[39]

The Report further asserts:

> We are not a policy committee, but among the steps Republicans take in the Hispanic community and beyond, we must embrace and champion comprehensive immigration reform. If we do not, our Party's appeal will continue to shrink to its core constituencies only.[40]

These represent only a small part of the overall recommendations from the report, yet they reflected the dominant thinking among GOP leaders on this issue as the 2016 nomination race began to heat up. Of the aspiring Republican candidates, all but one recognized this new political reality and tried, to varying degrees, to find a position on immigration reform that welcomed Hispanic voters but was also acceptable to their traditional base.[41] Immigration reform had nearly passed in 2013, when the *Border Security, Economic Opportunity, and Immigration Modernization Act of 2013* passed the Senate with Republican support before stalling in the House over concerns that its pathway to citizenship provision rewarded unlawful behavior. Most of the proposals focused on resolving these details in a way that seemed fair to all.

Trump saw things differently, and much to the dismay of his opponents, Republican voters agreed. Support for hardline immigration positions continued to gain traction throughout the 2016 cycle, and by election night Trump and his supporters had transformed the Republican stance on immigration and border security from one of expansion and inclusion to one of isolation and nativism. In the three years since, though several controversial executive orders have been blocked by the Courts and the wall along the southern border has yet to begin, support for these policies remains strong with the base of the GOP. In a survey conducted in June of 2016, more than three-fourths of pro-Trump Republicans indicated that they would like to see the number of immigrants to the U.S. decrease.[42] In 2019 polling from the Chicago Council on Global Affairs, 78 percent of Republicans view immigration as a critical threat, 78 percent believe that restricting immigration makes the United States safer, and 81 percent support the use of U.S. troops at the border to prevent illegal immigration. Eighty-two percent consider strict policy measures, such as arrests and deportations to be effective policies, and 83 percent support imposing new fines on businesses that hire illegal workers.[43]

Heading into 2020, demographic trends continue to work against the largely white, religious base of older rural and working-class voters that elected him in 2016. According to the American National Election Studies, the proportion of white voters in the electorate continues to decline, shrinking from 95 percent after World War II to around 74 percent in 2016.[44] According to the Pew Hispanic Center, this percentage continue to decrease, reaching 47 percent by 2050, while during the same period the proportion of Hispanics and Asians will increase to 29 percent and 9 percent respectively.[45] To this point, Trump has shown little inclination to change tracks, but instead has consistently worked to stoke fears and maximize participation from this segment of the population. In the long run, this strategy is clearly unsustainable, but it is clearly feasible that these voters could deliver a second term for Trump in 2020.

IMPLICATIONS FOR 2020

The #NeverTrump resistance to Donald Trump's domestic policy positions was slow to develop compared to the outrage generated by other aspects of his candidacy for a number of reasons. First, Mr. Trump was not viewed as a serious candidate by most Republicans. He had flirted with running before and his actions were easily dismissed as simple self-promotion. Second, he was not deeply invested in any specific ideological position, and frequently modified or contradicted prior positions on issues as diverse as healthcare, tax reform, and trade. Third, his inexperience with policy issues made his positions unpredictable and fluid and his populist streak made him critical and dismissive of expertise and bureaucratic institutions. Initially, establishment Republicans dismissed his claims and promises as empty rhetoric that voters would quickly see through, but were taken by surprise when it became apparent that these traits were admired by voters hungry for an alternative to the status quo. #NeverTrumpers were also slow to focus on domestic priorities because Trump was reasonably well-aligned with the rhetoric of U.S.

conservatives on core issues such as tax reform, the repeal of Obamacare, job growth, reducing regulation, gun rights, and perhaps most importantly, the appointment of a conservative judiciary. While there were many reasons for conservatives to oppose his candidacy, relatively few were founded on policy differences.

As it became clear that Trump was also wedded to several key issues that diverged from established conservative principles, opposition to his candidacy on the basis of his policies increased. Of concern to fiscal conservatives were his claims that citizens could expect dramatically expanded control over their health care as part of the "repeal and replace" of Obamacare. Of equal concern were exaggerated claims regarding the dangers from immigrants and his promise to build a great wall along the length of the southern border (and force Mexico to pay for it). He denounced NAFTA, TPP, and other multilateral trade agreements as "bad deals" in need of renegotiation, proposing instead "America First" protectionist trade policies that directly undermined decades of GOP support for free trade. Many establishment Republicans concluded that the gains were worth the costs as it became clear that Republican voters were, as Eric Cantor put it, "not as ideological as we thought they were."[46]

Since 2016, President Trump has continued to enjoy unwavering support from his base, fundamentally shifting the position of the Republican Party on these issues. Most officeholders who could not (or would not) adapt have retired, left the party, or been defeated. Ironically, as the consequences of Trump's policies on trade, immigration, and tax reform have developed, some Republicans have begun to remember why they opposed these positions in the first place. Many parts of the country heavily impacted by globalization have been among his most staunch supporters, yet in most of these places the jobs have not returned.[47] Worse, retaliatory tariffs on agricultural products have had profoundly negative effects on rural communities that are likely to continue for some time, even if new agreements are reached and trading relationships are restored.

Despite promising to balance the budget and even retire the national debt in eight years, Trump's tax reform package and budget deals have produced the opposite effect, nearly doubling the deficit in his first term with no end in sight. His proposed ban on Muslims, limits on refugees, elimination of DACA protections, and border wall policies run counter to all demographic trends and undermine bedrock American values.

Each of these issues offers opportunities for #NeverTrump resistance in 2020, both from within the Republican Party and from the Democratic nominee. The intra-party misalignment within the Republican Party documented in this volume has produced a durable block of support for positions that are, ultimately, untenable. #NeverTrumpers who are attentive will have opportunities to reshape the debates over these issues in the 2020 cycle and beyond, but they must assume that, at this point, President Trump is deeply invested in each of these issues and will use all the tools at his disposal to continue on the path he has chosen.

NOTES

1. Guy Benson, "Trump: I'm Capable of Changing to Anything I Want to Change To," *Town Hall*, February 12, 2016, https://townhall.com/tipsheet/guybenson/2016/02/12/trump-i-will-be-changing-very-rapidly-in-a-general-election-n2118062.

2. Benson, "Trump: I'm Capable."

3. "Donald Trump Announcement of Candidacy, Trump Tower, New York, NY," June 16, 2015, http://www.p2016.org/trump/trump061615sp.html.

4. "Here's Donald Trump's Presidential Announcement Speech," *Time*, June 16, 2015, https://time.com/3923128/donald-trump-announcement-speech/.

5. "Here's Donald Trump's Presidential Announcement Speech."

6. Cameron Joseph, "Romney Says US in a 'trade war' with China," *The Hill*, November 13, 2011, https://thehill.com/blogs/ballot-box/presidential-races/193221-romney-says-us-in-a-trade-war-with-china.

7. "Here's Donald Trump's Presidential Announcement Speech."

8. Kimberly Amadeo, "Comparative Advantage Theory and Examples," *The Balance*, https://www.thebalance.com/comparative-advantage-3305915.

9. See "H.R.3450 – North American Free Trade Agreement Implementation Act" https://www.congress.gov/bill/103rd-congress/house-bill/3450?q=%7B%22search%22%3A%5B%22nafta%22%5D%7D.

10. Tim Alberta, *American Carnage: On the Front Lines of the Republican Civil War and the Rise of President Trump* (New York: HarperCollins, 2019).

11. Uri Dadush and Laurence Kitlikoff, "Trump's Backfiring Trade Policy," September 11, 2019, *Forbes*, https://www.forbes.com/sites/kotlikoff/2019/09/11/trumps-backfiring-trade-policy/#d328db139be7.

12. James Pethokoukis, "For a Better America and World, Free and Open Trade," *American Enterprise Institute*, June 10, 2019, https://www.aei.org/economics/for-a-better-america-and-world-free-and-open-trade/; and Scott Lincicome, "The Case for Free Trade," *Cato*, May 2, 2019, https://www.cato.org/publications/commentary/case-free-trade.

13. Max Boot, "Our Great Patriot Leader Claims Another Illusory Win," *The Washington Post*, June 10, 2019, https://www.washingtonpost.com/opinions/our-great-patriot-leader-claims-another-illusory-win/2019/06/10/67859666-8b95-11e9-8f69-a2795fca3343_story.html.

14. Amy Bingham, "Donald Trump's Companies Filed for Bankruptcy 4 Times," *ABC News*, April 21, 2011, https://abcnews.go.com/Politics/donald-trump-filed-bankruptcy-times/story?id=13419250.

15. Steve Reilly, "USA Today Exclusive: Hundreds Allege Donald Trump Doesn't Pay His Bills," *USA Today*, June 9, 2016, https://www.usatoday.com/story /news/politics/elections/2016/06/09/donald-trump-unpaid-bills-republican-president -laswuits/85297274/.

16. Kimberly Amadeo, "US Budget Deficit by President," *The Balance*, https:// www.thebalance.com/deficit-by-president-what-budget-deficits-hide-3306151.

17. Kimberly Amadeo, "Obama's Stimulus Package and How Well It Worked," *The Balance*, https://www.thebalance.com/what-was-obama-s-stimulus-package -3305625.

18. Brad Bannon, "What Happened to the Tea Party?" *The Hill*, August 14, 2018, https://thehill.com/opinion/campaign/401820-what-happened-to-the-tea-party.

19. Jonathan Allen, "The Tea Party Finally Has Its Very Own Presidential Candidate: Donald Trump," *Vox*, August 7, 2015, https://www.vox.com/2015/8/7/9 115493/tea-party-donald-trump.

20. Bob Woodward and Robert Costa, "In a Revealing Interview, Trump Predicts a 'massive recession' but Intends to Eliminate the National Debt in 8 Years," *The Washington Post*, April 2, 2016, https://www.washingtonpost.com/politics/in-tu rmoil-or-triumph-donald-trump-stands-alone/2016/04/02/8c0619b6-f8d6-11e5-a3ce -f06b5ba21f33_story.html.

21. Reid Epstein, "Super PACS Launch Anti-Trump Ads in Florida, Illinois and Michigan," *Wall Street Journal*, March 2, 2016, https://blogs.wsj.com/washwire /2016/03/02/super-pacs-launch-anti-trump-ads-in-florida-illinois-and-michigan/.

22. Burgess Everett, "Club for Growth Warns Against Trump Endorsements," *Politico*, March 1, 2016, https://www.politico.com/story/2016/03/club-for-growth-trump-220020.

23. Jennifer Steinhauer and Alexander Burns, "Paul Ryan Says He Is 'Not Ready' to Endorse Donald Trump," The New York Times, May 5, 2016, https://www.nyt imes.com/2016/05/06/us/politics/paul-ryan-donald-trump.html.

24. David A. Fahrenthold, "Trump Recorded Having Extremely Lewd Conversation About Women in 2005," *Washington Post*, October 8, 2016, https://www.was hingtonpost.com/politics/trump-recorded-having-extremely-lewd-conversation-about -women-in-2005/2016/10/07/3b9ce776-8cb4-11e6-bf8a-3d26847eeed4_story.html.

25. Aaron Blake, "Paul Ryan Erases Any Doubt: 'We're with Trump,'" *The Washington Post*, November 8, 2017, https://www.washingtonpost.com/news/the-fix /wp/2017/11/08/paul-ryan-erases-any-doubt-were-with-trump/.

26. Bob Woodward and Robert Costa, "In a Revealing Interview."

27. "An Update to the Budget and Economic Outlook: 2019 to 2029," August 21, 2019, https://www.cbo.gov/publication/55551.

28. "An Update."

29. Charles J. Sykes, "Remember When Paul Ryan Was the Future of the Republican Party?" *The Washington Post*, December 20, 2018, https://www.washingt onpost.com/opinions/remember-when-paul-ryan-was-the-future-of-the-republican -party/2018/12/20/04d9686c-045e-11e9-b5df-5d3874f1ac36_story.html.

30. Jim Tankersley and Emily Cochrane, "Budget Deficit on Path to Surpass $1 Trillion Under Trump," *New York Times*, August 21, 2019, https://www.nytimes.

com/2019/08/21/us/politics/deficit-will-reach-1-trillion-next-year-budget-office-pred
icts.html.

31. "Donald Trump Announcement of Candidacy."

32. "Here's Donald Trump's Presidential Announcement Speech."

33. "Conservatives Against Trump," *National Review*, February 15, 2016, https://
www.nationalreview.com/magazine/2016/02/15/conservatives-against-trump/.

34. "Conservatives Against Trump."

35. "Growth and Opportunity Project," 2013, *Republican National Committee*,
https://online.wsj.com/public/resources/documents/RNCreport03182013.pdf, page 1.

36. "Growth and Opportunity Project," 2013, page 2.

37. "Growth and Opportunity Project," 2013, page 4.

38. "Growth and Opportunity Project," 2013, page 7.

39. "Growth and Opportunity Project," 2013, page 8.

40. "Growth and Opportunity Project," 2013, page 8.

41. "Presidential Candidates on Immigration," *The New York Times*, 2016, https:/
/www.nytimes.com/interactive/2016/us/elections/immigration.html.

42. Clare Malone, "The End of a Republican Party," *FiveThirtyEight*, July 18,
2016, https://fivethirtyeight.com/features/the-end-of-a-republican-party/.

43. Craig Kafura, "Republicans and Democrats in Different Worlds on
Immigration," The Chicago Council on Global Affairs, October 8, 2019, https://ww
w.thechicagocouncil.org/publication/republicans-and-democrats-different-worlds-i
mmigration.

44. "An Examination of the 2016 Electorate, Based on Validated Voters," *Pew
Research Center*, August 9, 2018, https://www.people-press.org/2018/08/09/an-ex
amination-of-the-2016-electorate-based-on-validated-voters/.

45. "Growth and Opportunity Project," 2013, page 7.

46. Alberta, *American Carnage*. 132.

47. Jim Tankersley, "Trump's Push to Bring Back Jobs to U.S. Shows Limited
Results," *The New York Times*, August 13, 2019, https://www.nytimes.com/2019/08
/13/business/economy/donald-trump-jobs-created.html.

Chapter 9

Never One of Us

The Battle for Conservative Purity in Trump's America

Christopher Paskewich

One interesting fallout of the candidacy and presidency of Donald Trump has been this: it has sparked a fight between conservatives—his supporters and his detractors—over what the heart of American conservatism is, and to what degree it has a core set of principles. If one politician is capable of throwing over sixty years of conservative political thought and practice into disarray, perhaps there were already some cracks in the foundation. Modern American conservatism, with its strong but cracked foundation, faces an immense test of philosophical principles with President Donald Trump, someone who appears to be like a political version of Schrödinger's cat, both conservative and not conservative at the same time.[1]

On the surface, conservatism should be able to easily absorb boundary-testing figures, just as any successful ideology does. Every ideology performs a type of self-policing, determining what is considered within bounds and what is out. Those who adhere to specific ideologies ask themselves a question: "What does it mean to truly be one of us?" Like other ideologies, modern American conservatism insists on a level of purity—a purity that is difficult for any ideology to meet once the actual work of governing begins. President Trump and his conservative opposition—#NeverTrump conservatives—make for an interesting case study in just what ideological purity means.

A casual look at President Trump's supporters would lead one to conclude that if anyone is conservative, surely it is them. An equally casual look at President Trump would show that, while certainly not left of center, he simply does not seem to fit any of the molds from which American conservatism makes their politicians. To use a more exact vocabulary, Trump exists in a liminal space in American conservatism: he lives between the border and the outside, acting as a wall that bars any on the outside from admittance.[2] While moderates who seek compromise positions seem to exist on the border, half in and half out, those moderates may never challenge the core principles of that ideology. Figures like Trump, on the other hand, really *do* operate in a kind of borderland, away from the intellectual stability of a capital city. The overall effect of this complicated dynamic is to give the ideological landscape a topsy-turvy quality. For this reason, this chapter will focus on untangling American conservatism prior to Trump, and how the current collection of #NeverTrumpers attempt to maintain these tenets. It also examines the twilight space that Trump occupies in American conservatism, and how he can appear to embody the spirit of it, if not the letter of it.

AMERICAN CONSERVATISM IN
HISTORICAL CONTEXT

Understanding Trump's challenge to the ideological foundation of the Republican Party requires us to look further back in time. American conservatism, especially after World War II, is an assemblage of smaller ideologically oriented groups, each with its own distinct priorities, goals, and policy preferences. In the big picture, they can give the sense of unanimity as they rally around certain philosophical ideals or political leaders. At the birds-eye view, the differences and disagreements among the various groups are obscured. Looking more closely, with an eye to policies and priorities, one spots the differences: one group desperately wants financial deregulation, while another wants to reshape Social Security and Medicare, while another seeks the government to define marriage based on their reading of the scripture, and yet another sees the most pressing issue to be one of Middle East foreign policy.

While these differences are real, the perceived conservative agreement at the birds-eye level is not an illusion. American conservatives find something approaching unity in some principles and policies that constitute a basic foundational canon or threshold, as well as in conservatism as a disposition. At this level, American conservatives are protective of their belief system and do not wish to see it polluted.

In looking at this decades-long consistency of values within American conservatism, one can easily see that Trump's political orientation has little in common with the last half-century of America's conservative ideas. It is the subjects of this volume, #NeverTrump conservatives, who could readily make the claim of continuity with America's conservative history. Going a step further, they also claim to be more than just purists who see Trump as an imposter, diluting the movement. #NeverTrump conservatives view him as harmful to liberal democracy in a way that transcends ideology and party politics. They also seem to be in the political minority on this, as most conservatives—elites and voters alike—support Trump. In this way, the question becomes whether American conservatism's consistent policies and principles—largely written about and articulated by elites—are what define conservatism, or whether those Americans who self-describe as Republican *and* who are supportive of Trump, truly reflect contemporary American conservatism.

American conservatism has had a complicated historical relationship to the broader ideological framework, as understood around the world. To the degree that one would want to trace American conservatism's connections across the ocean to Edmund Burke, "father of classical conservatism," conservatism has often aspired to having no ideology.[3] Burke rejected "abstraction," meaning political concepts and ideologies stripped from their specific context.[4] For example, Burke might find a discussion about freedom of press, in and of itself, to be a meaningless one. Such a discussion would need to focus on a specific country, with its own particular history and norms, during a particular time, and perhaps in regards to a particular event (e.g., reporting troop locations during wartime).

The main elements of Burke's views were adopted and interpreted by Russell Kirk, Burke's most public champion on the American right. Like Burke, Kirk understood conservatism to be more of a disposition than an ideology. Kirk's books on conservatism, including the famous *The Conservative Mind*, reflected this disinterest with ideology. Kirk focused on principles of conservatism, but did not stake out particular policy positions (such as privatizing public education).[5]

Burke and Kirk highlight one of the complicated aspects of conservatism: it can be a disposition (a set of attitudes without more specific political commandments), it can be a set of principles (which is a step further than a disposition, such as a list of guidelines for decision-making, without actual policies spelled out), or it can be policy positions (a typical ideology, with articulated policy preferences). The story of modern American conservatism is the story of individuals finding themselves yearning for different parts of their history: wishing to return to that disposition without ideological baggage, to return to those hallowed principles, and somehow also continue to support increasingly specific policy positions.[6] While American conservatives may have often struggled to put aside partisanship and ideological maneuvering to achieve their policy goals, they *did* always aspire to the noble "conservative disposition" and its attendant principles and elevation of institutions (e.g., the nuclear family, the military, the Constitution). This is one of the central breaks of Trump's conservatism from previous conservatism:

his conservatism has no appeal to restrain one's self to maintain a higher disposition, no principles to which one would return (especially after breaking them), and nothing beyond the man himself and his often transactional policies of the moment.

THE FRACTURED FOUNDATION OF
AMERICAN CONSERVATISM

One chief accusation that many #NeverTrump conservatives make to their fellow conservatives who support Trump is this: Trumpism is not the kind of principles or policies that we have pursued.[7] The typical starting place for this imagined conservative consensus is in the beginning of the 1950s. American conservatism emerged as an intentional grouping of different kinds of intellectuals and thought leaders who could all agree enough on certain conservative goals to elect a politician who would pursue them. There are three such pillars generally shared by these groups: a commitment to free markets, anti-communism, and traditional values.[8] This alliance also means that some adherents may be compelled to accept (or even endorse) positions they do not desire, simply because another group in the tent demands it. This vision of American conservatism, sometimes known as movement conservatism, means each conservative group should get some of their goals met, but will have to compromise with all of the other groups to keep such a large (and winning) coalition intact. For example, a conservative focused on traditional values may reluctantly support financial de-regulation as long as the movement agrees to support public school prayer. Movement conservatism emphasized the different groups found within American conservatism's big tent, the most important among them being traditionalists, libertarians, religious conservatives, and anti-communists. Perhaps the most helpful way of exploring the many groups of American conservatism, as specifically related to Donald Trump and the #NeverTrumper phenomena, is through the concept of fusionism, especially as pursued by Frank Meyer, William F. Buckley, and *National Review*.[9]

Frank Meyer, conservative thinker and associate editor for *National Review*, crafted the idea of fusionism—the sewing together of libertarianism and traditionalism.[10] This project was necessary because these philosophical outlooks were generally seen as in tension with one another. Libertarianism, therefore refers to a minimal government with few interventions into the lives of citizens beyond providing security (and few even then). Freedom is thus understood to be the government withdrawing from civil society and allowing people to make most of the important decisions for their own lives in both the moral and the economic realms. Traditionalists—those seeking the preservation of society's order and values—agree with this latter point. A free market with a minimal state is important for allowing people the ability to choose how to lead a virtuous life. But traditionalists are less enthusiastic about limiting the authority of government to impose moral order.

Fusionism attempts to bridge this gap in pursuit of the greater good of the conservative movement. It is the intellectual solution to the problem of conservative values appearing contradictory, and the New Right—with *National Review* at the forefront—used this to craft a new kind of conservatism. This conservatism, which is still largely the vision of conservatism held today, entails a shared commitment to the aforementioned three pillars: free markets, anti-communism, and traditional values. The New Right would use these two elements to create an electorally viable conservatism that could put politicians in office. This was different from older forms of conservatism that were without many unifying characteristics beyond a rejection of New Deal programs.

AMERICAN CONSERVATISM IN THE AGE OF TRUMP

Initially, it was easy to see that conservatives could view Donald Trump as an unreliable candidate for the presidency because of his long-standing identification as a Democrat, moderate to left policy positions on taxes, tariffs and otherwise, not to mention his brash New York celebrity persona, questionable personal relationships (both international and domestic), and problematic business practices. Conservatives found another problem beyond these: President Trump's approach to campaigning and governing challenged the New Right's fusion of traditionalism and libertarianism.[11]

Donald Trump's candidacy flew in the face of an elite conservative consensus that had been in place since Barry Goldwater's 1964 presidential campaign and the early days of the New Right. While many conservative groups were reluctant to embrace Trump, most eventually did. He was nobody's version of the most ideologically pure conservative, but perhaps that is not what conservative voters wanted. When discussing how a "good" and consistent conservative could support Trump for president, we should also ask why most conservative voters were *not* against Trump.

For Christian conservatives, Trump's own life did not meet the standards that previous Republican candidates had. His cavalier language about faith and his lack of humility did not indicate that he was someone who bore witness to the Good News of the New Testament. On the surface, about the most a Christian conservative could claim about Trump was that he might appoint some judges friendly to the cause, and perhaps take a few swings against perceived encroaching secularism.

For their part, traditionalists faced perhaps the least traditionally minded major Republican candidate of their lifetimes. Putting aside whether Trump understood (even on an intuitive level) the value of traditional American practices—political and otherwise—he sounded ominous notes against this form of received wisdom. Forging his own way, regardless of precedent, he seemed at times to have minimal understanding of and respect for the Constitution, institutions, the rule of law, and, more broadly, basic norms of liberal democracy. One glaring example was in the second presidential debate, when Trump suggested he might not concede the race if he lost.

Libertarians may see a closer kinship to Trump. As a billionaire and someone whose business practices reflected the mythic wild west, it would be easy to see him as a robust supporter of free markets. However, Trump the candidate and president frequently deviated from free markets. He promoted a trade war with China, general acceptance of protectionism, restrictions on immigration (and a source of cheap labor), and intervention in the energy sector to disrupt market forces putting pressure on certain sources of energy (such as coal).

Trumpism itself, as an ideology or merely one president's views on principles and policies, can be tough to pin down. There are those who view Trump as having few serious political convictions, instead treating his time in the White House as a cover for adding to his personal wealth (essentially ruling a crime syndicate with his family).[12] Others find Trump's policies and appointments as largely being water drawn from the "well constructed by the Republican Party and built to its specifications."[13] Nevertheless, Trumpism involves certain basic elements: nativism (and a skepticism toward those not from "here"), being antiestablishment (not in the Washington swamp), and populist (anti-intellectual, anti-expert, and channeling the righteous anger of some groups of people to finally shake things up).[14] Beyond this, some see an explicit rejection of the New Right's fusionism of "laissez-faire economic policies, social conservatism, and a hawkish foreign policy."[15] In its place, Trumpism reorients conservatism's focus: "Gathered to proclaim that big business is a greater threat to liberty than big government, that identity politics is a Freudian fraud and nation building is a chimera."[16]

This is not completely out of step with past conservatives. Many have been critical of corporate capitalism and regretted American interventions in the Middle East.[17] Trump's personality and policy positions were not necessarily inconsistent with elements of the Republican Party.[18] While many see Trump engaging in race-baiting and capitalizing on populist anger, so too have past conservatives (though modern American conservatism was not linked in any fundamental way to populism or race-baiting).[19] Trump's policies and rhetoric on immigration, foreign policy, and the economy—to say nothing of his general demeanor—were outside the boundaries of many conservative elites. But, therein lies the crux of this story.

Despite such reservations, many groups still embraced Trumpism, especially after he won the presidency. There is something about the history of American conservative ideas traced above that mapped onto the rich, the powerful, the famous, the insiders, and the establishment. This history often leaves out the average voter who is not familiar with many elements of conservatism that elites have considered: fusionism, Washington conventions, political precedents, the finer details about trade policy, arguments for when to tighten monetary policy, and so on. The emerging gap between conservative voters and conservative elites was made all the wider and more tense by one group in particular: neoconservatives.

NEOCONSERVATIVES AS CONSERVATIVE OUTLIERS

Neoconservatives represent perhaps the most prominent and most consistent group of #NeverTrump conservatives. The reason for this partly lies with the neoconservatives' own relationship to the American right at this time. Neoconservatism is a frequently misunderstood set of principles promoted by a group of conservatives who analyzed conservatism from both philosophic and social scientific lens. This led to a series of principles: a belief "in the fragility of social institutions, that all human enterprises will have monumental unintended consequences, that man has a moral responsibility to confront evil, and most of all, that the world is governed, in the end, by ideas."[20] This definition shows the ethical orientation of neoconservatism, and the concern it has for regimes, an approach will play a central role below. In essence, neoconservatism can be divided into two waves—the first from 1970 to 1990s, and the second from 1990 to 2000s.[21] Nathan Glazer, who made this observation, was a typical first-wave neoconservative. He focused on ways of rethinking domestic policy, especially the received wisdom of liberal positions. This meant that liberal thinkers, such as Glazer and Irving Kristol, reluctantly found that empirical social science research was not bearing out the success of big-government programs.

Neoconservatives thus found themselves, in the pursuit of methodological and intellectual consistency, migrating to the right of the political spectrum.[22] Because most first-wave neoconservatives had been socialized as liberals, and had supported liberal positions, they had to forge their own conservative policies and platforms. One example of this from Irving Kristol is the conservative welfare state.[23] Kristol argues that in this era of big government, there are no realistic strategies to reduce the size of government by any meaningful amount. Consequently, conservatives should make the best use of government. In this case, that means repurposing the welfare state so it encourages conservative values, such as independence, respect for families, and respect for the elderly.

The second wave of neoconservatives was led by a generation of younger thought leaders who were more focused on foreign policy. This wave includes familiar names, such as William Kristol, Charles Krauthammer, and Paul Wolfowitz. As Glazer himself observed, the two waves may have had little in common. However, one could not deny that both groups fulfilled Irving Kristol's goal of bending the Republican Party to their will.[24]

By the late 1990s, one could reasonably say that the neoconservatives were successful in remaking modern American conservatism in their own image.[25] One neoconservative, Norman Podhoretz, wrote a eulogy for neoconservatism, as he thought there was nothing left for it to accomplish.[26] Around the same time, the main scholarly journal for neoconservative policy, *The Public Interest*, ceased publication. The reasons were the same. Neoconservatism had so completely rewired the Republican Party that one did not have to maintain it as a separate group anymore.

Traditional conservative foreign policy, with the exception of aggressively opposing communism, otherwise sounded isolationist notes from the World War I era until the 1980s. During this time, it would be modern liberals who sought to intervene abroad to provide struggling states with support to enhance their democratic and cultural institutions. Neoconservatism would rewire conservative foreign policy to be far more interventionist beginning in the 1990s. Outside of a small, fringe contingent of isolationist conservatives like Pat Buchanan, neoconservative interventionism became the default Republican foreign policy position. From the Reagan administration through the first four years of the George W. Bush administration, neoconservatives seemed to have unchallenged dominance over the American right in both domestic and foreign policy. However, neoconservatism began falling out of favor toward the end of Bush's administration, just as the Tea Party began to ascend.

There are many ways to understand the Tea Party, one of which is through the lens of populism. Disenchanted and ignored conservatives felt outrage at their powerlessness to realize the changes they have been seeking.[27] Along with this populist read, one could say the Tea Party sought a pre-neoconservative American conservatism, one that simply limited government, did not have complex economic policies that favored corporations, and was more serious about acknowledging traditional conservative positions on social issues. Neoconservatives had purposely modulated the conservatism of the Republican Party, and now some conservatives wanted the earlier, sharper versions back.

NEOCONSERVATIVES AS #NEVERTRUMP CONSERVATIVES

Neoconservatism rose to power in the 1980s and beyond, many years after *National Review's* fusionism provided the intellectual vehicle for the New Right and modern conservatism. In some ways, its claim to fame was that it was putting pressure on mainstream American conservatism to modernize. Even with this view of American conservatism as being problematic enough to need saving, neoconservatives ended up defending traditional principles from Trump's scorched-earth treatment. As a result of this, many #NeverTrump conservatives—though not all—are neoconservatives or fellow travelers, while many of those conservatives skeptical of neoconservative elites would find themselves offering varying degrees of support toTrump and his policies.

#NeverTrump conservative intellectuals are those who reject Trump (the man), but also many of his policies, his demeanor, and ultimately his political loyalty (whether it is to himself or the republic). The #NeverTrump conservative presence found many prominent neoconservatives taking their stand against Trump. William Kristol—the son of Irving Kristol and Gertrude Himmelfarb, both first-wave neoconservatives—is a second-generation neoconservative. He is one of the most vigorous and highest profile #NeverTrump conservatives, and one of the most outspoken about Trump's lack of fitness for office.[28] One early conflict between Kristol and Trump was when the latter said that Senator John McCain was not a war hero (because he had been captured). On the air, the next day, Kristol said of Trump: "He's dead to me."[29] For Kristol, such apostasy confirmed that Trump had neither the respect for tradition (by denigrating military service) nor the disposition to claim the mantle of a conservative.

For Kristol, and other neoconservatives, Trump's criticism of President George W. Bush's Iraq War—largely seen as a neoconservative brainchild and vocally supported by them—was a concerning foreign-policy stance in the Age of Terror.[30] Trump not only mocked the logic behind the war, his supporters crafted rival foreign-policy directions, such as ending America's promotion of democracy abroad, and simply focusing on "the American effort to manage great power competition" around the world.[31] In a similar vein, Trump's criticism of NATO was unfathomable and unacceptable to neoconservatives. Kristol views Trump's brash demeanor, his trade protectionism, rejection of the Republican Party as an institution to be worked with in accomplishing conservative goals, and unconventional policy goals as decidedly anti-conservative. His rejection of Trump is unsurprising.

Like some other #NeverTrump conservatives we will examine, Kristol's main criticism of Trump is that he destabilizes the American regime, recklessly challenges established institutions and democratic norms, and is ultimately worse for the public good.[32] He admits that he hopes Trump's form of conservatism is nothing more than a "detour," to be abandoned once Trump is out of office and conservatism can continue as it did. His central point, however, is that Trump's presidency jeopardizes the United States and its liberal-democratic regime.

David Frum, a #NeverTrump neoconservative who supported Bush's Iraq War, is in a similar situation to Kristol. Indeed, Frum was a speechwriter for George W. Bush's administration during 9/11 and wrote the "Axis of Evil" phrase into Bush's speeches.[33] Frum also found Trump's rise deeply disturbing, and would go on to write a book criticizing Trump's presidency, *Trumpocracy*. Frum is not simply concerned with Trump's demeanor or policy positions, but also questions his basic decency and respect for democratic norms. His read of Trump is this: "Donald Trump will not set out to build an authoritarian state. His immediate priority seems likely to be to use the presidency to enrich himself."[34] Frum argues that Trump's time as president will gradually convert the American regime into an authoritarian one. Institutional norms will be ignored, politicians and administrators charged with holding illegal or improper behavior accountable will not do so, and powers of the office will be misused.[35]

Like Kristol, Frum's real worry with Trump is that of the American regime's health and well-being.[36] In this way, we will see that #NeverTrump neoconservatives end up playing the role of those conservative referenced above: traditionalists who seek preservation of the regime, those who value the conservative disposition (as opposed to Trump's perceived corruption) over policies (and many of Trump's policies are identifiably conservative). The key difference, then, is that Kristol and Frum see themselves having conservative dispositions and conservative policies, with Trump only having the latter. From their perspective, the disposition matters more—preserving one's regime and the rule of law is more important than court appointments or tax breaks.

Conservative columnist for *The New York Times* David Brooks also has openly opposed Trump, and for similar reasons as Kristol and Frum. One Trump supporter mocks Brooks' opposition, but perfectly summarizes the #NeverTrump neoconservative position:

> Brooks is one of those conservatives who isn't really concerned with politics so much as he is with assessing the 'character' and 'virtue' and 'principles' of every Republican who runs for something. And so winning an election or passing a conservative agenda in Congress is always kind of beside the point for Brooks. What's important to him is that even if every Republican who runs for president from now on loses, well, at least Brooks will be able to say each one of them was a good egg.[37]

Brooks, Frum, and Kristol have all written about electoral strategies, and how to ensure Trump is not reelected, but they are first and foremost concerned with the principles and disposition of conservatism, rather than electoral success or conservative legislation. While Trump has accomplished some conservative policy aims (tax reform and Supreme Court appointments), those victories are not worth the destruction Trump has wrought on the American republic.

The heart of the difference between Trump supporters and #NeverTrump conservatives is not whether conservative policy goals are achieved, but at what cost. #NeverTrump neoconservatives take a 30,000-foot view of the polity and are concerned about whether America is being nudged into authoritarianism. Brooks illustrates this birds-eye view here:

> For all the Sturm and Drang that surrounds Trump, populist Republicans and Democrats are gravitating toward the same foreign policy: We're in the middle of a clash of civilizations; the Middle East is so screwed up, we should just get out; we're too stupid/ineffective/racist/imperialistic to do any good there anyway. We fight viciously about Trump, but underneath, a populist left-right curtain is descending around America, separating us from the Mideast, China, even Europe. The real high-risk move is the one both parties are making together: that if we ignore the world it will ignore us. (It won't.)[38]

Brooks is writing about lurking populism on both sides of the aisle, with a backdrop of foreign policy concerns that are at stake if America's party system does not right itself. Brooks' vantage as a conservative is one that has expanded his vista from political positions to political philosophy.

Max Boot, #NeverTrump neoconservative, has effectively left the Trump-supporting right over similarly big-picture reasons: "We can readily survive a one-term Trump presidency. Second-Term Trump is more likely to inflict damage—to our democracy, our environment, our world order—that is incalculable and unfixable."[39] It is unsurprising that neoconservatives, like Boot and others discussed here, would find philosophical concerns most pressing, given their intellectual bent. It is important to note the ethical and regime-level critiques that are being made here: Trump endangers the broader functioning of America's liberal democracy, and also jeopardizes its moral compass. The latter situation could lead to a nation-wide decay in morals and the health of the polity.

CONSERVATIVE WINDS CHANGE

The rise of Trumpism can be seen as signaling a dethroning of neoconservatism.[40] The Tea Party had done this in part, but Trump openly questioned the neoconservative birthright to guide Republican policymaking. If one were to ask why so many different conservative groups would endorse Trump, one answer (but not the whole story) would be that this means reorienting the conservative dynamic described above. The central tension between traditionalists and libertarians can be expressed in many ways, and Trump's rise allows very different combinations, including abandoning the fusionism of the New Right altogether.

Not all conservatives are welcoming of this, however. While Trump represents a rebuke to neoconservatism, there are many conservatives who are not neoconservative also refuse Trump's iconoclasm. George Will has been one of America's most recognized conservative intellectuals for decades, and has found himself on the opposite side of Trump. Will's critique of Trump matches with many of the neoconservatives, in that Trump is seen as a vulgar, not entirely conservative, but also betraying many of America's ideals. In his writings on Trump's impeachment, Will used language that signaled his concern about America as a regime:

> Trump's gross and comprehensive incompetence now increasingly impinges upon the core presidential responsibility. This should, but will not, cause congressional Republicans to value their own and their institution's dignity and exercise its powers more vigorously than they profess fealty to Trump. He has issued a categorical refusal to supply witnesses and documents pertinent to the House investigation of whether he committed an impeachable offense regarding Ukraine. . . . [This] refusal attacks our constitutional regime. So, the refusal is itself an impeachable offense.[41]

Will has worked to craft an identifiably conservative ideology in this age of Trump Republicans that skews more to the right than the neoconservatives discussed above.

Another conservative writer who has also concluded that Trump represents an existential threat is Tom Nichols. Nichols resigned from the Republican Party, stating that "The Republicans, however, have now eclipsed the Democrats as a threat to the rule of law and to the constitutional norms of American society. They have become all about winning."[42]

Conservative author and biographer of Senator Mitch McConnell (R-KY), John David Dyche, also abandoned the Republicans for the Democratic Party, citing that Republicans are "beyond redemption," adding:

> Kentucky Republicans, what's your favorite part of Trumpist "conservatism"? Appeasing Putin after Russia attacked our election? Trillion dollar deficits? Trade wars to hurt ag, autos & bourbon? Hush money to porno mistresses? Calling neo-Nazis & white supremacists "fine people"? Caging children?

Family separations? Mocking POWs & Gold Star parents? Constant lying? Criminal convictions & guilty pleas? Insulting allies while praising butchers like Kim Jong Un? Cruelty, misogyny & racism? Tax fraud? Which part of Trumpist "conservatism" makes you proudest? [43]

He listed many grievances against Trump, some of which were policy positions, many of which were not. The underpinning theme of Dyche's statement is not that Trump failed to have consistently conservative policies, but that he lacked the principles or disposition to govern. His chief flaw is an ethical one, as opposed to an ideological one.

THE IMPACT OF #NEVERTRUMP CONSERVATIVES ON TRUMP AND THE AMERICAN RIGHT

It seems clear by now that #NeverTrumpism has had a loud bark but little bite when impacting conservative support for the president and his agenda. It is bad for any president to lose congressional seats and to have members of their party abandon the party. However, when it comes to ideological purity, a president with ardent support among voters can afford to lose the support of elite thought leaders who traffic in obscure ideological battles. The electoral success of Trumpism reframes the situation for career conservatives, who are all too aware of how much Trump is unaligned with many of the approaches to American conservatism. #NeverTrump conservatives reject a transactional conservatism, where support for Trump might secure some hoped-for conservative results. #NeverTrumpism is premised on the idea that the ends do not justify the means, that there is more than just winning, that the true conservative path is one that seeks a flourishing republic. Joe Walsh, who briefly challenged Trump for the Republican nomination in the 2020 election, observed this:

And despite what his enablers claim, Mr. Trump isn't a conservative. He's reckless on fiscal issues; he's incompetent on the border; he's clueless on trade; he misunderstands executive power; and he subverts the rule of law. It's his poor record that makes him most worthy of a primary challenge. [44]

Walsh identifies the core of #NeverTrump conservatism: whatever one thinks of Trump delivering conservative results, he simply cannot be said to have conservative principles or embody a conservative disposition.

One way to make sense of Republican Trump supporters is to follow Thomas Mann and Norm Ornstein in considering Republicans in terms of ideology and in terms of tactics. [45] These scholars argued that recent

Republican politicians have adopted harmful tactics that belie their conservatism, and damage our Constitutional democracy. They observe that the fault is not with the ideology itself (conservatism), but with how conservative goals are carried out in practice. This seems to be the heart of #NeverTrump conservatism: the goal is not *simply* to get as many conservative judges as possible, but to do so in a way that respects the rule of law, preserves the Constitution, and maintains basic integrity. Otherwise, one's conservatism is simply transactional.

#NeverTrump conservatives essentially function as the control group in a laboratory experiment. They are the conservatives who support global free trade, aggressive foreign policy (where appropriate), and implementing traditional community values without resorting to visible race-baiting. #NeverTrump conservatives also show everyone else what it looks like to be on the outside of the conservative inner circle by openly opposing Trump. They are ostracized, exert little influence within the White House, find their institutions and outlets marginalized, and are an example for others who dare question the new American conservatism as defined by Trump.

That so many conservative elites gradually joined Trump's side, even when they initially declared his candidacy an affront to conservatism, shows what #NeverTrumpers faced. They followed the road not taken—and paid for it. #NeverTrump conservatives thus remain the "other," who serve as the courageous conscience of those conservatives now on the inside. Former Speaker of the House Paul Ryan's (R-WI) story may be the most illustrative on this. Ryan rejected Trump's candidacy and, as he was seen to be one of the most relevant conservative voices of his generation, probably saw Trump as a pretender. Ryan ended up supporting Trump, at least publicly—especially because he had to work with him, and Ryan had a long agenda he wanted to accomplish in Congress. At that point, Ryan made quite a contrast with Trump. One writer observes of that time:

> [N]obody really saw Donald Trump coming. Or thought that Republican voters would so thoroughly reject Ryan's brand of conservatism in favor of Trump's nativism and nationalism. Or that voters would prefer Trump's bluster and pugilism over Ryan's personal decency and substantive approach to issues. Or that Ryan himself would surrender. . . . Ryan could have articulated an alternative vision of conservatism, untainted by Trump's ugly xenophobia, recklessness and isolationism. Had he led a principled opposition to Trumpism, Ryan might have emboldened others to find their spines and their voices.[46]

Instead of maintaining conservative principles, disposition, and policies, Ryan gradually sacrificed the former two for the latter. Eventually the tension between principles and policy became too much, and Ryan resigned from

Congress and gave up his position as the second most powerful Republican in the country.

LOOKING TO THE FUTURE

The ideological future of American conservatism is not obvious, but its past can provide some insight. Modern American conservatism has always been quite malleable. Despite appearances, the fusion of traditionalism and libertarianism has no clear equilibrium that perfectly satisfies both sides (and all the various groups emerging from these component parts). This means there is a long history of diverse conservative groups constantly sacrificing their priorities, receiving promises from politicians that go undelivered, and generally making some trade-offs.[47] One could read the rise of Trump in light of this: conservative groups that typically compromised some priorities to maintain success across the whole of the big tent are simply making one more compromise. It may not be a terribly profound choice, but simply another in a long line of conservative compromises to maintain proximity to power.

However, this malleability within conservative groups could also cut against Trump. The bargain by which some conservatives betrayed some of their values to support Trump, and in return gain outcomes they wanted, only works to the degree that Trump can provide conservative wins. If it seems that Trump can no longer deliver (or even manage to stay in office), the continual realignment between conservative groups would easily move on without Trump.

The more interesting question lies with the future relationship between #NeverTrump conservatives and the rest of the right. If Trumpism simply recedes after he leaves office and is not transferable to a dynasty of Trump's family who win the presidency, it seems plausible that #NeverTrump conservatives could easily find their way back to the rest of the conservative fold. However, *something* happened with Trump's election—relationships changed and so did party affiliations. The American electorate cannot go back to a pre-Trump era any easier than the Washington elites can.

Party realignment could be in our future and could offer an interesting alternative to American conservatives reconciling their differences. What seems most likely, though, is the least glamorous outcome of all: that #NeverTrump conservatives do not vote for Trump or Trump-related candidates, out of a sense of obligation to the health of the American regime. They simply do not share anything in common with those who are left of center, so it seems difficult to imagine #NeverTrump conservatives becoming leftists. Instead, it seems likely that #NeverTrump conservatives will become one more conservative group under the big tent, like libertarians, Christian conservatives, traditionalists, and so on. The difference is, this #NeverTrump group will likely prioritize conservative principles over all else—that is what their sacrifice thus far has been for and perhaps all they will have to show for it.

NOTES

1. Clare Malone, "The End of a Republican Party," *FiveThirtyEight*, July 18, 2016, https://fivethirtyeight.com/features/the-end-of-a-republican-party.

2. An interesting reflection on Trumpism being an awkward fit for America's right or left appeared via the Heritage Foundation. See David Azzerad, "America Divided: Trumpism Emerges Where Left and Right Fall Short," *Heritage*, October 23, 2017, https://www.heritage.org/conservatism/commentary/the-clash-ideologies-america-divided-trumpism-emerges-where-left-and-right.

3. Charles W. Dunn and J. David Woodard, *American Conservatism from Burke to Bush* (New York: Madison, 1991), 29–30.

4. Russell Kirk, *The Politics of Prudence* (Wilmington, Delaware: ISI Books, 1998), 9–11.

5. Russell Kirk, *The Conservative Mind* (Washington: Regenery, 2001), 8–9.

6. Matthew Continetti, "Making Sense of the New American Right," *National Review*, June 1, 2019, https://www.nationalreview.com/2019/06/new-american-right-schools-of-thought/.

7. Charles Sykes, "As a Conservative, I Despair at Republicans' Support for Trump," *The Guardian*, July 22, 2018, https://www.theguardian.com/commentisfree/2018/jul/22/conservative-despair-republicans-trump.

8. William F. Buckley, "Credenda and Statement of Principles," *The National Review*, November 19, 1955, https://www.nationalreview.com/1955/11/our-mission-statement-william-f-buckley-jr/.

9. Jeffrey Hart, *The Making of the American Conservative Mind* (Wilmington, Delaware: ISI Books, 2007), 376–77.

10. See Frank S. Meyer, "Freedom, Tradition, Conservatism," in *In Defense of Freedom and Other Essays* (Indianapolis, IN: Liberty Fund, 1996).

11. Peter Harris, "Trump and the Discrediting of American Conservatism," *National Interest*, December 15, 2019, https://nationalinterest.org/feature/trump-and-discrediting-american-conservatism-105207.

12. Sarah Kendzior, "Trump Played Nice for a Night," *QZ*, March 1, 2017, https://qz.com/922104/donald-trumps-joint-session-address-played-nice-for-a-night-in-front-of-congress-and-used-a-technique-straight-out-of-the-autocrats-playbook/.

13. Jamelle Bouie, "Donald Trump Is Not an Independent," *Slate*, September 11, 2017, https://slate.com/news-and-politics/2017/09/donald-trump-is-not-an-independent.html.

14. David Edward Tabachnick, "The Four Characteristics of Trumipsm," *The Hill*, January 1, 2016, https://thehill.com/blogs/congress-blog/presidential-campaign/264746-the-four-characteristics-of-trumpism.

15. Zack Beauchamp, "Trump and the Dead End of Conservative Nationalism," *Vox*, July 17, 2019, https://www.vox.com/2019/7/17/20696543/national-conserv atism-conference-2019-trump.

16. John Burtka, "Under Trump a Very Different Agenda for Conservatives Emerges," *The Washington Post*, July 22, 2019, https://www.washingtonpost.com/ opinions/2019/07/22/under-trump-very-different-agenda-conservatives-emerges/.

17. For a paleoconservative critique on this from the far-right, see Patrick Buchanan, "Whose War?" *The American Conservative*, March 24, 2003, https://ww w.theamericanconservative.com/articles/whose-war/.

18. Paul Waldman, "The Strange Ritual of Right Wing Race Baiters," *The Washington Post*, August 10, 2018, https://www.washingtonpost.com/blogs/plum-lin e/wp/2018/08/10/the-strange-ritual-of-right-wing-race-baiters/.

19. Conor Friedersdorf, "Conservatives See Race Obsession on the Left, but Never on the Right," *The Atlantic*, April 11, 2012, https://www.theatlantic.com/politics/ archive/2012/04/conservatives-see-race-obsession-on-the-left-but-never-on-the-right /255720/.

20. Mark Gerson, *The Essential Neoconservative Reader* (New York: Addison Wesley, 1996), xiv.

21. Nathan Glazer, "Neoconservative from the Start," *The Public Interest,* 159 (Spring 2005): 17.

22. Glazer, "Neoconservative," 15.

23. Irving Kristol, "A Conservative Welfare State," *Wall Street Journal,* June 14, 1993.

24. Irving Kristol, "The Neoconservative Persuasion," *The Weekly Standard,* August 25, 2003.

25. Irving Kristol, "An Autobiographical Memoir," *Neoconservatism: An Autobiography of an Idea* (Chicago: Elephant, 1999), 40.

26. Norman Podhoretz, "Neoconservatism: A Eulogy," *Commentary*, March 1996, https://www.commentarymagazine.com/articles/neoconservatism-a-eulogy/.

27. John B. Judis, *The Populist Explosion: How the Great Recession Transformed American and European Politics* (New York: Columbia Global Reports: 2016), 39–61.

28. Benjamin Wallace-Wells, "Bill Kristol Wanders the Wilderness of Trump World," *New Yorker*, February 2, 2018.

29. Michael Crowley, "Last Man Standing," *Politico*, July/August 2016.

30. William Kristol, "Trump Is Continuing Obama's Retreat from the World," *Fathom*, Autumn 2017, https://fathomjournal.org/trump-is-continuing-obamas-re treat-from-the-world-william-kristol-on-us-foreign-policy/.

31. James Jay Carafano, "Instead of Democracy Promotion, Sell Trumpism to the World," *Heritage*, March 1, 2019, https://www.heritage.org/defense/commentary/i nstead-democracy-promotion-sell-trumpism-the-world.

32. William Kristol, "A Time to Speak," *The Bulwark*, February 13, 2020, https:// thebulwark.com/a-time-to-speak/.

33. David Frum, *The Right Man: The Surprise Presidency of George W. Bush* (Random House, 2003), 235.

34. David Frum, "How to Build an Autocracy," *The Atlantic*, March 2017, https://www.theatlantic.com/magazine/archive/2017/03/how-to-build-an-autocracy/5 13872/.

35. For a more recent example, see David Frum, "Trump Is Defiling His Office," *The Atlantic*, February 5, 2020, https://www.theatlantic.com/ideas/archive/2020/02/ sotu/606142/.

36. David Frum, "Trump Is Defiling His Office," *The Atlantic*, September 29, 2019, https://www.theatlantic.com/ideas/archive/2019/09/realists-guide-impeachmen t/599056/.

37. Eddie Scarry, "David Brooks Makes Best Case for Reelecting Trump," *The Washington Examiner*, October 18, 2019, https://www.washingtonexaminer.com/ opinion/david-brooks-makes-best-case-for-reelecting-trump.

38. David Brooks, "Trump Has Made Us Stupid," *The New York Times*, January 9, 2020, https://www.nytimes.com/2020/01/09/opinion/trump-iran-media.html.

39. Max Boot, "Can American Democracy Survive a Second Trump Term?" *The Washington Post*, November 11, 2019, https://www.washingtonpost.com/opinions/ 2019/11/11/can-american-democracy-survive-second-trump-term/.

40. Michael F. Cannon, "How David Brooks Created Donald Trump," *Forbes*, February 11, 2016, https://www.forbes.com/sites/michaelcannon/2016/02/11/how-da vid-brooks-created-donald-trump/#282bfe34711e.

41. George Will, "The Spiraling President Adds Self-Impeachment to His Repertoire," *The Washington Post*, October 10, 2019, https://www.washingtonpost .com/opinions/the-spiraling-president-adds-self-impeachment-to-his-repertoire/2019 /10/10/8c1a739c-eb7c-11e9-9c6d-436a0df4f31d_story.html.

42. Tom Nichols, "Why I'm Leaving the Republican Party," *The Atlantic*, October 7, 2018, https://www.theatlantic.com/ideas/archive/2018/10/tom-nichols-why-im-l eaving-republican-party/572419/.

43. Caleb Ecarma, "Mitch McConnell's Biographer: Republicans Are 'Beyond Redemption,' 'Dems Only Viable' Option," *Mediaite*, November 23, 2018, https:/ /www.mediaite.com/online/mitch-mcconnells-biographer-republicans-are-beyond-re demption-dems-only-viable-option/.

44. Joe Walsh, "Trump Needs a Primary Challenge," *The New York Times*, August 14, 2019, https://www.nytimes.com/2019/08/14/opinion/joe-walsh-trump-primary .html.

45. Thomas E. Mann and Norman J. Ornstein, *It's Even Worse Than It Looks* (Basic Books, 2016), 8.

46. Charles J. Sykes, "Remember When Paul Ryan Was the Future of the Republican Party?" *The Washington Post*, December 20, 2018, https://www.washingt onpost.com/opinions/remember-when-paul-ryan-was-the-future-of-the-republican -party/2018/12/20/04d9686c-045e-11e9-b5df-5d3874f1ac36_story.html.

47. Paul Weyrich, "An Open Letter to Conservatives," *Conservatism in America Since 1930* (New York: New York University Press, 2003), 428–30.

Chapter 10

Conservative Character?

Donald Trump and the Corrosive Presidency

Martin Cohen

This is a chapter about Donald Trump and his corrosive presidency. The end. No, there is more. Character and decency, or public virtue, have been valued traits for politicians of all stripes in the United States since the nation's founding. In *Federalist 10*, Madison's argument in favor of ratifying the Constitution partially relied on the likelihood that the virtuous would fill the major offices and resist popular passions in favor of the common good.[1] Just to be sure the system worked, in *Federalist 51*, he made the case for the checks and balances in the Constitution because "men" rather than "angels" would govern.[2] Furthermore, in filling bureaucratic positions, early presidents sought to find the best person for each job which would help solve the principal-agent problem inherent in congressional and executive delegation to the bureaucracy. In 1796, in his farewell address, George Washington proclaims that "virtue or morality is a necessary spring of popular government."[3] As recently as 2000, George W. Bush ran an entire presidential campaign predicated on "restoring honor and dignity" to the White House after conservatives concluded that President Clinton had thoroughly debased the office.[4]

Indeed, traditional conservatives have always held personal morality high on their lists of essential candidate traits. Therefore, it is not surprising that the majority of #NeverTrump conservatives, regardless of their policy priorities, have arguably been most exercised over Trump's consistent flouting of political and social norms. For critics of President Trump, the roots of these transgressions have been his poor character and lack of basic, fundamental decency. Character is defined as moral or ethical quality. It is wrong to say the forty-fifth president of the United States lacks character. His has simply repeatedly proven to be deficient. What he may indeed lack is decency—any sort of conformity to the recognized standards of propriety, good taste, and modesty. His dearth of decency would be striking in any formal position, let alone in the leader of the free world. Another trait Trump is accused of being deficient in is integrity. Integrity is commonly taken to mean doing the right and moral thing when nobody is watching. Donald Trump has regularly behaved without virtue or morality when the *whole world* is watching. #NeverTrump conservatives shudder to imagine how he might act on the occasions when nobody is watching.

Republican and conservative #NeverTrumpism was partially born out of a revulsion to candidate Trump's many character flaws and frequent displays of indecency. It flourished and had legs due to the continuation of those contraventions through the entirety of his campaign and administration. This chapter will begin by introducing some of the major voices within the #NeverTrump movement. Although not exhaustive, I chose to focus on the individuals with the largest platforms from which to voice concern about Trump's poor character and lack of decency. Most, though not all, have remained steadfast in their opposition to the forty-fifth president of the United States.

How did these conservative Republicans become so disenchanted with their own party and ideological movement? What pushed them over the edge? I will argue that Donald Trump in his short political career has adopted the seven deadly sins as a personal to-do list. He has checked all the boxes multiple times; pride, greed, lust, envy, gluttony, wrath, and sloth. Trump has committed each of the deadly sins multiple times. The bulk of this chapter will be a recap of those transgressions with commentary from those #NeverTrumpers whom this book is about. The chapter will conclude with an analysis of how the #NeverTrump movement will impact American politics moving forward.

THE #NEVERTRUMPERS

The new darlings of some liberals are the conservative Republicans who have broken with their fellow partisans over Donald Trump's ascendance to the highest office in the land. Many have secured regular gigs on MSNBC, Real Time With Bill Maher, and CNN. Most have written full frontal assaults on the president that have landed on best seller lists and trended on social media. They are veterans of multiple GOP presidential campaigns and administrations. They are erudite, articulate, and mad as hell. David Frum, Rick Wilson, Charlie Sykes, and Max Boot are only some of the loudest and most acerbic voices in the #NeverTrump movement. Their criticisms carry increased weight because of the conservative pedigrees they bring to the table. Perhaps we will not know the full power of their collective voices until the 2020 presidential election results are examined in detail. But they have clearly made an impact on the current public discourse and their contributions are well worth studying.

One of the earliest manifestations of the #NeverTrump movement was a special issue of *National Review* dedicated to laying out the conservative case against Trump. It was published in early 2016 when the Republican presidential nomination was still up for grabs. On January 22, twenty-two prominent conservatives contributed to this diatribe against then-candidate Trump.[5] The goal of this edition of *National Review* was to derail the Trump train before it could get fully out of the station. Of course, it failed and Donald Trump cruised to the Republican nomination. But in this effort, some of the groundwork was laid for the #NeverTrump movement, especially in terms of questioning his fitness for office. Mona Charen, a well-known conservative columnist and television personality, said the following on the pages of *National Review*: "The man has demonstrated an emotional immaturity bordering on personality disorder, and it ought to disqualify him from being a mayor, to say nothing of a commander-in-chief."[6] Another well-known conservative commentator named Cal Thomas wrote, "Everyone has a temperament. The dictionary defines it as 'the combination of mental, physical, and emotional traits of a person.' Would Trump's 'combination' make him a good president? I think not."[7]

Even after Trump's nomination in Cleveland, the insults continued to be hurled at the real-estate mogul turned reality-TV star turned politician. The following is a non-exhaustive list of comments from Republicans about their *own* standard-bearer: "malignant clown," "national disgrace," "complete idiot," "a sociopath, without a conscience or feelings of guilt, shame or remorse," "graceless and divisive," "predatory and reprehensible," "flawed beyond mere moral shortcomings," "unsound, uninformed, unhinged, and unfit," "a character and temperament unfit for the leader of the free world," "a bigot, misogynist, fraud, and a bully."[8] With friends like that, who needs enemies? Yet, Trump prevailed in the end, defeating Hillary Clinton in a hotly contested general election. While Trump would win just enough votes to take the Electoral College, he did not get the votes of some prominent #NeverTrumpers who put their ballots where their mouths were in November of 2016. "I would sooner vote for Josef Stalin than I would vote for Donald Trump," wrote Max Boot, who happened to have emigrated to the United States from Russia at a young age.[9] Boot, the Jeane J. Kirkpatrick Senior Fellow in National Security Studies at the Council on Foreign Relations and a former *Wall Street Journal* editor and columnist continued:

> In the final analysis, the strongest case for Clinton is what she is not. She is not racist, sexist, or xenophobic. She is not cruel, erratic, or volatile. She is not a bully or an authoritarian personality. She is not ignorant or unhinged. Those may be insufficient recommendations against a more formidable opponent. But when she's running against Donald Trump it's more than enough.[10]

David Frum, a speechwriter for George W. Bush who inspired the "axis of evil" designation, also explained his voting calculus in a book published after Donald Trump was elected president:

> I was not voting for Hillary Clinton. I was voting for the American system. I was voting for the rules, the norms, the Constitution that I expected her to respect even as she implemented policies with which I disagreed—unlike Donald Trump, who would subvert those standards even in those cases where he did things I might approve. I am voting to defend Americans' profoundest shared commitment: a commitment to norms and rules that today protect my rights under a president I don't favor, and that will tomorrow do the same service for you.[11]

And Charlie Sykes, a stalwart conservative talk radio host said the following on the eve of the election, "Donald Trump is a serial liar, a con man who mocks the disabled and women. He's a narcissist and a bully, a man with no fixed principles who has the vocabulary of an emotionally insecure nine-year-old. So no, I don't want to give him control of the IRS, the FBI, and the nuclear codes. That's just me."[12] Also, long-time GOP consultant Mike Murphy believes Trump has driven the Republican Party into a moral and political ditch. Murphy elaborates, "Trump has gone so far—racial demagoguery and slurs, abuse of office, dictator appeasement, nepotism and family corruption, blazing incompetence, contempt for the rule of law, betrayal of public institutions, epic dishonesty, authoritarian thuggishness . . . the list never ends—that he is damaging public institutions and debasing the Presidency of the United States."[13]

Despite these high-profile defections, or maybe partially because of them, Donald Trump continued to captivate a large majority of the Republican base after the election. He continues to be very popular among Republican voters even while being despised by a majority of Democrats and independents.[14] As Trump's presidency has rolled along, the #NeverTrump movement has remained viable and voluble. Character and decency have been prominent fodder for this faction. I use the framework of the seven deadly sins to explore these criticisms. Trump has exhibited all of the sins and the #NeverTrumpers have been there every step of the way to catalog his shortcomings.

PRIDE

Perhaps Donald Trump's greatest sin is pride—and exaggerated sense of self-esteem. It is what leads him to lie and cheat more in one day than most of us do in a lifetime. Everything Trump does and is associated with has to be the biggest and the best. It's why he ordered Sean Spicer to lie about the size of his inauguration crowd.[15] It's why he bristles at estimates of the size of his hands.[16] Even if Trump does own some of the larger buildings and better golf courses in the world, *everything* has to be the largest and the best. That is, of course impossible, so lies must be told. In fact, he owes the start of his political career to the birther canard, arguing in spite of ample evidence that President Obama was not born in the United States. A deputy mayor of New York City once said that he would not believe Donald Trump if his tongue were notarized.[17] David Frum argues that no national political figure of any kind save Senator Joseph McCarthy has trafficked in more untruths than Donald Trump.[18] Rick Wilson believes he is a serial liar of such infamy that any promise he makes is at once conditional, ephemeral, and deniable.[19] Early in his presidency, Trump averaged almost five lies a day. Later in 2017, it was six and by May of 2018 he was lying nine times a day.[20]

Why does Trump always lie and cheat? The layman's answer comes from Rick Reilly, who wrote a book about Trump and golf called *Commander in Cheat*. Reilly believes Trump lies because it sounds better and sounding better is Trump's modus operandi.[21] The clinical version comes from Harvard psychiatrist Dr. Lance Dodes who is quoted at length in Reilly's latest book.

> Because he has to. He *needs* to be the best at everything. He can't stand not winning, not being the best. It had to have started very early in his development. To him, not being the best is like fingernails on the chalkboard to you. He can't live with it. . . . He exaggerates his golf scores and his handicap for the same reason he exaggerates everything. He has to. He exhibits all the traits of a narcissistic personality disorder. People with his disorder have no conscience about it. He has no sense of morality about things. He lacks empathy towards others. He's a very ill man. He doesn't get that other people have rights and feelings. Other people just don't matter to him.[22]

Whether it is golf or the presidency, Trump's pride and swollen ego drive his behavior. He always needs to be correct, which leads to some bizarre behavior, including, altering a NOAA weather map with a Sharpie to back up his claim that Hurricane Dorian was a threat to Alabama and fixating on former National Security Adviser John Bolton's notes. The information contained in those notes could potentially bolster the impeachment case against Trump, and maybe more galling to the president, contradict what he has said in public.[23]

David Boaz, in the special anti-Trump issue of *National Review*, was extremely troubled by Trump's idea of the presidency, which he argues stems from a fountain of unbridled narcissism. "Trump's promise that he is the guy, the man on the white horse, who can ride into Washington and fire the stupid people, hire the best people, and fix everything . . . he wants to govern by fiat, (to be) an American Mussolini."[24] Sure enough, during President Trump's first 100 days in office he had signed thirty executive orders, which was the most of any president since World War II.[25] It wasn't just the quantity of executive orders that bothered liberals and conservative #NeverTrumpers (the latter of whom had themselves railed against Barack Obama's use of only nineteen executive orders in his first 100 days). It was the quality of them. Many were challenged in court and a significant number were deemed violations of the U.S. Constitution.

GREED

On second thought, perhaps Trump's greatest sin is greed—his insatiable longing for material gain. Many accounts of the Trump campaign suggest that right up until he reached 270 electoral votes on November 8, 2016, Trump did not believe he was going to be elected president.[26] Running for the highest office in the land was merely an opportunity to build his personal brand, to put his name on a campaign the way he has always put his name on buildings, steaks, bottled water, and golf courses.[27] When he first announced, most elites saw his campaign in this way. His Republican rivals refrained from attacking him figuring that they could add his supporters to their coalition when he inevitably dropped out.[28] Of course, that strategy backfired spectacularly. When he trailed Hillary Clinton in the polls after the Access Hollywood tapes appeared, many speculated that he was only remaining in the race in hopes of creating a right-wing media channel that would rival Fox News—Trump TV.[29] Instead, Fox News has become President Trump's personal and political propaganda outlet, creating an unprecedented feedback loop between a presidential administration and a television channel the likes of which we have never seen.

Trump's greed has precluded him from divesting of his material holdings and led to the creation of a dubious "blind trust" run by his children. The president has given the appearance on multiple occasions that foreign visitors to this country can curry favor by staying at one of his properties.[30] Trump himself almost always vacations at his own establishments, essentially putting taxpayer funds in his own pocket and providing enormous publicity for his businesses. He also attempted to schedule the 2020 G7 Economic Summit at his Doral golf resort. When Republicans in Congress vociferously objected, Trump uncharacteristically reversed course.[31]

Of course, Trump's past was full of corporate bankruptcies, stiffed vendors, and shady ventures like Trump University that led to lawsuits and recriminations. Max Boot highlights Trump's ethical violations as president focusing on the unprecedented corruption and malfeasance of the Trump administration.[32] When the boss engages in quasi-criminal activity resulting from greed, his underlings will be emboldened to emulate those practices. Whether it is Ben Carson's $30,000 office furniture, Tom Price's insider trading, or Scott Pruitt's taxpayer-funded first-class travel, the examples are plentiful.[33] A president seeking to use the office to get rich was anticipated by the framers and they inserted the Emoluments Clause in the United States Constitution for that reason. None of the prior forty-four chief executives has tested it quite like President Trump.

LUST

While pride and greed have been front-and-center in Trump's administration, lust has not taken a back seat as one of Trump's seven deadly sins. An intense wanting and longing for an object, lust is often thought of first and foremost as sexual in nature. For Donald Trump, this is certainly a suitable definition. He has been married three times and engaged in countless extramarital affairs with a number of women, including adult entertainment stars and Playboy playmates. His affairs with Stormy Daniels and Karen McDougal became major legal headaches for the president when it was revealed that campaign funds were used to silence these women in the weeks prior to the 2016 election. Even before these indiscretions were reported, #NeverTrumpers had their doubts about the lust in Trump's heart. Many of these worries emanated from the Christian right leading to their general skepticism regarding his campaign during the nominating season. In the famous *National Review* anti-Trump issue, Russell Moore summarized the concerns of the values voter:

> One may say that Trump's personal life and business dealings are irrelevant to his candidacy, but conservatives have argued for generations that virtue matters, in the citizenry and in the nation's leaders. Can conservatives really believe that, if elected, Trump would care about protecting the family's place in society when his own life is—unapologetically—what conservatives used to recognize as decadent?[34]

Perhaps more troubling than the countless seemingly consensual affairs in which Donald Trump has engaged is the open bragging about sexual assault recorded in the Access Hollywood tapes. In addition to the braggadocio there have been multiple accusations levied at the president, including rape charges. President Trump's first wife Ivana famously used the word rape in their divorce proceedings and more recently E. Jean Carroll, a journalist and former television host, claims that in 1996 Donald Trump attacked her in a

Bergdorf Goodman dressing room. She contends she was raped by the future forty-fifth president of the United States.[35] While many evangelical leaders have overlooked the rape charges, the multiple divorces, the public fraternizing with porn stars, and the so-called locker-room talk, #NeverTrumpers have remained steadfast in their disapproval. They have often displayed this disapproval by calling out other Republicans who have countenanced this rhetoric and behavior. Rick Wilson argued that Sean Hannity's full-throated defense of Trump's "locker-room" talk told Trump that Hannity would never abandon him for anything as trifling as the truth, or morals.[36]

Charlie Sykes believes the Access Hollywood video foreshadowed the degree to which the right was willing to surrender its remaining principles and enable many of Trump's worst impulses.[37] And while hypocrisy is not one of the seven deadly sins, Sykes points out that the percentage of Republican voters who decried sexual misconduct by a president dropped from 70 percent during Bill Clinton's term to just 23 percent during Trump's.[38] It is worth noting that not all evangelical opinion leaders have been hypocritical regarding Trump's behavior. The explosive *Christianity Today* editorial by Mark Galli calling for the president's removal from office for withholding military aid from Ukraine was subtitled, "It's time to say what we said 20 years ago when a president's character was revealed for what it was."[39]

ENVY

For someone with an overinflated sense of self, Trump does display his fair share of the fourth deadly sin—envy. Trump is clearly envious, meaning he lacks another's qualities and wishes to have them. This has manifested itself in the bifurcated way in which he treats other world leaders. He insults ex-presidents and allies all the while praising dictators that oppose our national interests. Trump's envy accounts for this curious behavior. His main target, of course, has been President Barack Obama. He has intentionally sought to undo his legacy by scuttling the Iran Nuclear Deal and the Paris Climate Accord, as well as attempting to repeal Obamacare. And one must not forget that Trump owes the start of his political career to the birther hoax. More than other Republicans, Trump's supporters distrusted Barack Obama as alien and dangerous. Only 21 percent acknowledged that Obama was born in the United States and 66 percent of Trump voters believed that Obama was a Muslim.[40]

Besides the birtherism espoused by Trump when he was still a private citizen, the reality-tv star constantly sniped at Obama for everything from golfing too much to being weak in his dealings with our foreign adversaries. As president, the only policy coherence he has shown is a desire to do the opposite of what his predecessor in the White House did. It is not difficult to see what Trump envies in former president Obama. Obama is young, good-looking, and considered by most observers to be urbane and stylish. Trump, to put it bluntly, is none of those things. And to drive this point home, consider other world leaders with whom Trump has traded barbs during his term as president: Emmanuel Macron and Justin Trudeau. These are similarly younger, attractive, sophisticated world leaders. It is hard to overlook the possibility that Trump spars with those he envies.

Trump's bitter attacks on allies like Canada's Trudeau and France's Macron contrast sharply with his fawning praise of global thugs like North Korea's Kim Jong-un, Russia's Vladimir Putin, and Turkey's Recep Tayyip Erdogen. Envy is a good explanation for this curious behavior as well. Trump admires these strongmen because he wishes to be one. They are powerful men feared by friend and foe alike. Trump projects machismo and decisiveness but is often revealed to be a "Twitter Tiger" or someone who speaks loudly but carries a small stick. Whereas foreign dictators can rule with impunity, President Trump has found himself constantly constrained by the courts, the Congress, the free press, and public opinion.

Envy may also account for a darker side of Donald Trump. As Max Boot has pointed out, Trump evinces sympathy not just for dictators but for neo-Nazis, alleged child molesters, and accused wife-beaters.[41] Since he has a history of racist and anti-Semitic rhetoric and behavior, a stated desire to date his daughter, and numerous accusations of physical abuse from multiple women, one has to wonder if he doesn't secretly envy the worst of the worst in our society.[42]

GLUTTONY

While it may not have a lot to do with how he governs, Trump's gluttony certainly contributes to his lack of decency and poor character. Gluttony is defined as an overindulgence of food or other status symbols. The forty-fifth president's fast-food intake is legendary, as he is often photographed with McDonald's or KFC on the plate in front of him. His poor nutritional choices have led to speculation about his general health and for this reason, the president had his personal doctor put out a medical report that defied belief. Trump's health was lauded in breathless terms and it was speculated that the doctor exaggerated Trump's height just enough to keep his body mass index from classifying him as obese.[43] It is not just food that Trump overindulges in. His garish tastes have led him to gold plate whatever he can and place mammoth waterfalls on most of his golf courses. He has been known to refer to the White House as a "dump" presumably because it lacks gold and is not adorned with a waterfall of any size.

WRATH

While gluttony seems like one of the more harmless of the seven deadly sins that Donald Trump partakes in, his wrath has arguably led to some of the most damaging public policy efforts coming out of this administration as well as most of the toxic rhetoric that has so coarsened the public discourse. Wrathful behavior consists of a hostile response to hurt or threat. For Trump and his supporters, the threats come from Mexican immigrants, Muslim terrorists, Antifa, the free press, among others. This has led to policies and statements that have infuriated #NeverTrumpers since the very first day of his campaign for president. Max Boot's sensibilities were offended right from the beginning when Trump railed against Mexicans, "They're bringing drugs. They're bringing crime. They're rapists. And some, I assume are good people."[44] Trump's attacks on Senator John McCain also riled up #NeverTrumpers like Boot. "He's (McCain's) not a war hero. He was a war hero because he was captured. I like people who weren't captured."[45] From the stage, he advocated violence against anti-Trump demonstrators and openly hoped one in particular would be carried off on a stretcher.[46]

Also, from the campaign podium, he mocked a disabled reporter who dared question his bogus claim that thousands of Muslims in Jersey City cheered the destruction of the Twin Towers.[47] David Boaz had the following to say about Trump's 2016 candidacy: "Not since George Wallace has there been a presidential candidate who made racial and religious scapegoating so central to his campaign. Trump launched his campaign talking about Mexican rapists and has gone on to rant about mass deportation, bans on Muslim immigration, shutting down mosques, and building a wall around America."[48]

In the aftermath of the murderous, racially motivated riots in Charlottesville, VA in August 2017, 62 percent of Trump's retweets were of white supremacists and his response to this tragedy displayed at best an insensitivity to the horrible events that took place and at worst a tacit endorsement of them.[49]

Trumpian insensitivity to horrible events does not stop at the water's edge, as his response to critics of his administration's response to Hurricane Maria in Puerto Rico quite clearly shows. President Trump openly showed his disdain for the people of Puerto Rico and their leaders. He joked that relief efforts were throwing America's budget "out of whack," he tossed paper towel rolls to the crowd like a basketball player shooting 3-pointers, and he publicly savaged the mayor of San Juan.[50]

As president, of course, Trump has sought to put his racist, nativist, and Islamophobic rhetoric into practice. Pardoning Sheriff Joe Arpaio, insulting African American NFL players peacefully protesting police brutality, and demonizing illegal immigrants and Muslims have been some of the defining actions of his administration. According to Charlie Sykes, the heart-wrenching scenes of migrant children being separated from their parents at the border and held in cages drew widespread condemnation, but seemed a logical culmination of the Trumpian embrace of a policy of calculated cruelty.[51] Like any wrathful demagogue with fascist tendencies, the real danger comes from his ability to incite the same wrath in his supporters. Trump never fails to provoke outrage among his supporters toward those they feel are undeserving and overentitled. Sixty-three percent of Trump's supporters want to end birthright citizenship for the children of undocumented immigrants born on U.S. soil.[52] Rick Wilson pulls no punches when characterizing Trump supporters as racist and xenophobic. "Xenophobic fury at brown people coming here to live a better life doesn't motivate every person who voted for Trump, but every single person motivated by a xenophobic fury at brown people coming here to live a better life was a Trump voter, and he shamelessly, consistently, and viciously plays that card on the campaign trail and in office."[53]

There is plenty of Trumpian wrath to go around and a significant portion of it has been directed at the free press. According to Wilson, "Of all the norms Trump has shattered, of all the damage he's done to the Republic, the war on the press is the deepest affront to our traditions, values, and freedoms."[54] Leading chants of "Fake News" and "CNN Sucks," tweeting photoshopped images of him body-slamming a CNN reporter, and lauding a Republican politician who actually *did* body-slam a reporter has created a dangerous environment from which to practice the essential occupation of journalist.[55] Trump has called the free press the enemy of the people countless times and his supporters buy every bit of it. To #NeverTrumpers, the wrath of Trump has seemingly seeped into the deep recesses of the Republican Party and while this anger did not originate with Trump, he has institutionalized it. Max Boot senses the primary vibe of the GOP has become one of indiscriminate, unthinking, all-consuming anger.[56] David Frum sees the wrath extending to the conservative movement writ large. "By August 2017, what was left of the philosophy formerly known as conservatism beyond "f**k you, leftists?"[57]

In October 2019, the wrath of Trump and his supporters was neatly encapsulated by a violent video shown at a pro-Trump conference at the president's Doral resort. In the video, Trump's head is superimposed on the body of a character from a popular action film. This figure goes on to brutally murder roughly forty individuals whose heads had been replaced with the logos and faces of Trump's critics in the media and on the left. For instance, "Trump" drives a stake through the head of "CNN." Of course, the Trump campaign disavowed this video and campaign surrogates denied knowledge of the video being played on a loop during the conference.[58] The benefit of the doubt may have been afforded to another campaign and another public figure who had not openly advocated violence against protestors and crime suspects on multiple occasions, but in this case it is further evidence of the wrathful nature of this president and its corrosive effect on the body politic.

SLOTH

The seventh deadly sin Donald Trump engages in on an almost daily basis is sloth or laziness. Whether it is an unwillingness to read presidential briefings or a seemingly exclusive reliance on Fox News for policy ideas, Trump does not exactly give 100 percent to the office. The term "executive time" has become emblematic of the inattention that Donald Trump has shown to the job of president of the United States. His diligence and maximum effort only reveal themselves when it comes to golfing. According to www.trump-golfcount.com, as of January 17, 2020, he had visited golf courses 242 times playing on at least 112 occasions. The cost to the taxpayers has been roughly $121 million.[59] In another helping of hypocrisy, it is instructive to remember that Trump tweeted multiple times that Obama should golf less and spend more time governing the country.

Relatedly, Trump has shown no interest in rectifying his lack of basic knowledge about the workings of government. This ignorance first surfaced during the campaign when he did not know what the nuclear triad was during one of the Republican debates.[60] Considering the many insider accounts of the Trump White House, it is clear that his base of knowledge has not increased dramatically since taking the oath of office. Max Boot does not just take issue with President Trump's ignorance. "The real problem with The Donald is not that he is ignorant but that he is aggressively ignorant."[61] Ignorance in a world leader is bad enough. When one does not know anything, it can obviously lead to poor decision-making on extremely important issues. But we also know that Trump has an overinflated sense of his own abilities. He is extremely conceited. He always thinks he knows best. Jennifer Rubin, columnist for *The Washington Post*, zeroes in on this character flaw, "Trump's arrogant obliviousness . . . have blinded him to the multiple ways in which his own conduct . . . can be brought to light."[62] Ignorant and arrogant is an extremely bad and dangerous combination. You know nothing but at the same time you think you know everything. He exemplifies the Dunning-Kruger effect, where those most ignorant believe they are the most knowledgeable, and vice-versa. This is an annoyingly harmless trait for an uncle at Thanksgiving dinner—it is downright dangerous when the leader of the free world is too busy golfing to read an intelligence report.[63]

CONSERVATIVE INFIGHTING
CENTERED ON DONALD TRUMP

So far, this chapter has focused on the character flaws and lack of decency Donald Trump has displayed since even before he rode down that escalator in Trump Tower. #NeverTrumpers have bristled at the fundamental disrespect Trump has shown to his fellow Americans and to the office of the president. In this section, I address the impact of #NeverTrumpism within the Republican Party and how it will potentially affect American politics moving forward. It is hard to imagine the rifts created by Trump's rise will be closed any time soon. It would seem that the GOP and the conservative movement as a whole will be damaged considerably by the internecine warfare.

Leading members of the #NeverTrump movement have aimed their rhetorical cannons at Republicans who have countenanced and even enabled Trump's poor behavior. Rick Wilson faults Paul Ryan and his congressional cohorts for defending any outrage, arguing "This . . . gave Trump a sense that no line is too far, no outrage is too grand, no lie is too egregious. He didn't learn that the rule of law and the Constitution bind even the mighty powers of the President; he learned Dad and Mom were at the beach house and left the car keys and a credit card on the kitchen table."[64]

Similarly, Max Boot is furious at what Trump has been doing to our democracy and how he has demonized the most vulnerable among us. But he is also angry with all those people who are *not* angry, " . . . who are, in fact, complacent in the face of his attack on our institutions or even serve as his willing accomplices."[65]

Many conservatives have questioned their own movement's core principles and legitimacy in the wake of Trump's ascendancy. According to Charlie Sykes, the election of 2016 marked the abandonment of respect for gradualism, civility, expertise, intelligence and prudence. For Sykes, these were values once taken for granted by conservatives. Basic decency no longer needed to be advanced or even protected in the era of Trump.[66] Rick Wilson echoes the emphasis on decency. He believes decency "is not a liberal excuse but a foundational conservative value."[67] Max Boot defines conservatism as respect for character, community, personal virtue, and family.[68] Needless to say, the #NeverTrumpers mourn the loss of that respect and place the blame squarely on the shoulders of the man in the White House. Beyond decency but no less important, Trump drove a metamorphosis within the conservative movement on everything from personal character and public ethics to fiscal conservatism, crony capitalism, free trade, immigration, global leadership, human rights, and the rule of law. The conservative movement, with the exception of the #NeverTrumpers, abandoned decades-old policy positions when Donald Trump became president.

In addition to the #NeverTrumpers who have been critical from outside the halls of government, select Republicans inside the Beltway have shone a spotlight on Trump's boorish behavior. When the president began to attack former Republican Senator Bob Corker in 2017, Corker responded pointedly calling the White House an "adult day care center."[69] Corker's colleague in the Senate, Jeff Flake was also a frequent critic of the occupant of the White House before he retired in 2018. When he announced his impending retirement in the fall of 2017, Flake hit Trump hard, "Humility helps, character counts. Leadership does not knowingly encourage or feed ugly or debased appetites in us."[70] When he spoke at Harvard Law School commencement in May of 2018, he pummeled Trump, "Our presidency has been debased by a figure who has a seemingly bottomless appetite for destruction and division and only a passing familiarity with how the Constitution works."[71] And in his farewell speech on the floor of the United States Senate in December of 2018, he went after Trump again. "I believe that we all know well that this is not a normal time, that the threats to our democracy from within and without are real . . ."[72] Senator Mitt Romney (R-UT) even voted to remove Trump from office for abuse of power, emotionally explaining his decision in a moment that captivated the country, but did little to slow Trump's seizure of the GOP. While Trump has been able to count on the obsequiousness of most Republican members of Congress, a few members of his own party (albeit ones on their way out the door) have called out this president earning them the distinction of being at least an honorary #NeverTrumper.

WHAT WILL THE FUTURE BRING?

An ad produced and aired by a group of anti-Trump Republicans, including George Conway, husband of special adviser to the president Kellyanne Conway, gets to the heart of the matter. Included are biblical quotes, with a dire warning: "Beware of false prophets . . . If this is the best American Christians can do? God help us all."[73] Rick Wilson presents a similarly apocalyptic vision of the future of the conservative movement and the Republican Party if the alt-right virus injected by Trump spreads deeper into the political system. It is the single greatest risk to the party Wilson once called his own. He sees the rise of an overtly racist, overtly anti-Semitic tendency in modern American politics as revolting and disturbing and calls for "a pure, cleansing fire" to drive it back into the shadows.[74] Max Boot worries about fiscal irresponsibility emanating from Trump's GOP in the form of spending increases and tax cuts. He highlights Trump's hostility to democracy and free trade as major threats to the movement and the party.[75]

Clearly, much of this will depend upon whether Donald Trump is elected to a second term in November of 2020. A Trump victory will lead to four more years of the conservative apostasies alluded to throughout this chapter. A second term will leave the president unburdened by reelection concerns and presumably freed from Democratic threats to impeach him considering he survived their efforts surrounding the Ukraine scandal during his first term. One can only imagine the havoc Trump can wreak without these shackles that were hardly binding in the first place. For these reasons and others, four more years will likely damage the Republican Party and the conservative movement beyond repair. It figures to render the #NeverTrumpers meaningless and impotent since they will have gone 0-for-2 fighting against Trump and Trumpism (0-for-3 if you count the 2016 GOP nomination campaign).

On the other hand, a Democratic victory over Donald Trump in 2020 will be a cause for celebration for many of the #NeverTrumpers quoted in this chapter. The hard work of rebuilding the movement in their own image will begin. It will not be pretty but it will be necessary if the Republican Party is to begin to return to what it was before being taken over by President Trump. One can imagine much blame being foisted on Trump and his minions within the party and movement. The Republicans will be in the wilderness giving them an opportunity to truly conduct a reckoning over how the past five years came to be and how they can be avoided in the future.

For Rick Wilson, smarts, seriousness, and stature will need to make a comeback. "Our goal should be an end to the era of entertainment conservatism and to select candidates for their quality, not their celebrity."[76] But with the re-nomination of Donald Trump in 2020 in Charlotte, North Carolina, the GOP continues to be enthralled with the celebrity of Donald Trump. The lack of a serious challenge to his re-nomination proves just how much President Trump has taken over the Republican Party, and how much the #NeverTrumpers continue to be marginalized. They continue to play the role of Greek chorus, capable only of giving a running commentary on the comedy and tragedy that is Trump's presidency. They have not been able to derail that production and it remains to be seen if their rhetorical pounding of the president will leave him sufficiently battered so that he is denied a second act.

NOTES

1. James Madison, *Federalist 10*, https://billofrightsinstitute.org/founding-documents/primary-source-documents/the-federalist-papers/federalist-papers-no-10/#targetText=10%20(1787),be%20unresponsive%20to%20the%20people.

2. James Madison, *Federalist 51*, https://billofrightsinstitute.org/founding-documents/primary-source-documents/the-federalist-papers/federalist-papers-no-51/.

3. George Washington's Farewell Address, accessed January 11, 2020, https://bi llofrightsinstitute.org/founding-documents/primary-source-documents/washingtons -farewell-address/.

4. *Electing the President, 2000,* eds. Kathleen Hall Jamieson and Paul Waldman (Philadelphia: University of Pennsylvania Press, 2001), 103.

5. National Review Symposium, "Conservatives Against Trump," *National Review,* January 22, 2016.

6. Mona Charen, "Conservatives Against Trump," *National Review,* January 22, 2016.

7. Cal Thomas, "Conservatives Against Trump," *National Review,* January 22, 2016.

8. Max Boot, *The Corrosion of Conservatism* (New York: W. W. Norton and Company, 2018), 152.

9. Boot, *Corrosion,* 75.

10. Boot, *Corrosion,* 89.

11. David Frum, *Trumpocracy* (New York: Harper-Collins Inc., 2018), 234.

12. Charles J. Sykes, *How the Right Lost Its Mind* (New York: St. Martin's Press, 2017), xiv.

13. Chris Cillizza, "Can the Republican Party Survive Donald Trump?" August 21, 2018, https://www.cnn.com/2018/08/21/politics/donald-trump-republican-party/ index.html.

14. "Presidential Approval Ratings," Gallup Poll, accessed January 17, 2020, https ://news.gallup.com/poll/203198/presidential-approval-ratings-donald-trump.aspx.

15. Julie Hirschfeld Davis and Matthew Rosenberg, "With False Claims, Trump Attacks Media on Turnout and Intelligence Rift," *The New York Times,* January 21, 2017.

16. Stephen Hutcheon, "Downsized iPhone SE Plays into Trump's (tiny) Hands," *Sydney Morning Herald,* March 22, 2016, LexisNexis Academic.

17. Frum, *Trumpocracy,* 109.

18. Frum, *Trumpocracy,* 104.

19. Rick Wilson, *Everything Trump Touches Dies* (New York: Free Press, 2018), 87.

20. Boot, *Corrosion,* 128–32.

21. Rick Reilly, *Commander in Cheat* (New York: Hachette Books, 2019), 3.

22. Reilly, *Commander in Cheat,* 41.

23. Bill Tarrant, "Sharpie-Gate? Trump Shows Apparently Altered Hurricane Map," *Reuters,* September 4, 2019, https://www.reuters.com/article/us-storm-dorian -trump-idUSKCN1VQ00H; Jonathan Swain, "John Bolton Reportedly Kept Secret Notes About His Encounters with the President," *Business Insider,* November 11, 2019, https://www.businessinsider.com/trump-aides-reportedly-worried-about-john -boltons-notes-impeachment-inquiry-2019-11.

24. David Boaz, "Conservatives Against Trump," *National Review,* January 22, 2016.

25. Najja Parker and Ryan Stultz, "Here's Every Executive Order Trump Has Signed During His First Hundred Days," *Atlanta Journal-Constitution,* April 29,

2017, https://www.ajc.com/news/here-every-executive-order-trump-has-signed-d
uring-his-first-100-days/pHETsFIm2nYmj4VWlNHmbK/.

26. Nolan D. McCaskill, "Trump Tells Wisconsin: Victory Was a Surprise,"
Politico, December 13, 2016, 2019, https://www.politico.com/story/2016/12/donald
-trump-wisconsin-232605.

27. Rebecca Savransky, "Scarborough: Trump Didn't Think He Would Win,
Campaign Was 'Money-Making Scam,'" *The Hill*, August 29, 2017, https://thehill
.com/homenews/media/348370-scarborough-trump-never-thought-he-was-going-to-
win-campaign-was-a-money.

28. Michael Barbaro, Maggie Haberman, and Jonathan Martin, "Republican Party
Frets Over Trump; Officials Are Reluctant to Criticize Him, Fearing Independent
Candidacy," *The New York Times*, July 11, 2015, LexisNexis Academic.

29. Brendan James, "Trump TV: Is His Campaign Laying the Groundwork for the
Next Media Empire," *The Guardian*, August 31, 2016, LexisNexis Academic.

30. Steve Benen, "Foreigners Reportedly 'Curry Favor' with Spending at Trump
Properties," January 16, 2018, http://www.msnbc.com/rachel-maddow-show/forei
gners-reportedly-curry-favor-spending-trump-properties.

31. Maggie Haberman, Eric Lipton, and Katie Rogers, "Why Trump Dropped His
Idea to Hold the G7 at His Own Hotel," *The New York Times*, October 21, 2019, A1.

32. Boot, *Corrosion*, 132–37.

33. Eli Rosenberg, "Ben Carson Defends Purchase of New $31,000 Set: 'The
Dining Room Table Was Actually Dangerous,'" *The Washington Post*, March 20,
2018, https://www.washingtonpost.com/news/powerpost/wp/2018/03/20/ben-carson
-defends-purchase-of-new-31000-set-the-dining-room-table-was-actually-dange
rous/; Jayne O'Donnell, "HHS Nominee Tom Price Bought Stock, Then Authored
Bill Benefiting Company," *USA Today*, February 2, 2017, https://www.usatoday
.com/story/news/politics/2017/02/02/hhs-nominee-tom-price-bought-stock-then-auth
ored-bill-benefiting-company/97337838/; Anna Phillips, "Trump's ex-EPA Chief
Scott Pruitt Blew $124,000 on Travel, Audit Says," *Los Angeles Times*, May 16,
2019, https://www.latimes.com/politics/la-na-pol-pruitt-excessive-travel-costs-20
190516-story.html.

34. Russell Moore, "Conservatives Against Trump," *National Review*, January
22, 2016.

35. Alexandra Alter, "E. Jean Carroll Accuses Trump of Sexual Assault in Her
Memoir," *New York Times*, June 21, 2019, LexisNexis Academic.

36. Wilson, *Everything Trump Touches*, 209.

37. Sykes, *How the Right*, xi.

38. Sykes, *How the Right*, xii.

39. Mark Galli, "Trump Should Be Removed from Office," *Christianity Today*,
December 19, 2019, https://www.christianitytoday.com/ct/2019/december-web-only/
trump-should-be-removed-from-office.html.

40. Frum, *Trumpocracy*, 38.

41. Boot, *Corrosion*, 192.

42. Barry Levine and Monique El-Faizy, *All the President's Women: Donald
Trump and the Making of a Predator* (New York: Hachette Books, 2019).

43. Nick Allen, "Presidential Mystery May Be Solved . . . Is He 6 ft. 3 in. or 6 ft. 2 in.?" *The Daily Telegraph*, January 13, 2018. LexisNexis Academic.

44. Boot, *Corrosion*, xv.

45. Boot, *Corrosion*, xvi.

46. Boot, *Corrosion*, 67.

47. Boot, *Corrosion*, xvi.

48. Boaz, "Conservatives Against Trump."

49. Boot, *Corrosion*, 64.

50. David Jackson, "Trump Praises Puerto Rico Recovery, But Critics Assail Comments on Budget and Death Toll," *USA Today*, October 3, 2017, https://www.usa today.com/story/news/politics/2017/10/03/trump-puerto-rico-survey-hurricane-maria -damage/726352001/.

51. Sykes, *How the Right*, xviii.

52. Frum, *Trumpocracy*, 38.

53. Wilson, *Everything Trump Touches*, 252.

54. Wilson, *Everything Trump Touches*, 204.

55. Zeke Miller and Ashley Thomas, "Trump: Gianforte Is a 'Tough Cookie,'" *Chico Enterprise-Record*, October 20, 2018, LexisNexis Academic.

56. Boot, *Corrosion*, 179.

57. Frum, *Trumpocracy*, 48.

58. Paul LeBlanc, "Fake Video of Trump Shooting Media and Critics Played at His Resort," *CNN*, October 14, 2019, https://www.cnn.com/2019/10/13/politics/ trump-fake-video-shooting-media-critics-doral/index.html.

59. See https://www.trumpgolfcount.com/

60. Tom Jackson, "Latest Republican Debate a Nearly Forgettable Affair," *The Tampa Tribune*, December 20, 2015, LexisNexis Academic.

61. Boot, *Corrosion*, 63.

62. Douglas Perry, "The 21 Most Powerful GOP Critics of Donald Trump – And How They're Trying to Take Down the President," *The Oregonian*, July 26, 2017, accessed January 17, 2020, https://www.oregonlive.com/today/2017/07/the_21_mo st_powerful_gop_criti.html.

63. Faye Flam, "Trump's 'Dangerous Disability'? It's the Dunning-Kruger Effect," *Bloomberg News*, May 12, 2017, https://www.bloomberg.com/opinion/articl es/2017-05-12/trump-s-dangerous-disability-it-s-the-dunning-kruger-effect.

64. Wilson, *Everything Trump Touches*, 56.

65. Boot, *Corrosion*, 83.

66. Sykes, *How the Right*, xxx–xxxi.

67. Wilson, *Everything Trump Touches*, 297.

68. Boot, *Corrosion*, xix.

69. Philip Rucker and Karoun Demirjian, "Corker Calls White House 'An Adult Day Care Center' in Response to Trump's Latest Twitter Tirade," *The Washington Post*, October 8, 2017, 2019, https://www.washingtonpost.com/news/post-politics/ wp/2017/10/08/trump-attacks-gop-sen-corker-didnt-have-the-guts-to-run-for-reelec tion/.

70. "Full Transcript: Jeff Flake's Speech on the Senate Floor," *The New York Times*, October 24, 2017, https://www.nytimes.com/2017/10/24/us/politics/jeff-flake -transcript-senate-speech.html.

71. Katie Reilly, "Read Jeff Flake's Commencement Speech on the Rule of Law and Trump: 'We May Have Hit Bottom,'" *Time*, May 23, 2018, https://time.com/528 9380/jeff-flake-harvard-commencement-address-president-trump/.

72. Tucker Higgins, "Retiring GOP Sen. Jeff Flake Throws Shade at Trump in Farewell Address to Congress, Warns of Dangers to Democracy," *CNBC.com*, December 13, 2018, https://www.cnbc.com/2018/12/13/gop-sen-jeff-flake-warns-of-authoritarianism-in-farewell-address.html.

73. Anti-Trump Republicans Mock Evangelical Supporters with "MAGA Church" Ad, accessed January 11, 2020, https://www.foxnews.com/politics/anti-trump-republ icans-mock-evangelical-supporters-with-maga-church-ad.

74. Wilson, *Everything Trump Touches*, 249.

75. Boot, *Corrosion*, 137–48.

76. Wilson, *Everything Trump Touches*, 310.

Chapter 11

#NeverTrump Conservatives and the Corruption of Donald Trump

Beth Rosenson

Long before running for president in 2016, Donald Trump was dogged by legal and ethical quandaries. As a businessman, he was the target of numerous lawsuits, and as soon as he declared himself a candidate for the presidency, he faced questions about potential conflicts of interest relating to his sprawling domestic and international business empire. Concerns about law-breaking and corruption continued throughout the campaign and have not abated since he arrived at the White House.

The Founding Fathers were deeply concerned with assuring that the nation's top elected official refrains not only from bribery but also from less clear-cut forms of corruption. While illegality or law-breaking is a straightforward concept, corruption is a more nebulous one. David Bayley, writing in 1966, puts it succinctly: "Corruption, while being tied particularly to the act of bribery, is a general term covering misuse of authority as a result of considerations of personal gain, which need not be monetary."[1] Political theorist Dennis Thompson, who specializes in political ethics, emphasizes that the core of unethical or corrupt behavior is the perversion of the public interest by the personal interests of a public official. An official is corrupt when he/she makes decisions primarily based on the pursuit of private financial or political gain.[2] Financial gain refers to things of value in the private marketplace, while political gain refers to things of value in the electoral marketplace such as campaign contributions, endorsements, or electoral advantage. The pursuit of either type of gain is not improper in and of itself, Thompson argues; only when this pursuit becomes a significant influence over that official's behavior and impinges on the process of decision-making on the merits does it become improper.

Concerns about corruption preceded the American Revolution; royal governors such as New York's Benjamin Fletcher (1692–1697) took bribes to protect pirates, and customs officials were well-known for taking bribes.[3] Colonial governments had anti-bribery statutes, some specifically pertaining to election-related bribery—for example, the provision of money or meat to voters. The first federal anti-bribery statute, targeting customs officials, was passed in 1789.[4] In drafting the U.S. Constitution, the Founding Fathers were especially concerned with the possibility that the chief executive might be improperly influenced, particularly by foreign governments. Historian Gail Savage sums it up: "That a scheming, feckless leader might sell out his own country was a very real threat in the minds of those tasked to create a constitutional framework."[5] Washington, Jefferson, Adams, and Hamilton all spoke or wrote about the potential for foreign influence to undermine the security of the nation. This is why the drafters of the Constitution included the Emoluments Clause forbidding federal officials from receiving anything of value from a foreign government. This clause would become a matter of contention for Trump; indeed, numerous foreign governments continue to stay at the Trump Hotel and have not been shy about admitting that they hope to curry favor with the president by doing so.

At the most basic level, the founders were concerned with preventing tyranny and a president who might act like a king. Hence, they gave Congress the power to impeach presidents who put their own (or a foreign country's) interests above the interest of the nation. During the Constitutional Convention, the impeachment clause originally focused on the crimes of treason and bribery. The final draft was later broadened to include the phrase "high crimes and misdemeanors" or acts that "(involve) a president's abuse of the public's trust."[6]

Corruption charges have plagued various administrations, such as the Grant and Harding administrations, but typically the corruption has involved officials beneath the president. The exception, of course, is Nixon, for whom impeachment charges including the selling of ambassadorships to major campaign donors, and the use of federal agencies such as the IRS and FBI for political gain. Trump himself made the alleged illegality and corruption of his Democratic opponent Hillary Clinton a major campaign issue (distilled in the campaign rally phrase "lock her up").[7] Other Republicans before him had sought to weaponize and utilize the issue of corruption. Newt Gingrich, for example, made a point of attaching the term "corrupt" whenever he talked about Democratic speaker James Wright and the Democratic party in general in the early 1990s.[8]

There is no small amount of irony in the fact that Trump himself is now under near-constant attack for engaging in illegal and corrupt behavior. This chapter will address Trump's pre-presidency business activities, and then turn to his campaign activities, conflicts of interest, the Mueller investigation, Ukraine and impeachment, and the charges of corrupt, self-dealing behavior by his top aides and relatives. Throughout, we consider the response to them by congressional Republicans, other party members and conservative intellectuals and organized interests; it has been largely one of defending the president, with criticism of him sporadic and tepid up through the impeachment hearings and trial.

A BUSINESSMAN PUSHING THE LEGAL ENVELOPE

Long before he faced the impeachment charges of abuse of power and obstruction of Congress, businessman Donald Trump faced accusations of violating the laws and the rights of tenants, employees, and students. A 2018 *Rolling Stone* article sums up succinctly, "nearly every organization President Trump has led in the past decade is under investigation—his administration, campaign, transition team, private business and inaugural celebration."[9] Over a period of five decades, Trump was the target of numerous lawsuits and investigations into illegal behavior that involved his real estate properties, casinos, and Trump University. Additional charges of illegal behavior would arise during the campaign, for example involving the Trump Foundation and a payoff to an adult film actor.

The first time Donald Trump appeared in a *New York Times* article was in 1973; he was twenty-seven and being sued by the Department of Justice (DOJ) for racial discrimination. He and his father were charged with violating the Fair Housing Act of 1968 for refusing to rent to individuals because of their race or color and giving different rental terms and conditions because of race.[10] Trump responded by counter-suing the federal government. In the end Trump Management agreed to work with the New York Urban League to increase the number of black tenants. Over the years, Trump would make many such legal settlements.

Given the length of time since the racial discrimination incident, it is not surprising that Republicans have not spoken out against this charge of law-breaking. By contrast, Trump's reputation for stiffing contractors and other workers drew at least some response during the campaign from several Republicans, including two of his primary opponents. And #NeverTrumpers have attacked him for fraud involving Trump University. Before becoming president, Trump was sued by numerous contractors and employees for non-payment of wages and services. He has faced at least sixty lawsuits by people claiming they were shortchanged, including his personal driver of twenty-five years, a cabinet maker, a plumber, and the owners of a jewelry store, drapery business, and glass company.[11] A small businessman who signed a contract to sell Trump $100,000 worth of pianos for his new Atlantic City casino only received $70,000.[12] Some of the contractors who were underpaid settled, but others won their cases in court, such as a paint shop owner. *USA Today* in 2016 reported that Trump had twenty-four violations of the Fair Labor Standards Act since 2005 for failure to pay overtime or minimum wage.[13] The former president of the Plaza Casino in Atlantic City told *The Wall Street Journal* that it was common "when it came time to pay bills (for Trump to say) I'm going to pay you but I'm going to pay you 75 percent of what we agreed to."[14]

Senator Marco Rubio, running against Trump in the Republican primaries, in February 2016, said Trump had "spent forty years sticking it to the little guy . . . And every time one of those businesses of his failed, you know who didn't get paid? The little guy that was working for him."[15] Trump, however, was unrepentant. When asked by Hillary Clinton in a presidential debate about his failure to pay one contractor, he responded, "Maybe he didn't do a good job and I was unsatisfied with his work."[16]

A federal judge ruled in 1991 that Trump engaged in fraud by hiring undocumented immigrants to work on Trump Tower. He is also reported to have hired mob-connected firms to build Trump Tower and the Trump Plaza in Manhattan. Journalist David Cay Johnston wrote in 2016 that after twenty-seven years of covering Donald Trump, he "encountered multiple threads linking Trump to organized crime . . . top mobsters . . . (and) corrupt union leaders."[17] Thus Trump not only engaged directly in illegal activity by failing to pay employees, but also worked closely with individuals who engaged in illegal and often violent criminal activity.

Republicans have not spoken out on the subject of Trump's mob connections. As with his apparent tax schemes (discussed below), this may be due to the intricacies of the dealings that were involved, or because reporting on the matter, once Trump announced he was running for president, was limited to outlets without a large circulation, such as Politico.

An eighteen-month investigative reporting project by *The New York Times*, published in October 2018, concluded that Trump had "participated in dubious tax schemes during the 1990s, including instances of outright fraud."[18] The reporting was based on examination of confidential financial documents, including tax returns and public documents. It suggested that Trump helped set up a sham corporation with his siblings to disguise millions in gifts from their parents, and strategized to undervalue his parents' real estate holdings, which were ultimately transferred to their children. It also reported that Trump also received large loans from his father which were more like gifts—interest-free with no repayment schedule. A $3.5 million loan in 1990 for his casino, illegal under New Jersey gaming laws, resulted in a $65,000 civil penalty.

University of Florida law professor Lee-Ford Tritt said Trump "play(ed) around with valuations in extreme ways" and that Trump's activities in creating a company called All County were "highly suspicious" and could be considered criminal tax fraud.[19] It is likely that because of the highly technical nature of tax law, few potential Republican critics felt qualified to comment or pass judgment on the *Times* reporting on the matter (or even read that particular investigative reporting effort). Jennifer Rubin, a conservative *Washington Post* op-ed writer, was a rare and early voice who took on Trump's pre-presidency business practices. In an April 2016 piece, she referred to Trump as a "man who reportedly took advantage of every tax break, who as a business tactic sues at the drop of a hat, and who brags that he bought politicians."[20] This represented a turnaround for Rubin, who a year prior had said Trump had "an outstanding record as a businessman."[21] Since 2016, she has been a consistent critic of Trump with regard to his business dealings.

Additional lawsuits involved the now-defunct Trump University. In 2018, a federal judge signed off on a $25 million settlement in lawsuits filed by former students, who claimed they were bilked by the University's real estate program. The students said Trump committed fraud by promising to use "hand-picked instructors" and calling it a "university" when it was not an accredited school. Trump's attorney claimed the president did not run the university or get involved in its operation.[22]

In March 2016, the 2012 Republican presidential nominee Mitt Romney said of Trump, who was by then the Republican frontrunner, "His promises are as worthless as a degree from Trump University."[23] Sen. Marco Rubio, running against Trump for the Republican nomination, referred to Trump University, in a debate and an interview, as a "fake school" and called Trump a "world-class con artist" who scammed the people who signed up for Trump University.[24] Compared to tax evasion or organized crime connections, the operations of Trump University and non-payment for services rendered were easy acts of wrongdoing to comprehend and to communicate, and easy sound bites for a campaign opponent.

ILLEGALITY DURING THE CAMPAIGN: WIKILEAKS, STORMY DANIELS, TRUMP FOUNDATION, AND THE INAUGURAL COMMITTEE

During the 2016 the campaign, Trump came under fire from mainstream media and Democrats for encouraging the Russians to find Hillary Clinton's deleted emails. His comment during a press conference—"Russia, if you're listening, I hope you're able to find the 30,000 emails that are missing"— solicited, in plain sight, just the kind of foreign interference the Founding Fathers had warned against. Trump repeatedly praised Wikileaks, an organization that facilitates the anonymous leaking of secret information, for releasing thousands of Clinton campaign emails that were hacked by the Russian government. Special prosecutor Robert Mueller would later say of Trump's embrace of Wikileaks: "problematic is an understatement."[25]

Sen. Ted Cruz (R-TX), who like Rubio who was challenging Trump for the Republican nomination, said, "I think (WikiLeaks founder) Assange has done enormous damage to our national security. I would not be praising him under any circumstances."[26] Other Republicans were critical of Assange. Once Assange was arrested in April 2019, for example, Sen. Ben Sasse (R-NE) said, "He deserves to spend the rest of his life in prison."[27] Generally, Republicans did not criticize Trump directly for his apparent embrace of Russian interference, a pattern that would continue throughout his presidency.

Shortly before the election, it was revealed that adult film actress Stormy Daniels had been paid $130,000 by Trump's personal attorney, Michael Cohen, to sign a nondisclosure agreement about her affair with Trump a decade earlier. Cohen said he made the payment under Trump's direction. The political watchdog group Common Cause filed a complaint with the Federal Election Commission and Justice Department arguing that it amounted to an in-kind donation designed to affect the election outcome, which should have been reported under federal campaign law. Cohen would plead guilty to a campaign finance violation for his role in the payment.

Trump defended the payoff as "a simple private transaction." Even if he did break the law, said Republicans such as House Minority Leader Kevin McCarthy and Sen. Rand Paul (R-KY), it was not a serious issue. Paul commented, "If we're going to prosecute people and put them in jail for campaign finance violations, we're going to become a banana republic."[28]

Also during the campaign, it was reported that the non-profit Trump Foundation—which by law was supposed to operate as a charity and eschew political activity—had engaged in a wide range of activities that the New York Attorney General in a lawsuit called "a shocking pattern of illegality."[29] These activities included unlawful coordination with Trump's campaign. For example, the foundation spent money in Iowa right before the caucuses.[30] The New York AG's office charged that the foundation had engaged not only in "improper and extensive political activity" but also in "repeated and willful self-dealing," such as the purchase of a $10,000 portrait of Trump to display at his golf club. After initially saying he would not settle, Trump agreed to dissolve the foundation and put its remaining assets under court supervision. In November 2019, Trump was ordered to pay $2 million in restitution after the New York Supreme Court ruled that the foundation had misused charitable donations for Trump's personal benefit (such as buying a Tim Tebow helmet and settling personal lawsuits).[31] It is clear that the Trump Foundation was not a charity at all, but rather a front to promote the Trump brand.

Criticism of the foundation has come largely from Democrats and newspapers such as *The Washington Post* or *The New York Times.* Lonely criticism from #NeverTrumpers was offered by Richard Painter, a law professor and former chief ethics lawyer in the George W. Bush administration. Painter tweeted in July 2019 about "celebrat(ing) extravagant spending and say(ing) it is to benefit 'charity.' Example: The Trump Foundation."[32] Painter has been a sustained voice of criticism, arguing that the numerous investigations into Trump entities should be taken seriously and need to be assessed as an aggregate pattern of unethical conduct, not as individual misdeeds.

The charges of illegal behavior that dogged Trump since the 1970s, and throughout the campaign, did not end with his election. Even his inaugural committee came under fire, with federal prosecutors looking at whether foreigners from Middle Eastern nations illegally funneled money to the committee and a pro-Trump super PAC, using straw donors to hide their donations. Federal law prohibits foreign countries from donating to federal campaigns and political committees and inaugural funds.[33]

The inaugural committee did not draw notable criticism from Republicans, again with the exception of ethics lawyer Richard Painter. In a TV interview, Painter tweeted in December 2018, "Forty million unaccounted for? That is a telltale sign of fraud . . . Criminal activity is very likely."[34]

CONFLICTS OF INTEREST

Painter has also devoted substantial commentary to the conflicts of interest involving Trump's massive business empire. His view of the conflicts is summed up in the title of his April 2017 opinion piece, "Contempt for Ethics Hobbles Trump," coauthored with Norm Eisen, a lawyer who served in the Obama administration.[35] In it, they examine how Trump's conflicts influenced the policies he pursued in his first 100 days.

Among the potential conflicts Eisen and Painter highlight were loans from foreign banks and foreign governments, including the state-owned Bank of China and Deutsche Bank, which loaned over $2 billion to Trump projects and kept loaning even when Trump defaulted. The Deutsche Bank loans became the subject of an anti-money laundering investigation by the bank, and later a congressional investigation. Also, at issue were Trump's business ventures in twenty-five foreign countries with which he would have to deal as president, raising the question of whether his personal financial interests in countries where he already owned properties or hoped to develop properties, such as Russia, would affect his foreign policy decisions. Eisen and Painter noted the possible connection between Trump's Muslim ban and his overseas financial interests: "None of the countries subject to the ban are countries where the Trump Organization does business. And countries where Trump *has* done business, including Saudi Arabia, Egypt and the United Arab Emirates, are not on the travel ban list—even though they have a track record of exporting terrorism to the United States."[36]

Blind Trust

Painter has also expressed concern about Trump's domestic properties, which include at least seventeen residential real estate properties, golf courses, and hotels, most problematically the Trump Hotel, which is leased from the federal government and monitored by an agency whose head he appoints.[37] Trump's decision not to set up a blind trust is particularly problematic for Painter. Carter, the only recent president who owned a business, placed his peanut farm in a blind trust; former presidents Johnson, Clinton, Reagan, and both Bushes also created blind trusts.[38] While Trump did put his assets in a trust, the trustees were not truly independent (one was his oldest son). His two oldest sons took over management of the Trump Organization, the assets of which remain known to him and of which he maintains ownership.

Painter wrote an opinion piece a week after the election, urging that Trump "put all his conflict-generating assets in a true blind trust run by an independent trustee. The good of his own administration, and that of the country, demand nothing less."[39] Painter acknowledged that "Making a break with his complex U.S. and international interests would be a difficult and expensive sacrifice on his part," but said the alternative Trump was pursuing meant every decision he made as president would be subject to the charge that it was intended to benefit the Trump business. In another op-ed a few days later, Painter said even if the president were not engaging in self-dealing under the trust he had set up, "Americans have a right to a president who not only avoids corruption . . . but the appearance of corruption."[40]

Painter was a lonely Republican voice blasting the president's failure to set up a blind trust. Conservative lawyers David Rivkin and Lee Casey, who served in the Justice Department under Presidents Ronald Reagan and George H. W. Bush, disagreed with Painter's argument. They asserted that asking Trump to establish a blind trust was "unrealistic and unfair. . . . He would have to sell off business holdings that he has built and managed most of his life, and with which he is personally identified in a way that few other business magnates are . . . Liquidation would by definition take place in the context of a 'buyer's market,' and so Trump would also be required to accept a vast personal loss in financial worth."[41]

Emoluments

Painter argues that the president is exempt from one criminal statute, Title 18 U.S. Code 208, which bars executive branch employees from participating in matters in which they have a personal financial interest. But, he asserts, the president is not exempt from the Emoluments Clause of the Constitution (though it is worth noting that not all scholars agree). This clause says that no person holding federal office should accept any present, emolument, or office from any king, prince, or foreign state. Multiple federal lawsuits have argued that allowing foreign officials to patronize the Trump Hotel represents a violation of the Emoluments Clause, with two still in the courts.

Painter argued in his 2016 op-ed that "every time any foreign government or company controlled by a foreign government does business with a Trump entity, the president could be accused of . . . (violating) the Emoluments Clause."[42] He would reiterate this again two years later: "It is very clear the founders did not want anybody, including the president, receiving profits of benefits from dealings with foreign governments. He's ignored that."[43] The most obvious threat to the Emoluments Clause, Painter noted, is the Trump Hotel. As of January 2018, at least ten foreign governments had spent money there; at least twenty-two governments spent money at other Trump venues such as his golf clubs and restaurants, according to a June 2018 report.[44] Another critical Republican voice on the matter was conservative *The Washington Post* writer Jennifer Rubin who commented, "He taps foreign governments for emoluments."[45]

In October 2019, Trump reversed his plan to host the G7 summit at his Miami Doral resort, after blowback about him profiting off the presidency and violating the Emoluments Clause. The negative response came not just from "liberal media" or Democrats, but also from some *Fox News* personalities and Republicans who "complained to the White House that they couldn't defend another decision that's seemingly beyond the pale."[46] Rep. Tom Cole of Oklahoma told *The New York Times*, "I think there was a lot of concern. I'm not sure people questioned the legality of it, but it clearly was an unforced political error."[47] New Jersey governor Chris Christie commented, "It shouldn't have been done in the first place. And it's a good move to get out of it and get that out of the papers and off the news." Paul Rosenzweig, a former Department of Homeland Security official under George W. Bush and senior fellow at the R Street Institute, was more blunt in his criticism, focusing not just on optics but on the merits of the decision: "It is really just about him ordering the country to pay him money. It is just indefensible."[48] Even while dropping the idea, Trump blasted reporters: "You people with this phony Emoluments Clause" and insisted "it would have been the greatest G7 ever."[49]

Release of Taxes

When asked to release his taxes during the campaign so the public could see what kinds of conflicts he might have, Trump refused, saying he was under audit. He was the first presidential candidate not to release his taxes since 1976. A number of Republicans challenged him to release them, arguing for the virtue of transparency in government and saying he had no legitimate reason to refuse. These included South Carolina Governor Nikki Haley, who said in March 2016, "I'm an accountant; I'm telling you there's no audit that precludes you from showing your tax return . . . Donald Trump, show us your tax return."[50] Sen. John McCain (R-AZ) and Sen. Ted Cruz (R-TX) also said Trump should release his taxes. Cruz, running against him in the primaries, went further, arguing "He doesn't want to do it because presumably there's something in there that is bad. If there's nothing, release them tomorrow." Rep. Jason Chaffetz of Utah added, "If you're going to try to run and become the president of the United States, you're gonna have to open up your kimono and show everything: your tax returns, your medical records . . ."[51]

Richard Painter similarly argued in an April 2017 article for transparency, and raised what he called the "mother of all conflicts questions: Does Trump have financial ties to Russia that motivated his bizarre embrace of Putin? Donald Trump Jr. has . . . asserted the importance of 'Russian' money to the family business. The president denies that but has refused to disclose his tax returns."[52]

However, most Republicans remained silent on the matter of Trump's taxes or else took the stance of House Speaker Paul Ryan, who had run for vice-president on the Romney ticket in 2016: "I did release my returns. I'll defer to Donald Trump as to when he thinks the appropriate time is to release his returns. I know he's under audit."[53] Later, when the House subpoenaed the taxes (and California passed a law saying candidates must release their tax returns to appear on the ballot), some Republicans, such as Senator Chuck Grassley and House Minority Leader Kevin McCarthy defended the president, saying the demand was partisan and would set a bad precedent.[54]

PRESIDENTIAL PARDONS: TRUMP'S UNCONVENTIONAL EXERCISE OF HIS CONSTITUTIONAL POWER

Article 2 of the Constitution gives the president the power to pardon individuals for federal crimes; the Supreme Court has ruled this power to be unlimited with regard to such crimes. While previous presidents, such as Lincoln, Ford, and Clinton have issued controversial pardons, Trump has drawn attention for his unusual approach. Where other presidents relied on recommendations from the Justice Department's Office of the Pardon Attorney—an office that generally recommends pardons only after an expression of remorse—Trump has bypassed the office and appears to follow his own counsel. He is also unique in the extent to which he has used the pardon for seemingly political purposes. His first pardon, Arizona sheriff Joe Arpaio, was convicted of contempt of court for refusing to carry out a court order related to a racial profiling case. In November 2019, he pardoned three servicemen accused of committing war crimes. Most presidents also typically wait till near the end of their term to issue high-profile pardons of associates and supporters, as Clinton did with fugitive financier Marc Rich.[55]

As will be discussed later, special prosecutor Robert Mueller suggested that Trump dangled pardons as an inducement for individuals not to cooperate with prosecutors, such as his former personal attorney Michael Cohen, campaign chair Paul Manafort, and former National Security Advisor Michael Flynn, who were under investigation and possessed potentially damaging information about the president. Indeed, the fear of the pardon being used this way was expressed by George Mason, a delegate to the Constitutional Convention, who said, "The President ought not to have the power of pardoning, because he may frequently pardon crimes which were advised by himself. . . . [I]f he has the power of granting pardons before indictment, or conviction, may he not stop inquiry and prevent detection?" While Mason's concern was dismissed, it is illuminating that the response by James Monroe referenced Congress's impeachment power as a safeguard against the president abusing the pardoning power.[56]

Several high-profile Republicans warned Trump against a pardon of Manafort, including Senators Susan Collins, John Thune, Bob Corker, and Lindsey Graham. Collins said it would be a "misuse of power" and Thune and Graham said that a pardon should "be earned." Corker asserted that pardoning Manafort "would be very damaging to the presidency."[57] Some Republicans also spoke out against the pardon of Arpaio. They asserted that Trump had used the pardon it in a way it was not intended to be used by the Founders. Arizona's two Republican senators, John McCain and Jeff Flake, and New Jersey governor Chris Christie, all criticized the pardon. Ohio governor John Kasich said it was "out of bounds" to use the pardon power as a "political wedge." House Speaker Paul Ryan, through his spokesman, said "The speaker does not agree with the pardon. Law enforcement officials have a special responsibility to represent everyone in the United States."[58] Vice-president of the conservative think tank American Enterprise Institute Danielle Pletka also suggested it was "absolutely staggering that he . . . chose to use the power of the presidency in this way."[59]

Republicans also criticized the pardons of the servicemen accused of war crimes—which were opposed by the Navy and Army secretaries—that put a stop to disciplinary action by the military against the three men. Senators Susan Collins, Mitt Romney, and Lisa Murkowski all said the pardons set a bad precedent and would undermine the system of military justice. "I do not believe the president should intervene in the military criminal justice system," said Collins.[60] Sen. Lindsey Graham similarly stated, "I am concerned that the system will feel intimidated and that if you intervene too early and too often that it's going to have a chilling effect." Senator Thom Tillis commented, "I don't know what circumstances led him to do it, but any time you get into that level of command you always give pause because you've got to always preserve that command component."[61] Other Trump pardons that seem to have political implications were for former Governor Rod Blagojevich, Bernard Kerik, Dinesh D'Souza, along with a series of wealthy convicts with political connections.

MUELLER INVESTIGATION

The Mueller investigation represented a comprehensive and serious challenge to the legitimacy and legality of Trump's presidency. Mueller, a registered Republican nominated to the position of FBI director by George W. Bush, was appointed special counsel in May 2017. He was tasked with overseeing an investigation into charges of Russian interference in the presidential election and links between the Trump campaign and the Russian government. Mueller was allowed by law to pursue matters beyond the initial subject of the investigation, based on information discovered during the course of the investigation. Like Clinton special prosecutor Ken Starr, Mueller would look into possible presidential obstruction of justice. In particular, he examined Trump's firing of FBI director James Comey and Comey's testimony that Trump asked him to "let go" an investigation into fired National Security Advisor Michael Flynn.[62]

Both Democrats and Republicans have challenged Trump's apparent attempts to influence the Mueller investigation and his labeling of the investigation as a partisan "witch hunt." In December 2017, twenty-two former U.S. attorneys, some of whom had served under Republican presidents, wrote a letter to Trump that they made public, saying it was "critical" to the "interests of justice and public trust to ensure that those charged with conducting complex investigations are allowed to do their jobs free from interference or fear of reprisal."[63] A second letter to Trump, signed by twenty-two Republican former members of Congress and former high-ranking officials—including former defense secretary Chuck Hagel and former State Department counselor Eliot Cohen—said Trump's attempts to discredit Mueller's work "undermine the institutions that protect the rule of law and (the) nation."[64]

Mueller submitted his report to Attorney General William Barr on March 22, 2018, complete with summaries he had drafted for public release. Two days later, Barr issued a letter, addressed to the House Judiciary Committee, which did not include Mueller's summaries; it stated that the evidence in the Mueller report was "not sufficient to establish that the President committed an obstruction of justice offense."[65]

A month later, the DOJ released a redacted version of the report. It makes clear that Mueller investigated ten possible acts of obstruction of justice by Trump, including directing White House counsel Don McGahn to tell the acting AG to say that Mueller had conflicts that disqualified him from serving. In his report, Mueller said there was "substantial evidence" that such acts by Trump were linked to Mueller's investigation of the president's and his campaign's conduct and were aimed at preventing "future scrutiny" of that conduct. The report also examined the possible floating of presidential pardons and concluded that Trump wanted his campaign chair Paul Manafort "to believe a pardon was possible."[66]

Attorney George Conway, the husband of Trump staffer Kellyanne Conway—a Republican who had been one of Paula Jones's lawyers in her lawsuit against Bill Clinton—defended the Mueller investigation, and blasted the president for calling it "sick and unlawful." Conway tweeted in May 2019, "The Russia investigation was a legitimate investigation, with a legitimate basis, into how a hostile foreign power tried to interfere with and undermine our democracy. It was in the best interests of . . . all Americans, no matter who they voted for, that this investigation be allowed to proceed to its rightful conclusion, without improper attempts to obstruct it."[67] Conway also said Trump had committed perjury when he "repeatedly lied" from the outset of Mueller's investigation.

Mueller gave a public statement on May 29, 2019, in which he refused to clear Trump of criminal wrongdoing, saying "If we had had confidence that the president clearly did not commit a crime, we would have said so. We did not, however, make a determination as to whether the president did commit a crime."[68] George Conway would put the first sentence on his Twitter feed bio preceded by the words: "Favorite quote."

Over 1,000 former federal prosecutors, some of them Republicans, signed a petition stating their belief that if Trump were not president, he would have been indicted on multiple obstruction charges for trying to "stop, limit and interfere with the Mueller investigation and other federal investigations surrounding him."[69] In a video released by Republicans for the Rule of Law, a conservative group, three former Republican-appointed prosecutors explained how they believed Trump had obstructed justice. The trio, Donald Ayer, Paul Rosenzweig, and Jeffrey Harris (respectively appointed by George H.W. Bush, Ronald Reagan, and George W. Bush) said Trump started interfering in the Russia investigation shortly after taking office, and concluded, "The worst obstruction of all was the president actively being involved to affect the testimony and cooperation of critical witnesses (Manafort, Flynn and Cohen)."[70]

The lone Republican voice in Congress stating a similar view to that of the prosecutors was House member Justin Amash (R-MI). Amash, who said he had read all 448 pages of the Mueller report, tweeted, "Contrary to [Attorney General William P.] Barr's portrayal, Mueller's report reveals that President Trump engaged in specific actions and a pattern of behavior that meets the threshold for impeachment . . . Mueller's report identifies multiple examples of conduct satisfying all the elements of obstruction of justice, and undoubtedly any person who is not the president of the United States would be indicted based on such evidence."[71] Fellow Republicans such as Kevin McCarthy called Amash's support for impeachment "very disturbing . . . I think he's just looking for attention."[72] One senator, Mitt Romney, did call Amash "courageous." However, Romney said he did not agree with Amash's conclusion about obstruction of justice; his comments on the Mueller Report were more nuanced and mixed than Amash's. Romney called it "good news" that there was "insufficient evidence" to charge President Trump with conspiracy or obstruction, but said he was "sickened at the extent and pervasiveness of dishonesty and misdirection by individuals in the highest office of the land, including the President."[73] The senator also said he was "appalled" that those in Trump's campaign "welcomed help from Russia" and didn't inform law enforcement authorities.

Amash later announced he was leaving the Republican Party, and said, "fellow colleagues and other Republicans, high-level officials (contacted) me, saying, 'Thank you for what you're doing.'"[74] *Washington Post* journalist Jennifer Rubin raised the question of "why Amash stands alone" in his public assertions about the Mueller Report. She concluded that the failure of congressional Republicans to join Amash in challenging Trump's (and Barr's) interpretation of the Mueller report, was rooted in at least two factors: cynicism—accepting Trump's misdeeds because they like the policies or viewpoints he promotes—or fear, of losing office or future jobs.[75]

Former administration official Omarosa Manigault Newman, not similarly constrained, said in a television interview after the Mueller report was released, "I knew that Donald Trump was instructing people to do things unethical or immoral—it also confirmed what I suspected, that he was doing things that were illegal" and added, "I really believe Donald Trump is going to go to jail. When he is leading chants—'Lock her up! Lock her up!'—I see the irony of that, because . . . he has committed so many different crimes . . . but ultimately he will have to pay for those crimes."[76]

UKRAINE AND IMPEACHMENT

After he seemed to dodge a bullet when the House did not take up impeachment proceedings following the release of the Mueller report, Trump found himself back in the crosshairs in the second half of 2019. The charges: breaking the law and abusing his power by soliciting foreign (Ukranian) interference in the 2020 election and using the power of the presidency to gain political advantage over his likely rival Joe Biden. A whistleblower complaint, filed in August 2019, raised concerns that Trump, in a July 2019 phone call with the new president of Ukraine, Vlodymyr Zelensky, conditioned $400 million in military aid to Ukraine on Zelensky's willingness to announce publicly an investigation into corruption, but specifically into a Ukrainian national gas company that paid Biden's son Hunter handsomely for serving on its board of directors. The call transcript was placed in a highly classified system, leading to accusations of a cover-up.[77] The president was also alleged to have enlisted surrogates within and outside the administration, including his personal attorney Rudy Giuliani and Attorney General Bill Barr, to pressure Ukraine to investigate a conspiracy theory that it, not Russia, had hacked a DNC server in an attempt to influence the 2016 election.

In September 2019, House Speaker Nancy Pelosi announced a formal impeachment inquiry into the Ukraine matter by six House committees. Witnesses were deposed during the following months, including the former and current ambassadors to Ukraine, National Security Council staffers, and former and current staff of the president and vice-president. The White House counsel announced that the president would not cooperate with the investigation and the president directed several top aides and former aides not to testify under subpoena. Much attention during the hearings was devoted to the question of whether there had been a "quid pro quo" (a demand for the exchange of "this for that"). White House chief of staff Mick Mulvaney at first said in an interview, "We do that all the time. Get over it," then issued a correction saying there was "absolutely no *quid pro quo*" and that Trump had only withheld military aid to Ukraine over concerns about the country's corruption.[78] However, the U.S. ambassador to the European Union testified, "Was there a quid pro quo? The answer is yes . . . Everyone was in the loop. It was no secret."[79]

On December 10, 2019, the House Judiciary Committee passed two articles of impeachment, one for abuse of power and the other for obstruction of Congress. On December 18, a formal impeachment vote took place on the House floor. On abuse of power, all House Republicans voted against. Two Democrats also voted against and one voted present. On the obstruction of Congress charge, all Republicans again voted no, as well as three Democrats who also voted no and one who voted present. Republican-turned-independent

Justin Amash voted for impeachment on both charges, stating, "President Donald J. Trump has abused and violated the public trust by using his high office to solicit the aid of a foreign power, not for the benefit of the United States of America but instead for his personal and political gain."[80]

While House Republicans were clearly united against impeachment, there were also notable fissures within the party and among conservative opinion writers. The day after the impeachment vote, the evangelical magazine *Christianity Today* published an editorial that said Trump "attempted to use his political power to coerce a foreign leader to harass and discredit one of the president's political opponents. That is not only a violation of the Constitution; more importantly, it is profoundly immoral." Editor-in-chief Mark Galli added, "We believe the impeachment hearings have made it absolutely clear, in a way the Mueller investigation did not, that President Trump has abused his authority for personal gain and betrayed his constitutional oath."[81] In response, almost 200 evangelical leaders including Jerry Fallwell Jr. and Mike Huckabee blasted *Christianity Today* for its support of "entirely-partisan, legally-dubious, and politically-motivated impeachment," echoing Trump's labeling of the magazine as "far left."[82]

The sixty-four-year-old magazine *National Review*, one of the earliest voices of the #NeverTrump movement, also waited just one day after impeachment to publish an opinion piece, "Four Tests for Impeachment." It laid out the case for how advocates for impeachment had met all four: "the facts they allege are true . . . (the) pattern amounts to an abuse of power or dereliction of duty by the president . . . this abuse or dereliction is impeachable . . . (and impeachment) would produce more good than evil." Author Ramesh Ponnuru concludes, "The Constitution provides for impeachment and removal to protect us from officials, including presidents, who are unable or unwilling to distinguish between the common good that government is supposed to serve and their own narrow interests. Though he has done some good things in office, Trump is just such a president. Congress should act accordingly."[83]

Also within days of the House vote, the group Republicans for the Rule of Law (RRL) ran a TV ad urging their fellow citizens to call their senators to demand that four key witnesses be called in the Senate impeachment trial. Three of the four—Chief of Staff Mick Mulvaney, Trump's personal attorney Rudy Giuliani, and Secretary of State Mike Pompeo—had ignored subpoenas to testify before the House; the fourth, security adviser John Bolton, was not issued a subpoena by the House after his attorney said he would fight it in court.[84] Bolton eventually said he was willing to testify. However, the Senate decided against calling any witnesses at all.

On the webpage of the group RRL, under the heading "Conservative Consensus," are quotes from GOP officials such as Massachusetts Governor

Charlie Baker, Vermont governor Phil Scott, Ohio Rep. Mike Turner, and several U.S. Senators: Ohio Sen. Rob Portman, Maine Sen. Susan Collins, Alaska Sen. Lisa Murkowski, Pennsylvania Sen. Pat Toomey, and Utah Senator Mitt Romney. Romney is quoted as saying, "I did read the transcript . . . clearly what we've seen from the transcript itself is deeply troubling." Toomey is also assertive in his criticism, arguing "Look, it is not appropriate for any candidate for federal office, certainly, including a sitting president, to ask for assistance from a foreign country." Senator Portman, agrees, saying "The president should not have raised the Biden issue on that call, period. It's not appropriate for a president to engage a foreign government in an investigation of a political opponent."[85]

Although Republicans like those quoted in the paragraph above have indicated they were open to removing the president from office, the Senate Majority leader—a key player in deciding whether the process moves forward quickly or slowly, thoroughly or not—was strongly supportive of Trump's assertion that the impeachment was a partisan hit job. McConnell stated, "Everything I do during this, I'm coordinating with the White House counsel. . . . There will be no difference between the president's position and our position as to how to handle this to the extent that we can . . . I'm going to take my cues from the president's lawyers."[86]

Alaska Senator Lisa Murkowski responded to McConnell's comment with " . . . when I heard that I was disturbed."[87] Murkowski's public statement put her in the minority among Republican senators. Others expressed that they were on the side of the president; for example, Sen. John Kennedy of Louisiana said the president's stated concern about corruption means he cannot be proven to have had a corrupt intent.[88] Ultimately, the Senate voted to acquit the President on both articles of impeachment. The only person voting against their party was Mitt Romney, who became the first Senator in U.S. history to support removing a president from their own party from office when he voted to convict on the charge of abuse of power. In the aftermath of his acquittal, President Trump began to purge his administration of officials deemed insufficiently loyal.

THE TRUMP ADMINISTRATION: CORRUPTION
AND CONFLICTS OF INTEREST

In addition to illegal or corrupt behavior by the president, there are numerous examples of conflicts of interest and illegal behavior by Trump's top advisors. Richard Painter refers to a "plethora of unethical conduct across the administration."[89] Six months into the Trump presidency, Painter charged that Trump had brought a large number of lobbyists and other persons into his administration with a vast array of personal financial conflicts of interest (exceeded only by those of the president himself). "The swamp has become a cesspool. . . . A number of the high-ranking officials in Trump's administration . . . insist upon maintaining their investments in various businesses, while at the same time conducting official U.S. government policy."[90]

Writing in June 2019, Jennifer Rubin suggests that Trump's pattern of "self-enrichment . . . (has) become de rigueur for his underlings."[91] The worst "cabinet-level ethics mess," asserted Painter, was Betsy DeVos, whose "extensive financial holdings present significant—and unresolved—conflict of interest issues."[92] Another notable example of ethically problematic behavior is former EPA director Scott Pruitt, who resigned after multiple scandals. These included paying "cut-rate" rent to live in a condo owned by a lobbyist, spending over $100,000 on first-class travel in his first year of office, and installing a $43,000 soundproof booth in his office that the GAO said violated federal spending laws.[93] Treasury secretary Ryan Zinke and Treasury secretary Steven Mnuchin also engaged in "questionable travel expenditures," and HHS secretary Tom Price stepped down after reports of his use of private jets at taxpayer expense. Price also had a history of questionable actions as a member of Congress on behalf of companies in which he held stock.[94] Commerce secretary Wilbur Ross failed to divest assets after promising to do so, and after telling ethics officials he had done so.[95]

Perhaps the most repetitive example of law-breaking by a Trump staffer is Kellyanne Conway, who the White House ethics office reported in a letter to Mr. Trump, was a "repeat offender" of the Hatch Act, violating it for example by criticizing Democratic presidential candidates on social media and in interviews.[96] #NeverTrump journalist Jennifer Rubin stated, "When caught as a multiple Hatch Act offender, Conway contemptuously asks when her jail sentence begins, suggesting rules are for little people."[97]

On the other hand, since leaving the Trump administration, several former administration officials have gone public and charged Trump with illegal or corrupt behavior. One noted above was Omarosa Manigault Newman, speaking after the release of the Mueller report. Fired Secretary of State Rex Tillerson also commented, in a December 2018 interview, "Often the president would say, 'Here's what I want to do, and here's how I want to do it, and I would have to say to him, 'Mr. President, I understand what you want to do, but you can't do it that way. It violates the law.'"[98] After the House impeachment proceedings, former communications director Anthony Scaramucci said of Trump's actions toward Ukraine, "We know that it's completely impeachable and completely illegal."[99]

NEPOTISM

Nepotism and conflicts of interest involving the president's daughter Ivanka Trump and her husband Jared Kushner have also been the subject of much criticism, that started when they became unpaid advisors with broad domestic and foreign policy portfolios.[100] Not only *The New York Times* and *The Washington Post*, but also the more right-leaning *Chicago Tribune*, have editorialized and run hard news stories with a predominantly negative tone about the couple's lack of qualifications and the conflicts stemming from their couple's overseas business dealings.[101] For example, *Chicago Tribune* writer Rex Huppke said of Ivanka, "If she expected women in the workplace to cheer her elevation to the White House, I think she's going to find that respect is earned, not bestowed."[102] Both Ivanka and Jared were roundly criticized because they did not fully divest from their fashion and real estate businesses, which are entangled with countries including China and Qatar. Richard Painter has stated that like her father, Ivanka may be in violation of the Emoluments Clause if she accepted payments or gifts from foreign government while working in the White House.[103]

Writing in December 2017, journalist Jennifer Rubin called Ivanka a "walking advertisement for the dangers of nepotism" and a "con woman . . . who looks out for herself and only herself."[104] In an op-ed two months earlier, Rubin had suggested that she and her husband "must go" due to Kushner's failure to disclose his foreign contacts when he applied for security clearance and the use of private emails by the couple to conduct White House business.[105] Rubin also points out that despite the DOJ under Trump saying it was not a violation of the federal anti-nepotism statute for them to serve in unpaid White House positions, for decades Justice Department lawyers had argued the opposite.

CONCLUSION

Of the #NeverTrumpers who have criticized Trump and his aides for illegal and corrupt behavior, ethics lawyer Richard Painter, op-ed writer Jennifer Rubin, attorney George Conway (founder of the Lincoln Project, an anti-Trump super PAC), and the group RRL have been perhaps the most vocal and sustained voices. Although Senators Marco Rubio and Ted Cruz made some remarks about Trump's business and tax practices while running against him in the primaries, once Trump took office, they became less vocal in their criticisms of the president for illegal and corrupt dealings. Another strong voice against Trump has been Justin Amash, who in May 2019, alone among congressional Republicans, said he believed Trump should be impeached for obstructing justice. Two months later, Amash left the GOP and declared himself an independent.

But for the most part, congressional Republicans have been largely silent or else actively supportive of Trump when he calls investigations or charges of illegality or corruption against him partisan and unfounded. Those who have spoken out on issues such as on pardons or impeachment—have tended to be ideological or temperamental moderates or establishment Republicans, such as Senators Collins and Murkowski, or defenders of "purist" conservative principles, such as Amash or Romney. What they have in common is a belief that Trump's actions, and those of firebrand, take-no-prisoners fellow Republicans, are bad for the party brand as well as for the nation. They also tend to come from districts or states where Trump did relatively poorly in 2016 (e.g., Utah or Maine). As such, these individuals have less to lose than members whose voters supported and continue to support Trump. For many members from strongly pro-Trump districts, the battles lines are clearly drawn, and they are solidly on Team Trump, wholeheartedly echoing the president's claim that charges of corruption and illegality—and calls for impeachment—are driven by partisanship and lack merit. Interestingly, this includes not just Freedom Caucus members such as Rep. Mark Meadows and Rep. Jim Jordan, but also some members who before Trump's election were considered establishment or moderate Republicans, such as Senator Lindsey Graham.

Some of the most powerful attacks by federal officials on Trump for illegal and corrupt behavior have come from former federal prosecutors and other ex-government officials. The voices of former Republican prosecutors and former high-ranking officials on whether Trump obstructed justice carry a unique punch. They come across as relatively objective given that they are not running for office and indeed are no longer serving in government. This group of individuals also has the training to understand the complex legal issues at stake. It is not surprising that they would be moved to take a stand, since working in the legal profession involves a deep understanding of the centrality of rule of law to democratic government. This understanding makes it more likely that someone would be disturbed by actions that cross the boundary separating legal from illegal conduct and would feel an imperative to speak out to defend the rule of law.

As we move forward in the last year of Trump's presidency, electoral incentives will undoubtedly continue to motivate Trump's fellow Republicans. Reelection-motivated GOP members of Congress will continue to consider the possible electoral cost of speaking out, particularly if they are from districts where Trump remains relatively popular. Rubio and Cruz had an electoral incentive to highlight Trump's law-breaking during the primaries. It can also be argued that Painter, who ran for Senate in Minnesota in 2018 as a Democrat, has some electoral incentive, in addition to a professional one as a lawyer, to play up every possible instance of wrongdoing by the president. It seems that most Republicans in Congress applying cost-benefit analysis to attacking Trump for illegality and corruption come down on the side of active or passive public support of the president, even if in private they find his actions problematic.

The big question, of course, is whether the cost and benefit components of that analysis will change in response to new information and shifts in public opinion, leading members who silently question the president to move with the political winds (and/or their own consciences) to open opposition. This is what happened with President Nixon immediately after the release of the "smoking gun" tape showing he knew of the cover-up. That dramatic turning point led House and Senate Republican leaders in August 1974 to go to the White House and tell Nixon that he would lose the votes on impeachment and conviction, after which he resigned.[106] Trump is a different person than Nixon, however; he relishes conflict and does not back down from a fight, making it unlikely he will resign. As of January 18, 2020, less than half of Americans polled supported removing Trump for office, with 84.1 percent of Democrats and only 8.1 percent of Republicans in favor.[107] The partisan skew in public opinion was nowhere near as extreme in Nixon's case, before or after the "smoking gun." By contrast, Republicans today, particularly those from safe or gerrymandered districts, are much more attentive to Republican public opinion and may feel themselves to be insulated from Democratic public opinion.

What is certain is that #NeverTrumpers such as former government ethics official Richard Painter, former GOP prosecutors, journalists such as Rubin and *National Review*, and a core of moderate/establishment elected officials such as Collins, Murkowski, and Romney, will continue to speak out, with varying degrees of intensity, on impeachment and on ongoing investigations by various state prosecutorial authorities. They have little to lose by doing so. Given that Trump's conflicts of interest will continue to exist as long as his domestic and overseas businesses flourish—and given that there are still conflict or corruption-plagued members of the administration—criticism on those fronts is also unlikely to abate.

The long-term impact of corruption under the Trump administration is an open question. History tells us that ethics scandals often lead to reform. Organizations such as the non-partisan National Task Force on Rule of Law and Democracy, a group of former public officials and policy experts (including Republican ex-senator and former defense secretary Chuck Hagel and former Republican Governor Christie Todd Whitman) have proposed various reforms that may gather steam as a result of the issues discussed in this chapter. These include requiring the president to publicly disclose his or her tax returns, passage of a law that articulates what sorts of payments and benefits are prohibited by the Emoluments Clause, strengthening of the Office of Government Ethics, passage of legislation clarifying standards for how the White House should interact with law enforcement to guard against presidential interference for personal or political aims, and requiring the president to provide written justifications to Congress for pardons involving close associates. The group warned in an October 2018 report, "If the ethics precedents set by President Trump are not addressed now, they could also balloon in future administrations."[108]

NOTES

1. David H. Bayley, "The Effects of Corruption in a Developing Nation," *Western Political Quarterly*, 19, no. 4 (December 1966), 720.

2. Dennis F. Thompson, *Ethics in Congress: From Individual to Institutional Corruption* (Washington, DC: Brookings, 1995).

3. Paula Baker, Mary Berry, Daniel Czitrom, Barbara Hahn, James Kloppenberg, Naomi Lamoreaux, and David Witwer, "Interchange: Corruption Has a History," *Journal of American History*, 105, no. 4 (March 2019), 918.

4. Soren Schmidt, "The Most Dangerous Form of Bribery," *The Atlantic*, December 6, 2019, https://www.theatlantic.com/ideas/archive/2019/12/most-dange rous-form-of-bribery/603103/.

5. Gail Savage, "Why the Founders Feared Foreign Influence in American Politics," *The Washington Post*, July 19, 2018, https://www.washingtonpost.com/ news/made-by-history/wp/2018/07/19/why-the-founders-feared-foreign-influence-in -american-politics/.

6. Michael Sozan, "The Founders Would Have Impeached Trump for His Ukraine-Related Misconduct," *Center for American Progress*, September 26, 2019, https://www.americanprogress.org/issues/democracy/news/2019/09/26/475114/fo unders-impeached-trump-ukraine-related-misconduct/.

7. Rachel Frazin, "'Lock Her Up' Chant Breaks Out at Trump Rally," *The Hill*, August 1, 2019, https://thehill.com/homenews/campaign/455874-lock-her-up-chant -breaks-out-at-trump-rally.

8. Randall Strahan and Daniel. J. Palazzolo, "The Gingrich Effect," *Political Science Quarterly*, 119, no. 1 (Spring 2004), 89–114.

9. Jamil Smith, "Trump's Alleged Crimes Are Just the Tip of His Legacy," *Rolling Stone*, December 19, 2018, https://www.rollingstone.com/politics/politics -news/trump-alleged-crimes-771181/.

10. Morris Kaplan, "Major Landlord Accused of Antiblack Bias in City," *The New York Times*, October 16, 1973, https://www.documentcloud.org/documents/ 2186612-major-landlord-accuse-of-antiblack-bias-in-city.html.

11. Jeff Spross, "A Brief History of Trump's Small Time Swindles," *The Week*, July 11, 2018, https://theweek.com/articles/783976/brief-history-trumps-smalltime -swindles; Steve Reilly, "USA Today Exclusive: Hundreds Allege Donald Trump

Doesn't Pay His Bills," *USA Today*, June 9, 2016, https://www.usatoday.com/story /news/politics/elections/2016/06/09/donald-trump-unpaid-bills-republican-president -laswuits/85297274/.

12. J. Michael Diehl, "I Sold Trump $100,000 Worth of Pianos. Then He Stiffed Me," *The Washington Post*, September 28, 2016, https://www.washingtonpost.com /posteverything/wp/2016/09/28/i-sold-trump-100000-worth-of-pianos-then-he-stiffe d-me/.

13. Spross, "A Brief History of Trump's Small Time Swindles."

14. IBEW Media Center, "In Washington D.C., Another Contractor Stiffed by Trump," March 8, 2017, http://www.ibew.org/media-center/Articles/17daily/1703/ 170308_AnotherContractor.

15. David Wright, "Marco Rubio: Not Going to Turn Over GOP to 'con artist' Donald Trump," *CNN,* February 26, 2016, https://www.cnn.com/2016/02/26/politics/ marco-rubio-donald-trump-morning-show-attacks/index.html.

16. Diehl, "I Sold Trump $100,000 Worth of Pianos."

17. David Cay Johnston, "Just What Were Donald Trump's Ties to the Mob?" *Politico*, May 22, 2016, https://www.politico.com/magazine/story/2016/05/donald- trump-2016-mob-organized-crime-213910.

18. David Barstow, Susanne Craig, and Russ Buettner,"Trump Engaged in Suspect Tax Schemes as He Reaped Riches from His Father," *The New York Times*, October 2, 2018, https://www.nytimes.com/interactive/2018/10/02/us/politics/donald -trump-tax-schemes-fred-trump.html

19. Barstow, Craig, and Buettner, "Trump Engaged."

20. Jennifer Rubin, "Donald Trump Cannot Close," *The Washington Post*, April 16, 2016, https://www.washingtonpost.com/blogs/right-turn/wp/2016/04/11/donald-t rump-cannot-close/.

21. Jennifer Rubin, "Morning Bits," *The Washington Post*, August 19, 2015, https://search-proquest-com.lp.hscl.ufl.edu/washingtonpost/docview/1705412513/67 C55D8E08094834PQ/1?accountid=10920.

22. City News Service, "$25m Settlement Finalized in Trump University Lawsuit," April 9, 2018, https://fox5sandiego.com/2018/04/09/25m-settlement-fina lized-in-trump-university-lawsuit/.

23. CNN Wire, "Romney Implores: Bring Down Trump," March 3, 2016, https:/ /whnt.com/2016/03/03/romney-implores-bring-down-trump/.

24. Cbsnews.com, Interview, February 26, 2016, https://www.cbsnews.com /video/marco-rubio-trump-trying-to-pull-off-biggest-scam-in-american-political-his tory; Shahien Nasiripour, "Marco Rubio's Attacks on Trump Are Breathtakingly Hypocritical," *Huffpost.com*, March 3, 2016, https://www.huffpost.com/entry/rubio -trump-university-attacks_n_56d5e169e4b0bf0dab338856.

25. Li Zhou, "Mueller Offers His Most Direct Critique of Trump Yet," *Vox.com*, June 24, 2019, https://www.vox.com/policy-and-politics/2019/7/24/20721214/robert -mueller-testimony-trump-wikileaks-problematic.

26. David A. Graham, "The Astonishing Transformation of Julian Assange," *The Atlantic*, January 5, 2017, https://www.theatlantic.com/politics/archive/2017/01/as sange-man-in-the-news/512243/.

27. Alexander Bolton, "GOP Senator: Assange 'Deserves to Spend the Rest of His Life in Prison,'" *The Hill*, April 11, 2019, https://thehill.com/homenews/senate /438381-gop-senator-assange-deserves-to-spend-the-rest-of-his-life-in-prison.

28. Aaron Blake, "Trump's Bogus 'Simple Private Transaction' Defense," *The Washington Post*, December 10, 2018, https://www.washingtonpost.com/politics/ 2018/12/10/trump-gops-dishonest-minimizing-stormy-daniels-payment/.

29. David Goldmacher, "Trump Foundation Will Dissolve, Accused of Shocking Pattern," *The New York Times*, December 18, 2018, https://www.nytimes.com/2018 /12/18/nyregion/ny-ag-underwood-trump-foundation.html.

30. Noah Bookbinder, and Norman Eisen, "Trump Foundation Dissolves, but Trump Abuses and Pursuit of Personal Gain Live On," *USA Today*, December 20, 2018, https://www.usatoday.com/story/opinion/2018/12/20/trump-foundation-dis solves-trump-white-house-ethics-abuses-continue-column/2361880002/.

31. Philip Hackney, "Trump and His Foundation Were Just Forced to Admit Their Fraud. Now the IRS Needs to Act," *NBC News*, November 14, 2019, https:// www.nbcnews.com/think/opinion/trump-his-foundation-were-just-forced-admit-the ir-fraud-now-ncna1081906.

32. Richard Painter, @RWPUSA, Twitter Post, July 20, 2019. 7:22 AM, https:// twitter.com/RWPUSA/status/1156208395579514880.

33. Sharon Lafreniere, Maggie Haberman, and Adam Goldman, "Trump Inaugural Fund and Super PAC Said to Be Scrutinized for Illegal Foreign Donations," *The New York Times*, December 13, 2018, https://www.nytimes.com/2018/12/13/us/ politics/trump-inauguration-investigation.html.

34. OutFront CNN, @OutFrontCNN, Twitter Post, December 14, 2018, 7:59PM, https://twitter.com/OutFrontCNN/status/1073744400990101505.

35. Norm Eisen, and Richard Painter, "Contempt for Ethics Hobbles Trump," *USA Today*, April 26, 2017, https://www.usatoday.com/story/opinion/2017/04/26/ contempt-ethics-hobbles-trump-painter-and-eisen/100891776/

36. Eisen and Painter, "Contempt for Ethics Hobbles Trump."

37. Beth A. Rosenson, "Explainer: The Trumps' Conflict of Interest Issues," *The Conversation*, April 19, 2017, https://theconversation.com/explainer-the-trumps-c onflict-of-interest-issues-75761.

38. Matt O'Brien, "Donald Trump Won't Do What Ronald Reagan, George H.W. Bush, Bill Clinton, and George W. Bush Did," *The Washington Post*, November 15, 2016, https://www.washingtonpost.com/news/wonk/wp/2016/11/15/ronald-reagan-d id-it-george-h-w-bush-did-it-bill-clinton-did-it-george-w-bush-did-it-donald-trump -wont-do-it/.

39. Richard Painter, "Trump's 'Blind Trust' Is Neither Blind Nor Trustworthy," *The Washington Post*, November 15, 2016, https://www.washingtonpost.com/opin ions/trumps-blind-trust-is-neither-blind-nor-trustworthy/2016/11/15/6eeca1fc-aaa5 -11e6-a31b-4b6397e625d0_story.html.

40. Richard Painter, "Trump Must Address Conflicts of Interest," *CNN*, November 18, 2018, https://www.cnn.com/2016/11/16/opinions/trump-potential-conflicts-inte rest-painter/index.html.

41. David B. Rivkin, Jr., and Lee A. Casey, "It's Unfair and Unrealistic to Make Trump Use a Blind Trust," *The Washington Post*, November 22, 2016, https://www.washingtonpost.com/opinions/its-unrealistic-and-unfair-to-make-trump-use-a-blind-trust/2016/11/22/a71aa1d4-b0c0-11e6-8616-52b15787add0_story.html.

42. Painter, "Trump's 'Blind Trust' Is Neither Blind Nor Trustworthy."

43. "Ethics Report on Trump Administration: The Most Unethical Presidency," *NPR*, January 16, 2018, https://www.npr.org/2018/01/16/578247224/report-trump-administrations-first-year-has-been-unethical.

44. Shelby Hanssen and Ken Dilanian, "Reps of 22 Foreign Governments Have Spent Money at Trump Properties," *NBC News*, June 12, 2019, https://www.nbcnews.com/politics/donald-trump/reps-22-foreign-governments-have-spent-money-trump-properties-n1015806.

45. Jennifer Rubin, "The Oval Office Is Not a Throne Room," *Salt Lake Tribune*, June 3, 2019, https://www.sltrib.com/opinion/commentary/2019/06/03/jennifer-rubin-oval/.

46. Alison Durkee, "Trump Blasts 'Phony Emoluments Clause' in Post-Doral Meltdown," *Vanity Fair*, October 21, 2019, https://www.vanityfair.com/news/2019/10/trump-g7-doral-emoluments-clause-phony.

47. Durkee, "Trump Blasts."

48. Durkee, "Trump Blasts."

49. Durkee, "Trump Blasts."

50. Vera Bergengruen, "Nikki Haley to Donald Trump: 'Bless Your Heart,'" *McClatchy DC Bureau*, March 1, 2016, https://www.mcclatchydc.com/news/politics-government/election/article63390032.html.

51. Zach Montellaro,"Chaffetz to Trump: Release Your Tax Returns," *Politico*, August 24, 2016, https://www.politico.com/story/2016/08/chaffetz-trump-tax-returns-kimono-227387.

52. Eisen and Painter, "Contempt for Ethics Hobbles Trump."

53. Matt DeBonis, "Paul Ryan Suggests, but Does Not Demand, That Trump Makes His Tax Returns Public," *The Washington Post*, September 15, 2016, https://www.washingtonpost.com/news/powerpost/wp/2016/09/15/paul-ryan-suggests-but-does-not-demand-that-trump-make-his-tax-returns-public/.

54. Jonathan Chait, "Republicans Are Trashing the Law to Keep Trump's Taxes Secret," *The National Interest*, April 2, 2019, http://nymag.com/intelligencer/2019/04/trump-tax-returns-secret-congress-law.html.

55. Adam Liptak, "How Far Can Trump Go in Issuing Pardons?" *The New York Times*, Mary 31, 2018, https://www.nytimes.com/2018/05/31/us/politics/pardons-trump.html.

56. Paul Rosenzweig, "'Take the Land': Trump Promises Pardons for Law-Breaking," Lawfare Blog, September 3, 2019, https://www.lawfareblog.com/take-land-trump-promises-pardons-law-breaking.

57. Alexander Bolton and Jordain Carney, "Republicans Warn Trump Against Manafort Pardon," *The Hill*, August 22, 2018, https://thehill.com/homenews/senate/403062-republicans-warn-trump-against-manafort-pardon.

58. Peter Nicholas, "House Speaker Paul Ryan Critciizes Donald Trump's Pardon for Joe Arpaio," *The Wall Street Journal*, August 26, 2017, https://www.wsj.com/articles/house-speaker-paul-ryan-criticizes-donald-trumps-pardon-for-joe-arpaio-1503781921.

59. Molly Redden, "'Out of Bounds': Republicans Criticize Trump over Joe Arpaio Pardon," *The Guardian*, August 27, 2017, https://www.theguardian.com/us-news/2017/aug/27/republicans-criticize-trump-joe-arpaio-pardon.

60. Alexander Bolton and Rebecca Kheel, "Republicans Raise Concerns Over Trump Pardoning Service Members," *The Hill*, December 3, 2019, https://thehill.com/policy/defense/472910-republicans-raise-concerns-over-trump-pardoning-service-members.

61. Bolton and Kheel, "Republicans Raise Concerns."

62. William Saletan, "How William Barr Won," *Slate*, July 26, 2019, https://slate.com/news-and-politics/2019/07/mueller-hearing-william-barr-trump-investigation-winner.html.

63. Jill Colvin, "Former US Attorneys, GOP Officials Come to Mueller's Defense," *AP News*, December 22, 2017, https://www.apnews.com/beafb3028620497b97864e970fd7deca.

64. Colvin, "Former US Attorneys, GOP Officials Come to Mueller's Defense."

65. Saletan, "How William Barr Won."

66. Robert S. Mueller III, U.S. Department of Justice, Alan Dershowitz, *The Mueller Report* (New York: Skyhorse Publishing, 2019).

67. George T. Conway III, @gtconway3d, "Think of It," Twitter Post. May 12, 2019. 5:01AM https://twitter.com/gtconway3d/status/1127544265243070464?lang=en.

68. "Full Transcript of Mueller's Statement on Russia Investigation," *New York Times*, May 29, 2019, https://www.nytimes.com/2019/05/29/us/politics/mueller-transcript.html.

69. Alexandra Hutzler, "Former Federal Prosecutors Renew Statement That Trump Would Have Been Indicted If He Weren't President," *Newsweek*, May 30, 2019, https://www.newsweek.com/former-federal-prosecutors-trump-indicted-wasnt-president-1439716.

70. "Former Federal Prosecutors Speak Out Against President Trump's Obstruction of Justice," You tube video, 5:25, posted by Republicans for the Rule of Law, May 30, 2019, https://www.youtube.com/watch?v=bwnMpneFR34.

71. Editorial Board, "Could This Be … a Republican with Backbone?" *The Washington Post*, May 20, 2019, https://www.washingtonpost.com/opinions/could-this-be--a-republican-with-backbone/2019/05/20/5eb8fa7c-7b1f-11e9-8ede-f4abf521ef17_story.html.

72. Julia Musto,"Trump Impeachment Call from Rep. Amash 'Very Disturbing,' Kevin McCarthy Says," *Fox News*, May 21, 2019, https://www.foxnews.com/politics/trump-impeachment-call-from-rep-amash-very-disturbing-kevin-mccarthy-says.

73. Julia Arciga, "Romney: I Am 'Sickened' by 'Dishonesty' of Trump Outlined in Mueller Report," *Daily Beast*, April 29, 2019, https://www.thedailybeast.com/mitt-romney-i-am-sickened-by-dishonesty-of-trump-outlined-in-mueller-report.

74. Justin Wise, "Amash: 'High-level' Republicans Privately Thanked Me for Supporting Trump Impeachment," *The Hill*, July 7, 2019, https://thehill.com/homen ews/house/451882-amash-high-level-republicans-privately-thanked-me-for-supp orting-trump.

75. Jennifer Rubin, "Why Justin Amash Stands Alone," *Statesman*, May 21, 2019, https://www.statesman.com/opinion/20190521/why-justin-amash-stands -alone.

76. Celebrity News, "Omarosa: 'I Really Believe Donald Trump Is Going to Go to Jail," *Extratv.com*, April 25, 2019, https://extratv.com/2019/04/25/omarosa-i-real ly-believe-donald-trump-is-going-to-go-to-jail/.

77. Pamela Brown, "CNN: White House Says Lawyers Directed Moving Transcript to Highly Secure System," *CNN*, September 27, 2019, https://edition.cnn. com/2019/09/27/politics/donald-trump-ukraine-transcript-white-house/index.html.

78. Stefan Becket, Grace Segers and Kathryn Watson, "Mulvaney Links Delay in Ukraine Aid to DOJ Investigation into 2016," *CBS News*, October 18, 2019, https:// www.cbsnews.com/live-news/trump-impeachment-inquiry-latest-kurt-volker-gordon -sondland-testimony-2019-10-17/.

79. Marshall Cohen, Ellie Kaufman, and Lauren Fox, "Five Takeways from Gordon Sondland's Bombshell Testimony," *CNN*, November 21, 2019, https://www .cnn.com/2019/11/20/politics/gordon-sondland-hearing-takeaways/index.html.

80. EJ Montini, "Does Rep. Justin Amash's Vote Make Impeachment Bipartisan?" *Arizona Republic*, December 19, 2019, https://www.azcentral.com/story/opinion/op -ed/ej-montini/2019/12/19/rep-justin-amash-voted-impeachment-does-make-biparti san/2696156001/.

81. Editorial, "Evangelical Magazine Christianity Today Calls for Trump's Removal After Impeachment," *The Guardian*, December 19, 2019, https://www .theguardian.com/us-news/2019/dec/19/trump-evangelical-christian-magazine-impea chment.

82. Scottie Andrew, "Christianity Today Says It Saw a Spike in Subscriptions After It Called for Trump's Removal," *CNN*, December 23, 2019, https://www.cnn .com/2019/12/23/politics/christianity-today-mark-galli-trump-op-ed-trnd/index.html.

83. Ramesh Ponnuru, "Four Tests for Impeachment," *National Review*, December 19, 2019, https://www.nationalreview.com/magazine/2019/12/31/four-tests-for-impe achment/#slide-1.

84. Mary Papenfuss, "Witnesses 'Must Testify' at Impeachment Trial, Declares GOP Group, 'Call Your Senators,'" *Huffpost*, December 21, 2019, https://www.huf fpost.com/entry/republicans-for-the-rule-of-law-impeachment-witnesses_n_5dfec4af e4b0843d35fd0c00?.

85. "Conservative Consensus," *Republicans for the Rule of Law*, accessed on March 9, 2020, https://www.ruleoflawrepublicans.com/.

86. David Cohen, "Sen. Murkowski 'Disturbed' by McConnell's Approach on Impeachment," *Politico*, December 25, 2019, https://www.politico.com/news/2019/ 12/25/lisa-murkowski-impeachment-089767.

87. Cohen, "Sen. Murkowski 'Disturbed' by McConnell's Approach."

88. Ponnuru, "Four Tests for Impeachment."

89. Eisen and Painter, "Contempt for Ethics Hobbles Trump."

90. Eisen and Painter, "Contempt for Ethics Hobbles Trump."

91. Rubin, "The Oval Office Is Not a Throne Room."

92. Norm Eisen and Richard Painter, "The Ethics Case Against Betsy Devos," *The Hill*, February 6, 2017, https://thehill.com/blogs/pundits-blog/the-administration /317975-the-ethics-case-against-betsy-devos.

93. Oliver Millman, "A Scandal for All Seasons: Scott Pruitt's Ethics Violations in Full," *The Guardian*, June 10, 2018, https://www.theguardian.com/environment/ 2018/jun/10/scott-pruitt-epa-administrator-scandal-list.

94. Gregory Krieg, "The Trump Administration's Scandals and Embarrassments All in One Place," *CNN*, April 27, 2018, https://www.cnn.com/2018/04/27/politics/ trump-administration-scandals-and-embarrassments/index.html.

95. Center for Public Integrity, "'Not in Compliance': Wilbur Ross, The Trump Official Who Keeps Watchdogs Up at Night," *The Center for Public Integrity*, February 27, 2019, https://publicintegrity.org/federal-politics/wilbur-ross-ethics-trum p-commerce-oge/.

96. Grace Segers, "Federal Watchdog Recommends Kellyanne Conway Be Removed from Job Over Repeat Hatch Act Violations," *CBS News*, June 13, 2019, https://www.cbsnews.com/news/kellyanne-conway-hatch-act-violation-osc-federal -watchdog-special-counsel-trump-advisor-political-statements/.

97. Rubin, "The Oval Office Is Not a Throne Room."

98. Aaron Blake, "Rex Tillerson on Trump: 'Undisciplined, Doesn't Like to Read' and Tries to Do Illegal Things," *The Washington Post*, December 7, 2018, https://www.washingtonpost.com/politics/2018/12/07/rex-tillerson-trump-undiscipl ined-doesnt-like-read-tries-do-illegal-things/.

99. Jason Lemon, "Ex-Trump Official Anthony Scaramucci Warns of 'Crisis in Our Democracy' If Republicans Don't Remove President," *Newsweek*, November 4, 2019, https://www.newsweek.com/ex-trump-official-anthony-scaramucci-warns-cr isis-our-democracy-if-republicans-dont-remove-1469617.

100. Beth A. Rosenson, "Presidential Nepotism in Historical Perspective," Paper presented at the Southern Political Science Association conference, Austin, TX, January 7–9, 2019.

101. Rosenson, "Presidential Nepotism in Historical Perspective."

102. Rex Huppke, "Ivanka Trump's 'Seat at the Table' Not Inspiring Many Women in the Workplace," *Chicago Tribune*, March 24, 2017, https://www.chicagot ribune.com/business/careers/ct-ivanka-trump-women-huppke-work-advice-0326-biz -20170323-column.html.

103. Alexander Wong, "House Democrats Are Quietly Asking Questions About Ivanka," *Vanity Fair*, March 14, 2019, https://www.vanityfair.com/news/2019/03/ ivanka-trump-house-democrats-investigation.

104. Jennifer Rubin, "Ivanka Trump Is a Walking Advertisement for the Dangers of Nepotism," *The Independent*, December 22, 2017, https://www.independent .co.uk/voices/ivanka-trump-nepotism-incompetence-donald-trump-jared-kushner-w hite-house-a8123686.html.

105. Jennifer Rubin, "Jared Kushner and Ivanka Trump Must Go," *Salt Lake Tribune*, October 4, 2017, https://www.sltrib.com/opinion/commentary/2017/10/04/jennifer-rubin-jared-kushner-and-ivanka-trump-must-go/.

106. Richard Grier, "Richard Nixon's Resignation: The Day Before, a Moment of Truth," *Christian Science Monitor*, August 7, 2014, https://www.csmonitor.com/USA/Politics/Decoder/2014/0807/Richard-Nixon-s-resignation-the-day-before-a-moment-of-truth.

107. Aaron Bycoff, Ella Koeze, and Nathaniel Rakich, "Do Americans Support Removing Trump from Office?" *FiveThirtyEight*, December 25, 2019, https://projects.fivethirtyeight.com/impeachment-polls/

108. Brennan Center for Justice, "Proposals for Reform: National Task Force on Rule of Law & Democracy," October 2, 2018, https://www.brennancenter.org/our-work/policy-solutions/proposals-reform-national-task-force-rule-law-democracy.

Part III

CONCLUSION

Chapter 12

#NeverTrumpism and American Politics

Past, Present, and Future

Jeff R. DeWitt and Andrew L. Pieper

Donald Trump's shocking victory in the 2016 presidential election ushered in a profound reshaping of American politics and policy. His historic impeachment and subsequent acquittal exacerbated the already deep divisions between his supporters and critics. This collection focuses on the ways in which Donald Trump has reshaped the Republican Party and the conservative movement in the United States and how and why he has received an unprecedented level of pushback from a vocal group of prominent co-partisans and conservative thought leaders. Contributors detail the various ways that Donald Trump has accelerated shifts already underway in the GOP while he simultaneously undermines other long-standing elements of American conservative traditions. #NeverTrump critics discussed in these pages are mostly heretofore well-respected, establishment-oriented Republicans and stalwart conservatives who are appalled by Trump's policy positions, his behavior, and chiefly concerned about his potentially long-lasting impact on the GOP and the American democratic system.

This concluding chapter has several goals. First, we will summarize the overarching themes outlined by chapter contributors, placing them in the larger context of the prevailing conflict between Trump and his #NeverTrump adversaries. Second, we will explore some key opportunities and challenges that Trumpism poses for the Republican Party broadly speaking, with particular focus on the counter policies and principles espoused by #NeverTrump conservatives. Finally, we will assess the potential short-term and long-term impact of the Trump era on American politics and policy, paying particular attention to shifting party systems and ideological cleavages.

KEY FINDINGS

It serves us well to first highlight the broad themes explored in the previous pages. Chapter contributors analyzed #NeverTrumpers from a variety of academic perspectives. Although disparate in important ways, we note that several refrains emerged. First, we will discuss motivations that have fueled #NeverTrump opposition, and the resulting impact on the future of the Republican Party and American politics more generally. At the same time, the undeniable reality is also that many, if not most, Trump skeptics eventually came to embrace the mad genius of Trump. As such, we will highlight the varying explanations for "Eventual Trumpism" in order to glean lessons from their apparent change of hearts.

Why #NeverTrumpers

The core finding of this volume is that #NeverTrumpers are motivated by a variety of factors. Some critics, especially conservative institutionalists, libertarians, and intellectuals in the Burkean tradition, view Trump's ignorance of the Constitution—and unappreciation of its constraints—as a threat to democracy in the United States and around the world. Various interest groups, think tanks, and anti-Trump legal societies, such as Defending Democracy Together and the Lincoln Project, make this case. They are led by disenchanted Republican thought leaders, legal practitioners and scholars such as William Kristol and George Conway III. As highlighted in chapters 10 and 11, many consider Trump's character to be so deficient that the United States as a whole—and the GOP in particular—is being corroded by having such a detestable leader at the helm. As *Christianity Today* put it, "Can we say with a straight face that abortion is a great evil that cannot be tolerated and, with the same straight face, say that the bent and broken character of our nation's leader doesn't really matter in the end?"[1]

Initially, many #NeverTrumpers were also driven to action out of deep concern for both the short-term and long-term prospects of the Republican Party, as they viewed Trumpism as a sure fire way of destroying it from within.[2] A key component of their fear was the stark realization of just how far Trump and his small circle of loyalists had strayed from the collective wisdom of party elites such as those who, with an eye toward electoral viability, drafted the Growth and Opportunity Project Report (GOPR) in 2013. Trump's anti-immigrant messaging and often politically incorrect, inflammatory campaign rhetoric may have helped create the populist fervor necessary to catapult him to victory. However, as discussed throughout this volume (see chapter 6, in particular), establishment-oriented #NeverTrumpers believe that such rallying cries are obstacles to sustained electoral success. Results from recent elections serve to validate fears that by tethering itself to blatant ethnic nationalist messaging (under the guise of "populism"), the GOP creates a barrier, a "wall" if you will, between the party and success given imminent demographic shifts within the American public.

One of the principal concerns expressed by conservative thought leaders was that the Trump era would represent a destruction of bedrock, tried-and-true, principles and policy positions upon which the movement, and in turn the Republican Party, has been built. Some critics have left the party, which they claim represents Trump the man more than the values upon which the GOP had flourished, electorally and ideologically, under previous presidents. As chronicled in chapter 1 and by Johnson and Amira in chapter 4, no moment of the 2016 campaign signaled the American Right's discomfort with Donald Trump more than the publication of a special edition of the conservative magazine *National Review*. In February 2016, as candidate Trump was gaining momentum, the longtime stalwart of traditional Burkean-style conservatism published an entire issue detailing the reasons it could not support the Trump campaign effort. Other important conservative media outlets and writers joined the chorus, and figures such as George Will and William Kristol bemoaned the rise of Trump and his takeover of the Republican Party and conservative movement. Three years later, in 2019, former Republican congressmember and presidential candidate Joe Walsh similarly questioned Trump's conservative bona fides. He argued:

> And despite what his enablers claim, Mr. Trump isn't a conservative. He's reckless on fiscal issues; he's incompetent on the border; he's clueless on trade; he misunderstands executive power; and he subverts the rule of law . . . Enough, sir. We've had enough of your indecency. We've had enough of your lies, your bullying, your cruelty, enough of your insults, your daily drama, your incitement, enough of the danger you place this country in every single day. [3]

Donald Trump's message resonated powerfully with rural officeholders who embraced his populist tirades against big banks, international trade deals, and loose borders. However, as outlined by Anthony Sparacino in chapter 3, Republican officeholders from states with large populations of color and significant international trade agreements were alarmed by Trump's rhetoric and policy proposals. Many were also concerned with how his candidacy would affect down-ballot races in purple and blue states. His tenure as president did little to assuage these fears, as even rural areas were damaged by trade wars and unfulfilled promises of infrastructure plans. Several state lawmakers from suburban districts, in particular, have abandoned the GOP with one, in particular, announcing: "My core values that originally drew me to the

Republican Party, have not changed, but the party which once echoed the vision of Ronald Regan no longer exists."[4]

As detailed by Heather Yates in chapter 5, conservative-leaning think tanks faced a major conundrum with the Trump candidacy and presidency, a conundrum characterized by tremendous political uncertainty. Donald Trump's abject lack of consistent positions or conservative principles meant that think tanks did not know where to best initiate and nurture their relationship with the newly elected Republican president. They were also hampered because many of the traditional actors engaged in Washington politics were not only excluded from the orbit of the Trump campaign and White House but were derided as part of the problem itself, part of the "swamp." Some groups were able to overcome these challenges, as they calculated the best way forward was to simply embrace and engage with his transactional political instincts where loyalty is the premium commodity. Others, however, remain sidelined, either by choice or by unforgiving political circumstances, viewing his policies as damaging to the conservative cause or they are weary of embracing a president so unwilling to engage in traditional norms of relationship-building. It should be noted that most of these groups are rarely outwardly hostile toward Trump, preferring instead to wait patiently or otherwise pick their moments, engaging in limited strategic ways in order to protect or advance their interests.

Among policy experts and observers, President Trump's inexperience in foreign affairs was among the most alarming deficiencies in his knowledge. His campaign adopted mainstream Republican positions on key issues, including immigration policy, commitment to Israel, and steadfast expressions of adherence to the "peace through strength" doctrine. On other issues, such as free trade, U.S. involvement in NATO, and commitment to multilateralism, Trump ignored traditional conservative norms. Many questioned whether his temperament and off-the-cuff, provocative style might lead to frayed relationships or plunge the nation into poorly planned or even accidental military engagement. Moreover, President Trump's dismissal of the U.S. intelligence community and apparent willingness to embrace authoritarianism abroad left conservatives both flabbergasted and scrambling to contain any eventual real-world fall-out. In chapter 6, Wes Renfro explores how establishment conservatives recoiled from the policy and stylistic shibboleths that President Trump shattered and expressed concern that his temperament and impulsiveness could detrimentally impact international security.

Establishment-oriented Republicans also questioned the wisdom of a variety of Trump's domestic policies. Of particular concern were his claims that citizens could expect dramatically expanded control over their health care as part of "repeal and replace," as well as occasional statements that taxes should be raised on the wealthy, and exaggerated claims regarding immigrants and U.S. immigration policy. Broadly speaking, Trump seems aligned with the rhetoric of U.S. conservatives but with a defiant populist streak that seemed at times imprudent and unpredictable. In chapter 7, Robert (Bo) Wood examines how Trump's policy inexperience, populist tendencies, and uneven temperament drove away reticent conservatives and moderate Republicans on the issues of trade policy, fiscal responsibility, and immigration and border security, in particular.

Since the Reagan-era marriage of Burkean-style conservatives and free market libertarians, the Republican Party has championed central tenets of an internationalist foreign policy, free market, and small government economic policies rooted in deregulation, and "family values" oriented social policies. President's Trump's long-standing association with progressive-minded Democratic policy positions, in addition to his brash New York celebrity persona, questionable personal relationships (both international and domestic) and business practices meant that many conservative Republicans viewed him as far too unreliable to trust with the presidency. Paskewich, in chapter 9, details how traditional conservatives feared Trump's impact on the movement and expressed unease with his apparent willingness to blow wherever the political winds may take him. Along these lines, Senator Jeff Flake (R-AZ) laments how his party has strayed from its moorings, and its adherence to ideological principle:

> Rather than fighting the populist wave that threatened to engulf us, rather than defending the enduring principles that were consonant with everything that we knew and had believed in, we pretended that the emperor wasn't naked. Even worse: We checked our critical faculties at the door and pretended that the emperor was making sense. . . . It is a testament to just how far we fell in 2016 that to resist the fever and to stand up for conservatism seemed a radical act.[5]

Supporters and detractors alike agree that we have never seen a candidate or president quite like Donald Trump. Fans applaud his tendency to flout, and even mock, polite society and "speak his mind" without regard for "political correctness." More traditional conservatives (in terms of ideological orientation as well as personal respect for measured temperament in general), however, view his willingness to routinely engage in provocative and incendiary rhetoric, and his tendency to find comity with fringe conspiracy theories, openly disparage even his fellow Republicans, and inability to restrain damaging impulses, to be disqualifying. In chapter 10, Martin Cohen discusses conservatives who were particularly troubled by Trump's tenuous connection with truth, eagerness to thrust extreme beliefs into the mainstream, and inability to conform to what they view as the inherent dignity of the office. Cohen chronicles, accordingly, how Trump has shattered countless norms of good character we have grown to expect from our leaders—indeed, he has violated all seven of the deadly sins—to the consternation of those in the conservative movement and the Republican Party.

Donald Trump—before and after becoming candidate and the forty-fifth president of the United States—has exhibited a tenuous relationship with the law. Claims of housing discrimination, broken contracts, and connections to organized crime dogged his pre-political life. As a candidate, his campaign was accused of encouraging (perhaps even coordinating with) Russian operatives to distribute embarrassing stolen emails from the Clinton campaign. As president, he found himself under investigation by Special Counsel Mueller, various congressional committees, and been accused of numerous malfeasance, including violations of the public trust, and of impeachable and even criminal actions. Soon after taking office, government ethics experts noted that the president and those around him, such as Jared Kushner and his daughter Ivanka Trump, failed to properly distance themselves from business interests. Some even suggest he has used his position to benefit financially. His administration has been beset not only by two historic investigations—the Mueller investigation into Russian interference and an impeachment inquiry, which resulted in two articles (abuse of power and obstruction of Congress) approved of in the House and, ultimately, acquittal in the Senate—but also claims of rampant misuse of government funds by staffers and cabinet appointees. Beth Rosenson, in chapter 11, addresses the many questions about illegality and corruption that have plagued Trump and those around him, and how conservatives have been some of the most vocal critics, sounding alarms.

Rise of the Eventual Trumpers

Even amid that wide array of principled critiques from Republicans and conservatives, however, the fact remains: many of those who launched into opposition mode—some as early as 2015—would eventually come to defend or even embrace Trump and his presidency. *Washington Post* columnist Jennifer Rubin seeks answers to the pressing question: "Why are Republicans such quivering sycophants, willing to lie and debase themselves in support of an unpopular president who is repudiating many of the principles they have spent their lives advancing?" She identifies several categories of these eventual or reluctant Trumpers, including "cynics" who resort to working with Trump to generate whatever favorable outcomes they can, the "scaredy-cats" who sacrifice principle for the purpose of political or professional self-preservation, and the "cranks, the zealots, the racists, and the haters" who see themselves as victims, relishing the opportunity to strike back at society from a place of bitter resentment.[6]

Indeed, "eventual Trumpism" has become a common "fall back" position for several reasons. Simply put, Trump as president has ended up serving as a suitable deliveryman for the GOP agenda from a few key policy perspectives (though he was not nearly as effective as he could, or perhaps should, have been, as Lazarus details in chapter 2). He has appointed judges, signed tax bills, and supported regulatory reforms that largely align with conventional Republican priorities. For some skeptics who were concerned about his reliability in the areas of domestic policies, this became reason enough to hop aboard the Trump train. Rich Lowry, editor in chief of *National Review*, and likely author of the original "Against Trump" editorial salvo, clarifies "One of the giant ironies of this whole phenomenon for us is that Trump represents a cartoonish often exaggerated, version of the direction we wanted to see the party go in."[7] However, much of the early (and later) opposition was so fundamental that mere policy victories cannot explain the evolution of former critics.

For many, the simplest explanation is the best; it is about survival. President Trump has overtaken the Republican Party—he now *is* "the establishment"—and anyone who expresses public, or even private, criticism risks losing her or his position not only as an elected official, but also in the broader community of the GOP. A long understood "canonical claim is that lawmakers are single-minded seekers of re-election."[8] Lawmakers engage in persistent "position-taking" in order to better ensure they maintain positions in power.[9] The reality is simple: "You can't get elected in the Republican Party today being opposed to Trump."[10] Only a small number of public officials, especially at the national level, have held onto their status while exhibiting anything other than sheer obedience to him.

In chapter 2, Jeffrey Lazarus explores the remarkable conversion to support status by numerous congressmembers who were once very outspoken in their criticism. While many legislative leaders and rank-and-file lawmakers expressed opposition to Donald Trump during his candidacy, since his inauguration as president outspoken defiance has been at best sporadic and most often muted. We all recall the historic moment when Senator McCain delivered the decisive "thumbs down" verdict on the president's signature domestic policy item—repeal of Obamacare. Similarly, Senators Flake, Collins (R-ME), and Murkowski (R-AK) stood up to Trump in rejecting the "fast track" vote on Justice Kavanaugh until the FBI could conclude an investigation of new allegations. However, only Murkowski withheld support from the nominee in the end. Collins, in particular, has become the benchmark by which "Eventual Trumperism" is considered. After explaining "Why I cannot support Trump" in the pages of *The Washington Post* in August 2016, it has become increasingly clear that she has "gambled her legacy" on him, frequently expressing "concern" and "disappointment" for the president's behavior while claiming he "learned his lesson" as she voted to acquit on both articles of impeachment.[11] As of this writing, the senator has declined to say whether she will support Trump's reelection bid.[12]

The pattern of wayward lawmakers voicing tepid disagreement or simply staying silent while failing to offer viable alternative courses of action was commonplace. "Scaredy-cat" congressmembers would almost always fall in line as a result of a crude political calculus—concerns about getting publicly and harshly shamed by Trump, losing support among constituents, and ultimately facing a viable primary challenge in the next election cycle. Several legislators, such as Marco Rubio (R-FL), Lindsey Graham (R-SC), Dean Heller (R-NV), and Mike Lee (R-UT) opted to set aside #NeverTrump status entirely and became some of the president's most ardent advocates in Congress. This support is out of expediency, not conviction. According to long time GOP consultant Michael Murphy and former Republican senator Jeff Flake, if there had been secret ballots, Trump would have been removed from office by his Republican senators.[13]

Tim Alberta, Politico's chief political correspondent, provides further insight. Even non-officeholders must maintain appearance of allegiance, noting that Republicans risk not only electoral defeat but also social and financial ostracization if they dare oppose Trump openly.[14] Indeed, the same trend toward eventual Trumpism was evident in conservative media. For example, talk radio host and conservative columnist Erick Erickson, who was once one of the president's most vocal critics, effectively caved and pledged his support. "Some of my concerns about President Trump remain. I still struggle on the character issue and I understand Christian friends who would rather sit it out than get involved. But I also recognize that we cannot have the Trump Administration policies without President Trump and there is much to like."[15]

Some observers claim the movement has "flamed out" as potential opponents failed to gain traction, or even a place on the ballots.[16] Rick Wilson, stalwart conservative critic, offers the counter argument as "NeverTrumpers have seen their profiles soar in disproportion to their actual influence among Republicans." He asserts, "There is merit in maintaining a rebel army . . . there is a moral case to be made for standing up for nonauthoritarian conservatism."[17] Charlie Sykes, a conservative former radio host in Wisconsin whose umbrage over Trump has gained him cable ubiquity and a book of his own (titled *How the Right Lost Its Mind*), echoes this sentiment. "I'm not going to pretend that I'm not disappointed that we've had this attrition . . . It's been this rolling, soul-crushing disappointment, watching people that you thought you knew." Sykes adds that this has only strengthened his conviction. "It's really not a hard choice," he said. "There are advantages to being an only child."[18] At the end of the day, NeverTrumpers may not so much represent a political movement as they are a "slingshot army aimed at a single target."[19]

A major assumption that motivated this project from its original inception is that the two-party system is an essential feature of American politics, and that if it is true that Donald Trump is a threat to the viability of the Republican Party, then the two-party system itself is also in jeopardy. While liberals and Democrats may cynically celebrate this as a desirable outcome, most objective observers would view the implosion of the GOP with trepidation. As it stands now, Republicans seem to have weathered the storm of the 2018 midterms, and remain united behind the president. A more careful consideration, however, makes clear that the Republican Party's position as anything other than a permanent minority status is due at least in part to the hyper-effective gerrymandering in the states it controls, the undemocratic allocation of Senate seats, and rural state tilt of the Electoral College.[20] Regardless, Trump's victory has both re-energized the Republican Party and shaken its core foundations. In the following section, we highlight some opportunities and challenges that the GOP must navigate in the age of Trump and beyond.

OPPORTUNITIES FOR THE TRUMP-ERA GOP

President Trump's 2016 victory presents the Republican Party with three key opportunities. The first—alignment of both governmental and nongovernmental institutions for the pursuit of the GOP's long-term goals—has been in motion for a couple decades but is now nearly fully realized. Specifically, we have seen conservative media, including mainstay behemoths such as Fox News, talk radio, *The Wall Street Journal*, and smaller outlets like RedState, Breitbart, and Sinclair Broadcasting, largely coalesce around Trump and his supporters. An additional part of GOP-friendly institutional alignment is that the party, for all practical purposes, has secured control of the federal court system for the foreseeable future. Neil Gorsuch, rather than Merrick Garland, replaced Antonin Scalia, and dependable conservative Brett Kavanaugh has replaced reluctant moderate Anthony Kennedy on the U.S. Supreme Court. Barring something drastic, conservatives will dominate the Supreme Court for a generation, likely overhauling national jurisprudence in a way not seen since the Warren Court. Lower courts are now dominated by conservative justices as well, many of them protecting Trump and the GOP through their rulings, which promote executive power and conservative interests.

Finally, the GOP's status is bolstered by impressive gerrymandering efforts, which is of course not new but has reached a level of professionalism through the skilled use of modern technology, systematically sorting, stacking, and packing based on well-defined geographic patterns. Many experts believe the Republican Party could regularly win U.S. House majorities even when they lose the overall U.S. House vote.[21] State officials are more willing (and able, thanks to the courts) to construct obstacles to voting for those less inclined to pull the lever for the GOP. These entrenched advantages were developed over a long period of time but were cemented with Trump's victory and his continued ability to command the allegiance of other conservatives.

A second opportunity for the GOP was not necessarily guaranteed at the beginning of 2016, but now seems assured—an engaged, mobilized base of supporters. The 2016 Republican primary field was the largest ever and was populated by Republicans from across the spectrum (even George Pataki was resurrected from the twentieth century). The party was divided over whether to pursue more moderate policy positions to appeal to changing demographic and economic realities, as promoted in the GOPR, or whether to double down on the culture wars and anti-government rhetoric. Such divisions no longer exist, and the GOP has Trump to thank for clarifying the "correct" positions to take and, in doing so, unifying the party. Donald Trump—his rallies, the devotion he has cultivated in the conservative media, the domination of the Trump brand throughout the GOP—has answered the question. The party of Reagan has become the party of Trump. Conservative thinker Victor Davis Hanson makes "The Case for Trump," asserting "In counter intuitive fashion, the provocative and often off-putting Trump proved to be a far more effective uniter of his party than had any prior elected populist maverick."[22] Damon Linker agrees, proclaiming that "The faction that ran the show from 1981-2016 . . . is finished, caput, dead, and buried."[23] He adds that [#NeverTrumpers] "Jonah Goldberg, Michael Gerson, and George F. Will could talk the ghost of Ronald Reagan himself into challenging Trump in 2020, and Trump would trounce him."[24]

For the foreseeable future, the GOP will find millions of votes ready to be activated and mobilized with cries of defiance against open borders, persecution of Christians, political correctness, (non-white) identity politics, and internationalism. Many Republicans who may have once been skeptical of nativist anti-conservative populism have since largely adopted it as fundamental to Republicanism today (thus their inclusion in the "Eventual Trumper" camp). Fractured by intra-party infighting as recently as 2016, the GOP now finds itself far more unified, if slightly smaller, as 2020 unfolds. While, as contributors to this volume point out, there is no consensus about what it means to be a "conservative." However, appeals rooted in festering perceptions of "status threat" and fueled by symbolism and "negative ideology" (that is, opposition to that which conservatives perceive to be "liberal") should pay political dividends by encouraging ideological loyalty, if not operational integrity.[25] Institutional advantages, as discussed, above also mitigate the GOP's slightly smaller size.

A third opportunity that Trump presents the Republican Party is the ability to reinvigorate its once stale policy paradigms. While corporate tax cuts and free trade still assume maximal status, Trump's emphasis on immigration, trade restrictions, foreign policy isolationism, and "insurance for everybody" indicates shifting rhetoric and priorities that are clearly popular at his rallies and also play well on conservative media.[26] It is not clear whether these new policy priorities will be engaged by other policymakers, as tax cuts, deregulation, and anti-government vengeance—rather than fundamental trade reforms, permanent immigration fixes, and genuine health care reform—have dominated GOP policymaking during Trump's term. It could well be that as time passes, Republican Party policymaking, insofar as a coherent agenda is evident, will better reflect the priorities and will of its base. Trumpsim, as defined, would provide it cover.

CHALLENGES FOR THE TRUMP-ERA GOP

The GOPR (2013) was written in the wake of the 2012 elections by veteran party members and conservatives intimately familiar with the strengths and weaknesses of the party's position given the state of play in national politics. Donald Trump has certainly reinvigorated the GOP base and mobilized loyalists that had largely felt disenchanted and directionless. In this age of extreme polarization, he has also ginned up the opposition, and, as a result, cost the party support among educated white voters, especially women in the suburbs.[27] The future of the GOP is brighter than it was in October 2016, but policy and political challenges remain.

On the policy front, one of the simplest obstacles to long-term success—beyond an election or two—is simple math. Despite a broad ideological preference for balanced budgets and restrained taxes and spending, the GOP has not been effective, in any measurable sense, at implementing its penchant for fiscal responsibility. Under Trump, budget deficits (even before Covid-19 economic stimulus) have skyrocketed to levels never seen outside of major economic downturns in the postwar era.[28] The Republican Party continues to cut taxes, while not implementing the fundamental entitlement reforms required to offset those tax cuts. It may very well be that, as many critics argue, Republicans only care about deficits when there is a Democrat in the White House.[29] At some point, however, rising deficit levels will become too unsustainable to ignore any longer; Former GOP congressmember and Governor Mark Sanford (R-SC) pulls no punches, asking why his fellow Republicans make excuses for Trump's deficits. "He is driving the country to financial ruin. And his own party is letting it happen."[30]

If Republicans are successful at cutting the deficit, it may come at the cost of losing elections, a price supposedly rational parties are unwilling to pay. Discretionary spending has been cut so deeply since the 1990s that there little fat left. As such, the GOP will need to decide between their "go to" policy instincts of tax cuts on the one hand and firmly grasping the "third rail" of entitlement spending on the other hand. The former is clearly popular, but the latter has proven to be a difficult sell. The simple fact is that voters and states that elect Trump and other Republicans benefit tremendously from entitlement spending, and less so from tax cuts. Ledgers do not lie, even if politicians do, and a Republican Party that successfully wins elections will be responsible for deficit spending unless they make hard choices—choices that will likely upset many in the GOP base.

Math also formed the impetus for the GOPR—the party must acknowledge and adapt to evolving demographics. As reported in a variety of outlets, the United States is becoming more diverse by a variety of measures. The GOP's base under Trump is more mobilized, but also smaller, and shrinking by the year. Young people in 2020 are abandoning the Republican Party—and conservative policies more generally—in waves.[31] These demographic realities were a dilemma in 2013 when the GOPR was written. They have only worsened.[32] These demographic changes are mitigated by the friendly allocation of voters in rural red states, which artificially inflates the party's electoral performance in terms of balance of power in the House of Representatives, the Senate, and in the Electoral College.

Without question, demographic challenges that existed prior to Trump are made worse by his policy proposals, rhetoric, and political tactics, which have driven away young moderates, voters of color, and women. In this way, the GOP writ large is a victim of Trump's success. To build a coalition large enough to effectively govern, it will need to figure out how to win in places where elderly, rural, white voters are not dominant. Former GOP Congressman David Jolly (R-FL) argues, "The Republican Party is in longterm trouble. The demographics of the nation are shifting away from hardcore Republican conservatism and they're basically doubling down on that while relying on these rigged elements of the system to help them keep power."[33] #NeverTrump Republican Mike Murphy agrees, suggesting that "only true suckers fight demography."[34]

Finally, as much as Trump has reinvented the Republican Party, it remains to be seen whether it can survive without him as a candidate. In other words, one of the greatest challenges is to maintain a party driven by Trumpism without Trump. His political skills, personal connection to voters and activists, ability to dominate the media, intimidate rivals, and, frankly, lie so convincingly and brazenly without remorse or blowback, are unique and unrivaled. Will the voters who flock to rallies and to polling booths to support Trump do the same when he is no longer on the ballot? His policies and priorities have changed the party, but can Marco Rubio convincingly rail against undocumented immigrants, or embrace authoritarian regimes? Will

Ted Cruz or Mike Pence bring enough personality to political rallies or be able to dominate a media cycle for weeks at a time?

The dilemma of a party built on the charisma of one individual is that eventually the person is gone. The Republican Party may be left with the wreckage of the policy and political challenges that Donald Trump wrought, but not have the "cult of personality" to hold it all together.[35] Mike Murphy agrees, and says "like all cults, it'll end badly" adding "The GOP went on a wild, stupid bender with Trump and now the hangover will be very painful."[36] Judging by the popularity of Trump family members with his base, it is conceivable that the Republican Party embraces a Trump family dynasty in the early twenty-first century to rival the Bush dynasty of the late twentieth century. The question is whether Republican senators and governors will put aside their pride (and ambition) to serve Ivanka or Donald Jr. the way Mitch McConnell and Lindsey Graham have for Donald J. Trump.

CONSEQUENCES OF TRUMP PRESIDENCY ON AMERICAN POLITICAL SYSTEM

In Spring 2016, John Judis reflected on the political lay of the land. "This year's election may not realign the parties, but it could be one of key's "critical" contests."[37] Indeed, in the immediate wake of the heated presidential contest, with Donald Trump claiming a stunning victory, some observers predicted a period of Republican resurgence—a partisan realignment—as a substantial number of voters who had cast ballots for Barack Obama four years prior, including many "working class" Democrats, supported Trump for president while the GOP maintained control of both chambers of the U.S. Congress. However, a closer reading of the political environment and review of more recent election results suggests that the Republican Party is, in fact, less emergent than it is in a state of inner turmoil. While Trump garners seemingly heretofore unshakable support from the rank-and-file Republican base, the rising tide of defiant anti-Trump opposition expressed by a cadre of prominent conservative elites and establishment-oriented Republicans portends undeniable short-term and long-term challenges for the GOP. This volume has diligently worked to describe the way Donald Trump has upended conservative politics in the United States and overtaken the Republican Party. But his impact is not simply on the inner-workings of the GOP. Separate from the policy implications of the Trump presidency (of which there are many), he has clearly changed the U.S. political system in ways impossible to overstate.

One major impact relates to how Trump has dramatically altered the alignment of the political parties. If the analysis found in these pages is correct, Donald Trump has aligned the Republican Party solidly with the identity—if not the interests—of non-college educated rural white voters, especially men. His policy positions and rhetoric have destroyed any ambitions Republicans laid out in the GOPR of 2013 of gaining the support from voters of color and increasingly progressive young voters. He may have also alienated well-educated, suburban women, pushing them to the Democratic Party fold. To be sure, these shifts began before Trump, but it seems likely that he cast them in bronze. What he exposed is a prevalent "misalignment" between GOP elites and the base that has grown since at least the 1990s. According to *The Economist*, Trump's election revealed "the *mismatch* (emphasis ours) between the ruthless economics Republican leaders preached and the economic security their voters wanted."[38] The "GOP coalition of downscale Reagan Democrats and the Republican business class" has been undeniably disrupted.[39]

This book describes the reaction of those elites to the usurpation of the party and movement they led for at least a generation. Trumpism, such as it can exist after Trump, will need to cater to the "insurgent" masses who are guided less by a coherent, conservative ideology than by resentment against elites who have promised them prosperity and cultural dominance. As one #NeverTrumper argues "I think this is where the party is," adding "I'm curious who follows Trump because the politics aren't going to change so dramatically . . . Anyone who wants to win in this party will have to appease the Trumpist base one way or the other."[40] The challenge is whether it can win general elections with a base that is a shrinking minority of the country. This becomes increasingly true as the base of the Democratic Party is growing and the Democratic-friendly territory is, by most accounts, thriving economically. On the other hand, some observers suggest the Democratic Party appears to be "breaking" in a manner similar to the GOP.[41]

Democrats are themselves, of course, impacted by Trump's victories. The presidential primaries of both 2016 and 2020 show that Democratic elites are also struggling to match an insurgent base. These insurgents view mainstream liberalism as insufficiently responsive to the challenges of twenty-first century economic decline and insufficiently confrontational with the ascendancy of religious and cultural conservatives in the culture wars. Conflict between insurgents in each party and the elites they hope to overthrow will likely be the dominant political paradigm for the years to come. As one report written collaboratively by conservatives and liberals on the status of the American political system concludes:

> The task for America's political establishment is nothing short of revolutionary change—change that realigns the establishment with the demands of alienated political bases but eschews anti-democratic populism. In the United States, extreme partisanship and unresponsive government is a driver of the gridlock,

frustration, and extreme populism that has developed over the past quarter century.[42]

Conservative elites highlighted in this volume seem to hope that a devastating loss for Republicans will mitigate and even reverse the damage they think Trump has done to the GOP. One suggests that 2020 will "be our McGovern '72 and out of that rubble the 2023-4 GOP primary race will redefine the party, hopefully back to opportunity conservatism."[43] Another adds that "The GOP will only change when white-grievance politics is consistently rejected at the ballot box, as it is in California."[44] Libertarian-leaning Conor Freidersdorf agrees, writing that "Sooner or later, the GOP will face a backlash over the unsavory forces they've allied with and unleashed, just as they faced a backlash after Pete Wilson's embrace of Proposition 187 in California . . . The GOP will deserve every bit of its next fall from power. And only Never Trumpers will have the credibility to pick up the pieces and rebuild."[45] Both parties will have to contend with the intra-party divisions he has exacerbated. Because Democrats have the numerical advantage nationally, and Republicans have the advantage institutionally (through the Senate and the Electoral College), such a stinging defeat seems unlikely to occur for either party. If it does, polarization and negative partisanship makes it unlikely that the insurgents will give up the fight to more "reasonable" elites in response.

A second major result of Donald Trump on the broader political system is a deep acceleration of a long-term trend that Arthur Schlesinger Jr. termed the "Imperial Presidency."[46] Trump has expanded the use of executive action in ways that President Obama's critics only imagined. Unilaterally, Trump has changed U.S. immigration policy, altered asylum policy, shifted significant funds for the border wall construction, and engaged in clear violations of the emoluments clause, nepotism laws, and use of government resources for political gain.

Recent polls indicate that Republicans are more open to the idea of expanded presidential power.[47] Perhaps more troubling, however, is that Trump's allies in Congress and his appointees to the federal judiciary were unwilling to exercise their Constitutional authority to halt such developments. His acquittal on impeachment articles was opposed by the assembly of #NeverTrumpers discussed in this volume but supported by all GOP Senators except Mitt Romney, who has perhaps rightly been singled out as "best positioned to pry the Republican Party from Trump's hands."[48] Republicans associated with the Lincoln Project note that "this president's actions are possible only with the craven acquiescence of congressional Republicans" adding that "They have done no less than abdicate their Article I responsibilities."[49] It remains to be seen whether Democratic presidents will continue the tradition of unilateral executive excesses, but several of the 2020 Democratic candidates indicated they would enact policies unilaterally if needed. History tells us that presidents rarely give up those powers their predecessors have gained, and Trump's gains for the executive branch may be an impressive bequeathal for his successors.

Finally, Donald Trump inherited a political culture that had become—through the growth of cable television news, social media, partisan polarization, and the expansion of moneyed interests—coarse and confrontational. He took that inheritance and exacerbated it tenfold. Politicians and public figures had for some time tried to push the boundaries and skirt the norms of basic decency. The conservatives highlighted in this book decry above all else the way Donald Trump has erased those boundaries and obliterated the moral norms that governed public life in liberal democracy. As Peter Wehner writes, "Mr. Trump's behavior isn't governed by moral standards; he doesn't seem to believe objective moral standards even exist."[50] *Christianity Today*, an evangelical Christian publication long supportive of Republicans, wrote an editorial supporting Trump's removal from office, and echoed Wehner. "None of the president's positives can balance the moral and political danger we face under a leader of such grossly immoral character."[51] Former George W. Bush speechwriter and current *Washington Post* conservative columnist Michael Gerson has consistently bemoaned the obsequiousness of his fellow evangelical Christians toward Trump. These leaders think Christians should simply accept "the proposition that a political coalition with ethnonationalists, led by a malicious, immoral buffoon, is good for the cause of justice and for the cause of Christ."[52]

Trump began his campaign by calling Mexican immigrants rapists and continued breaking norms until there seemingly were none left to break. He then found norms in a long-locked closet and brought them out to trample on them as well. He did this with such efficiency that his party, his opponents, and the public at large eventually became numb to how devastating his words and behavior became. He shattered specific norms with such brutality that eventually people stopped believing that there were things we should accept as norms. He attacked federal judges. He insulted his own political appointees. He curtailed the independence of the Department of Justice. He bragged about sexual conquests. He bullied the Federal Reserve. He politicized diplomatic relations with Ukraine. He praised totalitarian autocrats. He condemned the free press. He gave shelter to neo-Nazis and white supremacists. He lied . . . "constantly, extravagantly, incontinently," and without remorse, regret, or consequence.[53]

Over the course of the last four years, it has become clear that the Republican Party is the party of Donald Trump and his most ardent supporters. Individuals who initially opposed Trump (much of the GOP) eventually acquiesced, if reluctantly, to his leadership. This project was conceived in the aftermath of the 2018 midterm election, when #NeverTrumpers held out hope that the GOP's devastating losses might wake up traditional conservatives, both inside and outside the corridors of power, to Trump's corrosive impact on civil discourse and Constitutional restraints. For the most part, few have woken up. In fact, as this project evolved, it became clear that there were only a handful of #NeverTrump conservatives left in the modern Republican Party—almost all have abandoned the GOP as it has folded its big tent and doubled down on Trump-style populism and pugilism. Nonetheless, NeverTrumpism remains impactful. As Jay Nordlinger, Senior Editor at *National Review* points out: "I see that "Never Trump" is trending. It is ever-trending, so to speak. On one hand, "Never Trumpers" are few and irrelevant—barely a pimple on the butt of the body politic. On the other, they are a scourge, a menace. Their antagonists cannot stop talking about them. Odd."[54]

To be clear, the rise of Donald Trump did not occur in a political vacuum. As Dionne, Ornstein, and Mann discuss, the process of shifting party dynamics has long been underway. "It involves the decline of basic norms in politics, governing and the media as well as the decay of institutions that are central to republican government. The radicalization of the Republican Party and its primary electorate began three decades ago. Absent these forces, Trump would still be a loudmouthed developer and brand-peddler far removed from the levers of power."[55] Indeed, many of the very same #NeverTrumpers who now complain so stridently about a Republican Party rife with anti-intellectual attitudes, strains of bigotry and xenophobia cloaked in nationalist populism, and a president who routinely promulgates inflammatory, divisive, anti-establishment rhetoric had ignored, dismissed, or even helped plant the seeds of discontent which have now fully developed into the movement. For all the courage and conviction that motivates many in the #NeverTrump movement at present, the truth is this: had they simply stood up on principle, and opposed, rather than encouraged, the increasingly strident rhetoric of their fellow partisans at any other time during the 1990s and early 2000s, then they might have stemmed the rise of Trumpism. These individuals— George Will, Max Boot, Jennifer Rubin, Jeff Flake—once seemed content to stoke the warm embers of a small campfire fueled by anti-liberal hysteria and grievance-based "take no prisoners" politics. Now that the raging forest fire has engulfed the country and the party they once claimed as their own lies in ruins, they fume that their warnings have thus far gone mostly unheeded.

Eric Alterman of *The Nation* highlights the apparent hypocrisy. "Former Fox News pundits had no problem chasing the paychecks when, for instance, Glenn Beck insisted that President Obama had a 'deep-seated hatred for white people,' and . . . that [Bill] Kristol, together with Never Trumper hero John McCain . . . elevated Sarah Palin."[56] Alterman notes that Trump is the "symptom, not the cause." Matthew Dallek of George Washington University amplifies this point:

> Ultimately, Trump was the logical consequence of a posture followed for decades at the top echelons of the conservative movement; The batty screeds are silly, but since they help us, we won't work zealously to purge them. Trump's conspiracy-based capture of the GOP has less to do with him and his perspective than with a party that sought and often won the support of people who believe those notions.[57]

Charlie Sykes clarifies the critical choice: "The crisis of conservative media is deciding whether or not it's going to become a tool of Trumpism."[58] Fellow #NeverTrumper Rick Wilson argues that it already has, which is at least partly the fault of the GOP. "The way we were able to build a set of tools to persuade conservative voters . . . this package of messages and these channels we reached, whether it was Fox, or social media or talk radio . . . we presumed wrongly that no one would ever take the keys to those tools." Wilson adds that "When Trump got ahold of them, he used them way outside the boundaries, and he's using them purely for his own personal power."[59] Columnist George Will went so far as to ridicule Lindsey Graham as a "political windsock," emblematic of how the once proud party has lost its way, effectively sacrificing its moral foundation at the altar of Trump. Will bemoans the trade-off. "Today, Graham, paladin of conservatism and scourge of opportunism, says building the border wall is an existential matter for the GOP: 'If we undercut the president, that's the end of his presidency and the end of our party.'"[60] So it goes. Clearly, the onus is also on principled actors within the Republican Party to step up, repair the damage done and right the ship, as Rauch and Wehner argue in a blistering *New York Times* op-ed:

> The most troubling—and from our point of view the most disappointing—development of the Trump era is not the president's own election and subsequent behavior; it is the institutional corruption, weakness, and self-betrayal of the Republican Party. The party has abandoned its core commitments to constitutional norms, to conservative principles and even to basic decency. It has allowed itself to be hijacked by a reality television star who is a pathological liar, emotionally unsteady, and accountable only to himself. And Republicans have embraced presidential conduct that, had it been engaged in by a Democrat, they would have denounced as corrupt, incompetent, and even treasonous.[61]

In conclusion, the conservative tradition in the United States—and indeed, throughout the Western political tradition—demands the recognition and maintenance of norms, at least until a strong consensus emerges to shift those norms. Conservatism stresses adherence to a concept channeled by comedian Dana Carvey, who was not a conservative but played one on TV—prudence. The conservatives and Republicans we focus on in this book are distraught by many developments in the Trump era, but above all they mourn the loss of prudence in their party. They believe that under the right circumstances, with the right leaders, conservatism may be made prudent again. They have staked their careers and reputations on such a return. But the damage to the Republican Party—and American democracy—may already be done. Our goal in this book was to highlight those #NeverTrump conservatives who fought to prevent such damage. Any chance the Republican Party has to break free from Trumpism will rely on the principles of these conservatives to guide the way.

NOTES

1. Mark Galli, "Trump Should Be Removed from Office," *Christianity Today,* December 19, 2019, https://www.christianitytoday.com/ct/2019/december-web-only/trump-should-be-removed-from-office.html.

2. Chris Cillizza, "Can the Republican Party Survive Donald Trump?" *CNN,* August 21, 2018, https://www.cnn.com/2018/08/21/politics/donald-trump-republican-party/index.html.

3. Joe Walsh, "Joe Walsh: Trump Needs a Primary Challenge," *The New York Times,* August 14, 2019, https://www.nytimes.com/2019/08/14/opinion/joe-walsh-trump-primary.html.

4. Alan Greenblatt, "Some Suburban State Lawmakers Are Leaving the GOP," *Governing,* January 29, 2019, https://www.governing.com/topics/politics/gov-california-kansas-party-switch-lawmaker.html.

5. Jeff Flake, *Conscience of a Conservative* (New York: Random House, 2017), 79.

6. Jennifer Rubin, "Why Justin Amash Stands Alone," *The Washington Post,* May 19, 2019, https://www.washingtonpost.com/opinions/2019/05/19/why-justin-amash-stands-alone/.

7. Eric Alterman, "Never Trumpers Never Mattered," *The Nation,* May 3, 2018, https://www.thenation.com/article/archive/never-trumpers-never-mattered/.

8. Lauren R. Johnson, Deon McCray, and Jordan M. Ragusa, "#NeverTrump: Why Republican Members of Congress Refused to Support Their Party's Nominee in the 2016 Election," *Research and Politics,* 5 (January 2018): 1–10; David Mayhew, *Congress: The Electoral Connection* (New Haven, CT: Yale University Press, 1974).

9. Gregory L. Bovitz and Jamie L. Carson, "Position Taking and Electoral Accountability in the U.S. House of Representatives," *Political Research Quarterly,* 59, no. 2 (June 2006): 297–312.

10. Sam Stein and Asawin Suebsaeng, "The #NeverTrump Movement Has Been Neutered," *The Daily Beast,* December 27, 2019, https://www.thedailybeast.com/the-nevertrump-movement-has-been-neutered.

11. Susan Collins, "GOP Senator Susan Collins: Why I Cannot Support Trump," *The Washington Post*, August 8, 2016, https://www.washingtonpost.com/opinions/gop-senator-why-i-cannot-support-trump/2016/08/08/821095be-5d7e-11e6-9d2f-b1a3564181a1_story.html; Rebecca Traister, "The Immoderate Susan Collins: After a Long Career Voting Across the Aisle, Why Did the Maine Senator Gamble Her Legacy on Trump?" *The Cut*, February 20, 2020, https://www.thecut.com/2020/02/susan-collins-moderate-legacy-trump.html; Griff Witte, "Republican Sen. Susan Collins Finds It's Lonely in the Middle," *The Washington Post*, February 2, 2020, https://www.washingtonpost.com/national/republican-sen-susan-collins-finds-its-lonely-in-the-middle/2020/02/02/6e4b3964-45c2-11ea-8949-a9ca94a90b4c_story.html.

12. Manu Raju and Alex Rogers, "Susan Collins Declines to Say Whether She'll Support Trump," *CNN*, March 3, 2020, https://www.cnn.com/2020/03/03/politics/susan-collins-trump-reelection/index.html.

13. Juleanna Glover, "There's a Surprisingly Plausible Path to Removing Trump from Office," *Politico*, November 19, 2019, https://www.politico.com/magazine/story/2019/11/12/path-to-removing-donald-trump-from-office-229911.

14. Zach Beauchamp, "Lamar Alexander and the Power of Right-Wing Political Correctness," *Vox*, January 31, 2020, https://www.vox.com/policy-and-politics/2020/1/31/21116689/trump-impeachment-lamar-alexander-witness-bolton

15. Erick Erickson, "I'll Be Voting for President Trump and Vice President Pence in 2020," *The Resurgent*, February 11, 2019, https://theresurgent.com/2019/02/11/ill-be-voting-for-president-trump-and-vice-president-pence-in-2020/.

16. Alex Isenstadt, "Never Trumpers Flame Out," *Politico*, January 18, 2020, https://www.politico.com/news/2020/01/18/never-trump-2020-walsh-weld-100665

17. Mark Leibovich, "President Trump Is Overwhelmingly Popular with His Base, But a Handful of Dissident Republicans Think They Know How to Defeat Him in a Primary Contest. Are They Wrong?" *The New York Times*, April 24, 2019, https://www.nytimes.com/2019/04/24/magazine/republican-primary-trump-resistance.html.

18. Leibovich, "President Trump Is Overwhelmingly Popular."

19. Leibovich, "President Trump Is Overwhelmingly Popular."

20. David Wasserman, "The Congressional Map Has a Record-Setting Bias Against Democrats," *FiveThirtyEight*, April 7, 2017, https://fivethirtyeight.com/features/the-congressional-map-is-historically-biased-toward-the-gop/.

21. Ian Millhiser, "America's Democracy Is Failing. Here's Why," *Vox*, February 13, 2020, https://www.vox.com/policy-and-politics/2020/1/30/20997046/constitution-electoral-college-senate-popular-vote-trump.

22. Paul Bedard, "Book: Never Trumpers Have 'Failed,'" *The Washington Examiner*, March 1, 2019, https://www.washingtonexaminer.com/washington-secrets/book-never-trumpers-have-failed.

23. Damon Linker, "The Death Rattle of the Never Trump Republicans," *The Week*, November 13, 2019, https://theweek.com/articles/878011/death-rattle-never-trump-republicans.

24. Linker, "The Death Rattle of the Never Trump Republicans."

25. Diana C. Mutz, "Status Threat, Not Economic Hardship, Explains the 2016 Presidential Vote," *Proceedings of the National Academy of Sciences of the United States of America*, 115, no. 19 (April 23, 2018); Michael Barber and Jeremy C. Pope, "Conservatism in the Era of Trump," *Perspectives in Politics*, 17, no. 3 (September 2019): 719–36; Alan Abramowitz, *The Great Alignment: Race, Party Transformation, and the Rise of Donald Trump* (New Haven: Yale University Press, 2018).

26. Henry C. Jackson, "6 Promises Trump Has Made About Health Care," *Politico*, March 13, 2017, https://www.politico.com/story/2017/03/trump-obamacare-promises-236021.

27. Sheryl Gay Stolberg, "Trump Republicans Invigorate, and Complicate, Party's Fight for Senate," *The New York Times*, August 29, 2017, https://www.nytimes.com /2017/08/29/us/politics/senate-trump-lou-barletta-.html.

28. Heather Long and Jeff Stein, "The U.S. Deficit Hit $984 Billion in 2019, Soaring During Trump Era," *The Washington Post*, October 25, 2019, https://ww w.washingtonpost.com/business/2019/10/25/us-deficit-hit-billion-marking-nearly-p ercent-increase-during-trump-era/.

29. Max Boot, "Republicans Are Making a Mockery of Their Reputations," *The Washington Post*, February 11, 2018, https://www.washingtonpost.com/opinions/ republicans-are-making-a-mockery-of-their-reputations/2018/02/10/866aefe0-0eaa-1 1e8-8890-372e2047c935_story.html.

30. Mark Sanford, "Why Do My Fellow Republicans Make Excuses for Trump's Deficits?" *The New York Times*, February 18, 2020, https://www.nytimes.com/2020 /02/18/opinion/trump-budget.html.

31. Emily Badger and Claire Cain Miller, "How the Trump Era Is Molding the Next Generation of Voters," *The New York Times*, April 1, 2019, https://www.nyt imes.com/2019/04/01/upshot/trump-era-molding-young-voters.html.

32. For a through debate of how demographic issues affect both parties, see Ronald Brownstein, "Are Demographics Really Destiny for the GOP?" *The Atlantic*, May 31, 2017, https://www.theatlantic.com/politics/archive/2017/05/trump-2016-e lection/528519/; Ramesh Ponnuru, "How Republicans Can Ward Off Demographic Doom," *Bloomberg*, April 17, 2018, https://www.bloomberg.com/opinion/articles/20 18-04-17/demographics-don-t-doom-republican-party; Rob Griffin, William H. Frey, and Ruy Teixeira, "States of Change: How Demographic Change Is Transforming the Republican and Democratic Parties," July 1, 2019, https://www.brookings.edu/rese arch/states-of-change-2019/.

33. Sean Illing, "A Former Republican Congress Member Explains What Happened to His Party," *Vox*, December 6, 2019, https://www.vox.com/policy-and -politics/2019/12/6/20993403/impeachment-hearing-trump-congress-david-jolly.

34. Chris Cillizza, "Can the Republican Party Survive Donald Trump?" *CNN*, August 21, 2018, 2020, https://www.cnn.com/2018/08/21/politics/donald-trump-re publican-party/index.html.

35. Jeff Flake, "Republicans Must Move Beyond the Cult of Trump's Personality," *The Washington Post*, November 8, 2018, https://www.washingtonpost.com/opin ions/jeff-flake-republicans-must-move-beyond-the-cult-of-trumps-personality/2018 /11/07/b6432414-e2a1-11e8-8f5f-a55347f48762_story.html.

36. Cillizza, "Can the Republican Party Survive Donald Trump?"

37. John B. Judis, "After 2016, Will the Political Parties Ever Look the Same?" *The Washington Post*, March 11, 2016, https://www.washingtonpost.com/opinions/after-2016-will-the-political-parties-ever-look-the-same/2016/03/11/07a18da6-e709-11e5-bc08-3e03a5b41910_story.html.

38. "'Never Trump' Republicans Could Have Their Revenge," *The Economist*, August 9, 2018, https://www.economist.com/united-states/2018/08/09/never-trump-republicans-could-have-their-revenge.

39. Judis, "After 2016."

40. Illing, "A Former Republican."

41. Derek Thompson, "The Democratic Party of 2020 Is Broken," *The Atlantic*, February 14, 2020, https://www.theatlantic.com/ideas/archive/2020/02/democratic-party-2020-broken/606547/.

42. Dalibor Rohac, Liz Kennedy, and Vikram Singh, "Drivers of Authoritarian Populism in the United States," *The Center for American Progress*, May 10, 2018, https://www.americanprogress.org/issues/democracy/reports/2018/05/10/450552/drivers-authoritarian-populism-united-states/.

43. Cillizza, "Can the Republican Party Survive Donald Trump?"

44. David Roberts, "Never-Trump Republicans Face an Obvious Choice. They're Not Going to Like It," *Vox*, April 27, 2018, https://www.vox.com/policy-and-politics/2018/4/24/17269600/trump-republicans-vote-democrats.

45. Conor Friedersdorf, "'Never Trump' Will Be the Only Faction Still Standing When He's Gone," *The Atlantic*, December 27, 2017, https://www.theatlantic.com/politics/archive/2017/12/never-trump-is-conserving-decency-on-the-right/549197/.

46. Arthur M. Schlesinger Jr., *The Imperial Presidency* (Boston: Houghton Milton, 1973).

47. PEW Research Center, "Republicans Now Are More Open to the Ida of Expanding Presidential Power," PEW, August 7, 2019, https://www.people-press.org/2019/08/07/republicans-now-are-more-open-to-the-idea-of-expanding-presidential-power/.

48. Sarah Longwell, "Mitt Romney, It's Time: The Senator Is Best Positioned to Pry The Republican Party from President Trump's Hands," *The Atlantic*, October 23, 2019, https://www.theatlantic.com/ideas/archive/2019/10/mitt-romney-versus-trump/600508/.

49. George T. Conway III, Steve Schmidt, John Weaver and Rick Wilson, "We Are Republicans, and We Want Trump Defeated," *The New York Times*, December 17, 2019, https://www.nytimes.com/2019/12/17/opinion/lincoln-project.html.

50. Peter Wehner, "What's the Matter with Republicans?" *The New York Times*, September 30, 2019, https://www.nytimes.com/2019/09/30/opinion/republicans-trump-impeachment.html.

51. Galli, "Trump Should Be Removed from Office."

52. Michael Gerson, "Evangelicals Need to Follow Christianity's Morals, Not Trump's," *The Washington Post*, December 23, 2019, https://www.washingtonpost.com/opinions/evangelicals-need-to-follow-christianitys-morals-not-trumps/2019/12/23/34e74ef6-25d3-11ea-9c21-2c2a4d2c2166_story.html.

53. Quin Hillyer, "Why I Remain a Never Trumper, and What It Means," *The Washington Examiner*, March 11, 2019, https://www.washingtonexaminer.com/opini on/columnists/why-i-remain-a-never-trumper-and-what-it-means.

54. Jay Nordlinger, @jaynordlinger, "I see that "Never Trump" is trending. It is ever-trending, so to speak." Twitter, February 23, 2020, https://twitter.com/jaynordlin ger/status/1231706426055315457.

55. E. J. Dionne, Norman Ornstein, and Thomas E. Mann, *One Nation After Trump* (New York: St. Martin's Press, 2017), 4.

56. Alterman, "Never Trumpers Never Mattered."

57. Matthew Dallek, "Swamp Fever," *The Washington Post,* January 2, 2020, https://www.washingtonpost.com/outlook/2020/01/02/dont-blame-trump-rise-right -wing-conspiracy-theories/?arc404=true.

58. Sean Illing, "How Conservative Media Became a 'Safe Space,'" *Vox*, January 19, 2019, https://www.vox.com/2019/1/18/18175582/trump-fox-news-conservative -media-charlie-sykes.

59. Davis Richardson, "Why 'Never Trump' Godfather Rick Wilson Started Carrying a Gun in Public," *Observer*, August 13, 2018, https://observer.com/2018/08 /rick-wilson-never-trump-strategist-death-threats/.

60. George Will, "Why Do People Such as Lindsey Graham Come to Congress?" January 23, 2019, *The Washington Post*, https://www.washingtonpost.com/opinions/ why-do-people-such-as-lindsey-graham-come-to-congress/2019/01/23/9830a174-1 e68-11e9-8e21-59a09ff1e2a1_story.html.

61. Jonathan Rauch and Peter Wehner, "Republicans Got Us into This Mess, and They Have to Get Us Out of It: The Idea Sounds Crazy—Until Suddenly It Doesn't," *New York Times*, February 8, 2019, https://www.nytimes.com/2019/02/08/opinion/su nday/trump-impeachment-resignation-republicans.html.

Epilogue

It would be inadequate to characterize the Trump candidacy and presidency as unprecedented. Some of the division and chaos is not necessarily driven by Donald Trump. The economic and social upheaval wrought by the coronavirus pandemic, for instance, would have taken place in some form or another under any president (though #NeverTrumpers discussed in this volume have made the case that competent leadership could have mitigated the impact). But other shocks to the system—impeachment investigations, openly courting foreign interference in U.S. elections, violations of long-standing political norms and constitutional guardrails—must be placed squarely at the feet of Donald Trump. His campaign and presidency have been an inconceivably tumultuous ride, and if there is anything that conservatism eschews, it is tumult.

Even still, the political ground continues to shift dramatically, as relevant events unfold almost daily. Since the chapters herein went to print, the nation has been forced to confront three monumental challenges—the underestimated and mismanaged COVID-19 pandemic, the sharpest and deepest economic collapse in generations, and a widespread grass roots movement to address systemic racial disparities which were highlighted for all to see in the tragic killings of George Floyd, Ahmaud Arber, Breonna Taylor, and Rayshard Brooks, among too many others. In all four cases, President Trump has failed to rise to and meet these challenges as one should expect from a U.S. president. To the contrary, he has mismanaged and misled, instead choosing to use his bully pulpit to divide rather than unite Americans. The public has taken note. His approval ratings have slipped and #NeverTrump critics, such as those involved with groups like The Lincoln Project and Republican Voters Against Trump, are feeling even more emboldened, and have ramped up devastating ad campaigns opposing him.

Moreover, Trump's former National Security Advisor, John Bolton, has penned *The Room Where It Happened: A White House Memoir*, which includes dramatic revelations of corruption and incompetence, and implied that Trump was indeed guilty of the charges brought forth in the Articles of Impeachment. President George W. Bush, former GOP presidential candidate Mitt Romney as well as Colin Powell, Carly Fiorina, and John Bolton have gone public with their opposition to Trump's reelection.

We also now know that Joe Biden has won the Democratic nomination and will face Donald Trump in November 2020. Biden clearly represents the safest choice that Democrats could have made; at the same time, it is telling and ironic that some question his candidacy because insurgents on the left flank of the Democratic Party view him as part of the out of touch political "establishment," part of the "swamp" to be drained. While Biden seems to have secured full support from across all parts of the traditional Democratic coalition, and has also made significant inroads with critical swing voters, questions remain. Will Biden excite the Democratic Party base enough to turn out in droves, or will many of them stay home as they did when Hillary Clinton was on the ballot? Will Biden appeal to coveted swing voters, such as "working class" (Obama to Trump) whites and suburban women?

It is clear, however, that he was almost universally the preferred Democratic candidate of #NeverTrump conservatives, some of whom warned that Bernie Sanders or Elizabeth Warren would be as big a threat to the republic as Donald Trump. During the 2020 primary election season, many of the individuals described in this volume took to social media, providing proud public pronouncements of their first ever vote for a Democratic candidate—Joe Biden. It is less clear how many rank-and-file Republicans are also disgruntled enough to follow their example, or will in November.

Part of the dilemma that traditional conservatives face in the era of Donald Trump is that the modern system is marked by excessive partisan and ideological polarization. In another political world—indeed, in almost every other political era in American history—copartisans who were skeptical of Donald Trump would have simply switched sides. This is particularly true for elected officials, who are described in this book as those *least* likely to oppose Donald Trump. In another time, as recently as the 1990s under Bill Clinton, officeholders would flip to the other party if they feel their current one does not reflect their values, or if they sense strategic advantage in making the switch. In the United States in 2020, however, the ideological means of the parties are simply so far apart that switching is not a viable option. Though a select few state and local Republicans flipped to become Democrats, not one Republican member of the U.S. Congress has followed suit (though Justin Amash abandoned the GOP for "Independent" status). Simply put, there is not a "conservative" wing of the Democratic Party in which #NeverTrump

Table 13.1   Prominent #NeverTrumpers

Justin Amash	David French	Colin Powell
Max Boot	David Frum	Jennifer Rubin
David Brooks	Michael Gerson	Mitt Romney
George H. W. Bush	Jonah Goldberg	Mark Sanford
George W. Bush	Steven Hayes	Joe Scarborough
Jeb Bush	Larry Hogan	Steve Schmidt
Laura Bush	David Jolly	Brent Scowcroft
Linda Chavez	Elise Jordan	Michael Steele
Mona Charon	John Kasich	Charlie Sykes
Eliot Cohen	Bill Kristol	Joe Walsh
George Conway	Matt Lewis	Nicolle Wallace
Bob Corker	John McCain	John Weaver
S.E. Cupp	Mike Murphy	Bill Weld
Ross Douthat	Ana Navarro	George Will
Carly Fiorina	Peggy Noonan	Christine Todd Whitman
Jeff Flake	Richard Painter	Rick Wilson

Source: Compiled by the authors. Not intended to be exhaustive.

conservatives could find a home. They are quite literally a movement without a party.

The epigraph of this book is a quote (or commonly represented as a quote) by a godfather of conservative thought, Edmund Burke. Burke is well-known for his theories of trustee representation and treatise on cultural and institutional norms. This phrase—"The only thing necessary for the triumph of evil is for good men to do nothing"—emphasizes the importance of active engagement with the world of politics and policymaking. It is a well-known proclamation, referenced by civic-minded individuals of all political stripes. We emphasize it because, as we note in the preface, we would run short of material in a volume featuring "profiles in courage." There were simply not enough conservatives and Republicans—especially elected officials—who consistently and adamantly opposed Trump to fill such a volume. It is perhaps the great tragedy of the American political system, one which punishes courageous leadership and instead rewards those who sacrifice principle, choosing instead to strategically "go along to get along" and chase public acclaim campaign dollars and primary votes. That said, we would be remiss if we did not identify, for the record, those individuals who have defied their president, their partisan affiliation, popular opinion, and even risked their careers, in order to do the "right" thing, and sleep well at night. The individuals above, as well as others unmentioned, channeled their inner William F. Buckley, Jr., stood athwart history, and yelled "Stop!"—March 10, 2020.

Index

About the Contributors

Andrew L. Pieper is an associate professor in the School of Government and International Affairs and coordinator of the political science program at Kennesaw State University in metro Atlanta. He teaches courses in American politics, including the U.S. Presidency, U.S. Congress, research methods, and political behavior. His research revolves around the intersection of religion and American politics, particularly the culture wars between the American left and right. He has published in numerous outlets, including the *New England Journal of Public Policy*, the *Journal of Media and Religion*, and *American Politics Research*.

Jeff R. DeWitt is a professor of political science in the School of Government and International Affairs at Kennesaw State University, where his primary field of study is American political behavior with research interests in electoral politics, political communication, and public opinion. He has published in various academic journals, including *Politics & Policy*, *Journal of Political Science*, *American Review of Politics*, *Journal of Official Statistics*, *Journal of Public Administration Research and Theory*, *Journal of Faculty Development*, and *Place Branding and Public Diplomacy*. Dr. DeWitt teaches courses in American government, mass media and politics, research methods, and senior seminar, is coordinator for certificate programs in both professional politics and political communication, and is also a member of KSU's Honors faculty.

Karyn A. Amira is an assistant professor of political science at the College of Charleston. She specializes in political psychology and political behavior with a focus on ideology, partisanship, candidate perception, and voting. She has also coauthored research on resistance to Donald Trump among his Republican copartisans in Congress. Her work has been published in *The Journal of Politics, Perspectives on Politics, Political Behavior, The Journal of Experimental Political Science, American Politics Research, Social Science Quarterly, The Journal of Political Science Education*, and *International Journal of Politics, Culture and Society*. She is a voracious consumer of political news media—probably to an unhealthy degree—and lives in Charleston, SC, with her husband Nathan and their dog Eddie.

Jason S. Byers is a visiting assistant professor at the University of North Georgia. His research areas are Congress, the presidency, the separation of powers, congressional elections, and quantitative methods. His research has focused on congressional primary and general elections, the confirmation process of presidential nominees, and presidential campaign politics. His work has been featured in *Congress & the Presidency, Political Behavior*, and the *Forum*.

Martin Cohen is an associate professor of political science at James Madison University. He teaches classes on political parties, religion and politics, and the role of evangelical Christians in the Republican Party. He is the author of *Moral Victories in the Battle for Congress* published in 2019 by the University of Pennsylvania Press and the coauthor of *The Party Decides: Presidential Nominations Before and After Reform*. Martin is also the coauthor of "A Theory of Political Parties," which won the Jack Walker Award for its outstanding contribution to research on political organizations and parties.

April A. Johnson is an assistant professor in the School of Government and International Affairs at Kennesaw State University. Her current research emphasizes the intersection between political psychology and electoral behavior. She has published articles in the *Journal of Politics, Political Studies, State Politics and Policy Quarterly, Policy Studies*, and the *Journal of Health Politics, Policy and Law*.

Jeffrey Lazarus is professor of political science at Georgia State University. His research focuses on Congress, elections, and political parties, and much of it focuses on how Congress members use perquisites of office to help themselves win reelection. He has published numerous book chapters and articles in scholarly journals including *The American Journal of Political Science, The Journal of Politics, Political Research Quarterly, Legislative Studies Quarterly*, and others. His coauthored book *Gendered Vulnerability: How Women Work Harder to Stay in Office* is available from University of Michigan.

Christopher Paskewich is associate professor of politics at Centre College. He teaches courses on political theory, political ideologies, and mass incarceration. Dr. Paskewich has written about the political thought of Leo Strauss, as well as management theory.

Wesley B. Renfro is an associate professor of political science and an associate dean in the College of Arts and Sciences at Quinnipiac University in Hamden, Connecticut. He earned a BA in history and philosophy at Heidelberg College and a MA and PhD in political science at the University of Connecticut. His research has appeared in numerous journals and edited volumes. Renfro's scholarship is on the modern American presidency, U.S. foreign policy and strategy, and empire.

Beth Rosenson is associate professor of political science at University of Florida, specializing in American politics. She received her PhD from the Massachusetts Institute of Technology in 2000. She has published extensively on political corruption and on ethics and campaign finance regulation at the state and national levels, with a particular focus on ethics in Congress and state legislatures. She also does research on political communications, most recently on media bias and media coverage of state legislators. Current research projects examine presidential nepotism in historical perspective and how gender affects perceptions of political courage.

Anthony Sparacino is a visiting lecturer at the University of Richmond. He received his PhD from the University of Virginia. His research is broadly within the field of American political development with particular emphases on the origins of political party organizations and ideology. He is the author of "Compassionate Conservatism in the Spiral of Politics," published in *American Political Thought*, and coauthor (with Sidney M. Milkis) of "Pivotal Elections" in the *Wiley Companion to the Gilded Age and the Progressive Era*. He is currently working on a book project on the origins and development of the Democratic and Republican Governors' Associations as well as paper projects on the Democratic and Republican mayoral conferences and state attorneys' general organizations.

Robert (Bo) Wood is a professor in the Department of Political Science and Public Administration at the University of North Dakota. He is the director of the Master of Public Administration program at UND and serves as the Policy Lead for UND's Research Institute for Autonomous Systems (RIAS). He was the director of the Bureau of Governmental Affairs at UND from 2006 to 2016. He received his PhD in political science from the University of Washington in 2003. His most recent publications focus on policymaking processes at the local level, how public services are best delivered in rural communities, bureaucratic behavior and regulatory policy. Dr. Wood has presented his work at such conferences as the annual meetings of the American Political Science Association, Midwest Political Science Association, and the Association for Public Policy Analysis and Management. His research has been published in the *Journal of Public Administration Research and Theory*, the *Policy Studies Journal*, *Urban Affairs Review*, *Review of Policy Research*, *Environmental Communication*, *The Journal of Environmental Policy and Planning*, and *State and Local Government Review*.

Heather E. Yates is an assistant professor of political science at the University of Central Arkansas where she teaches courses on women and gender in politics, race in American politics, and the American Presidency. Dr. Yates researches political behavior and is the author of two books linking voters' emotions with their appraisal of campaign issues during presidential elections and is co-editor of *The Hollywood Connection: The Influence of Fictional Media and Celebrity Politics on American Public Opinion*.

www.ingramcontent.com/pod-product-compliance
Lightning Source LLC
Chambersburg PA
CBHW031351290326
41932CB00044B/976